UP THE
CUT

AN ANTHOLOGY OF
INLAND WATERWAYS

UP THE CUT

CUT

AN ANTHOLOGY OF
INLAND WATERWAYS

IVAN E. BROADHEAD

ALAN SUTTON PUBLISHING LIMITED

BRITISH WATERWAYS

First published in the United Kingdom in 1994
Alan Sutton Publishing Limited
Phoenix Mill · Far Thrupp · Stroud · Gloucestershire
in association with British Waterways

First published in the United States of America in 1994
Alan Sutton Publishing Inc
83 Washington Street · Dover · NH 03820

British Library Cataloguing-in-Publication Data

A catalogue record for this book is available from the British Library.

ISBN 0–7509–0585–9

Library of Congress Cataloging-in-Publication Data applied for

Typeset in 10/13 Sabon
Typesetting and origination by
Alan Sutton Publishing Limited.
Printed in Great Britain by
Butler and Tanner, Frome, Somerset.

Dedication

To Ed Smalle, who first broadened my horizons, and all my American friends.

Contents

Acknowledgements   ix

Map   x

Introduction   xi

1.   TIDES OF JOY   1

Two Centuries of a Water Highway Sponsored by Bradford Merchants
One Hundred and Fiftieth Anniversary of the Caledonian Canal,
1822–1972 — The Chesterfield Canal, 1777–1977 — The Trent and
Mersey Canal – 200 Years of Service, 1777–1977 — Yorkshire Ouse –
River of Destiny

2.   BEYOND THE LOCKS   20

An Inland Voyage — Five Girls and One Man . . . On a Boat
Honeymoon on the Canals in 1908 — Two Nice Ladies went Astray
Summer Cruise Inland Cruising Sixty Years Ago

3.   OF CASTINGS, CHOCOLATE AND CONJUGAL BLISS   43

Severn Merchant Adventurer — Charlie and His Chocolate Boat — A
Barge-load of Elvers — Trent Trade was Marriage Making — By Tanker to
Leeds — Carrying Giant Castings with *Confidence* on the SSYN

4.   STAIRWAYS TO HEAVEN   61

Canal Inclined Planes of Shropshire — Canal Tunnels — Staircase to the
South – The Story of Foxton — Canal Lighthouses — Opening Day at
Pontcysyllte — Stairway to Heaven

5.   DOWN THE SLIPWAY   76

The Scottish 'Puffers' — The Story of Fly-boats — Vital Link – The Story of the Thames Steam Tug and Lighterage Company — When 'Tom Puddings' Took a Trip by Train — Inn Signs Tell of Forgotten Craft — One of the Aire and Calder Navigation's Successful Operators — York Had the First Iron Boat

6. ARISTOCRATS TO TILLER GIRLS 93

A Pioneer of Island Waterways — A Scot Across the Border — Colour on Canals — There's Romance on Canals — People and Craft of the Narrow Canals — The Leisurely Life

7. FLOTSAM AND JETSAM 111

Commemorating the Canal Cutters — On the Wave of a Crest — Canal Curio Tells of Coal Tax — Mystery Monument at Ripon — Missive with a Message Tragedy of Christmas Carollers — Maud Heath's Causeway

8. STREAMS OF WAILS 128

The Black Jack Mystery — Lock Bubbles for Sale — The Lady in the White Gown — Saturday Night Fever for Juliet's Ghost — The Human Sacrifice

9. ALL KINDS OF WATER 144

The Great Frost of 1895 — Rudyard, Stanley and Knypersley — Are We in Danger of Losing the Severn Bore? — Day of the 'Iceberg' — That Water Shortage

10. FOR THE COMMON GOOD 159

A Waterway Built for War — Life on the Canals in Wartime Britain — Dad's Waterborne Army — An Aire and Calder Boatman of the War Years

11. ON REFLECTION 175

Craft-y Nonsense — A Standard Craft — Grand Union — Where's the Typist Cartwright's Grey Mare — Who? — Thoughts at the Clubhouse Window The Last 'Number One' — Our Lovely Heritage — Peace – and Plenty Can You? — Rochdale Canal — Trent Waters — Something New in London Fly-boats — Ducking for Joe — Canal Journey — A Saga of Canals — Will This Make 'em Think? — Sale of a Boat — On retiring — The River by Night November Holiday — Pennine Reservoir — The Leeds and Liverpool Canal The Canal — Narrow Boat — Polluted Canal — A Black Spider Gloucester and Sharpness Canal — We Shall Return — A Working Day Unbelievable — Hard Work — Into a Tunnel — Waterways

Acknowledgements

This book could not have been produced without the permission, approval and assistance of British Waterways, which runs the country's canals, and in particular Claire Keane, Sara Ansell and Roy Jamieson, so it is particularly gratifying to find it warrants identification with their Canals 200 celebrations.

The contents include some of my own contributions but also those of the undermentioned, who I hope are pleased to see their efforts preserved in a more permanent form than the ephemeral newspaper. I am therefore indebted for the literary efforts of: D.R.M. Adams, Mick Anthony, Carolyn Artis, K.W. Ashberry, Denis J. Aston, Philip Baker, R. Baldwin, Monica Bennett, F.G. Birden, Mrs Bowman, C.P. Carrdus, Emily Case, J. Chatwin, Kenneth Clew, Josephine (Jo) Coles, Martin Cooper, Courtney Dainton, Philip Daniell, Andre Drucker, H. Dunn, Margaret Evans, Frank Fernyhough, Roger Ford, J.F. Farm Machines Ltd, John Fox, Emma G., C.W. Godden, C.S.R. Hall, Peter Hall, Wilfred Harper, Elsmere Harris, Rose Hildebrand, Sir Reginald Hill, George E. Horton, Jack Howard, Bill Hutton, A.W. Knight, Tom Lawrence, Henry Mottram, Stan Nelson, Martin Jonathan Orson, Val Oxley, Frances Pratt, W.H. Pryce, G.H. Pursell, P.J.G. Ransom, H.A. Roberts, Sylvia Rudkin, Alfred Sapsford, R.C. Scriven, Malcolm Sellers, Victoria Smallpiece, Alma Starrett, John M. Sully, E. Taylor, Mike Taylor, Alfred Thomas, F.G. Tracey, Celia Turner, Pat Waldron, C.P. Weaver, C.R. Weaver, Ron Whatley, Arthur Wheeler, W. Howard Williams, Cyril Wills, Reginald Wood.

Photographs include some from my own collection but also others supplied by British Waterways, Newark Local History Library and Cadbury Limited, as well as drawings by Brian Hales.

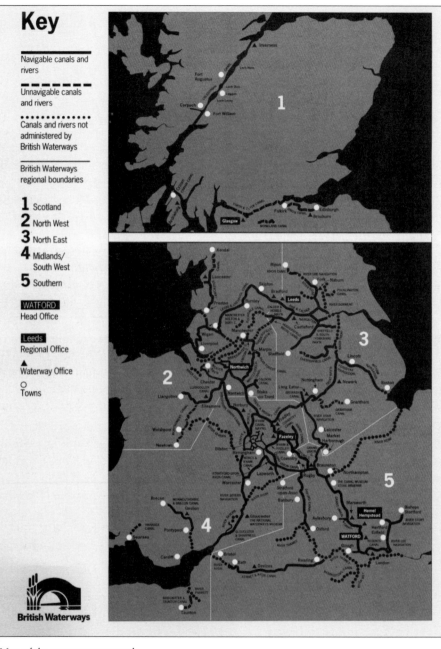

Map of the waterways network

Introduction

Sir Walter A. Raleigh (1861–1922) once wrote that 'An anthology is like all the plums and orange peel picked out of a cake.' I hope that the same criterion is met by the contents of this anthology, which are taken from the pages of news publications created for employees of the inland waterways network that was brought together by the Transport Act of 1947.

In September 1949 *Lock & Quay* was first published by the Docks & Inland Waterways Executive for its employees, but under a 1955 reorganization separating inland waterways from dock activities *Waterways Magazine* was launched. This was superseded in 1971 by *Waterways News*, in newspaper format, until regionalization of British Waterways in 1989, when it was retitled *New Ways*.

Collected here from these publications are contributions that were produced largely with topicality in mind and designed to have an immediate impact, usually being read in circumstances not allowing the maximum concentration, with the result that they were soon forgotten. Yet they can be read later with interest, enjoyment, amusement and even profit.

Unlike Britain's motorways, which belong entirely to the twentieth century, inland waterways offer a glimpse into the past and provide the finest opportunities for seeing the most beautiful and remote parts of our countryside. The charm of travelling slowly along a canal, sometimes high above the surrounding fields or through deep, tree-lined cuttings, has no equal. In adjacent villages or alongside the towpath, rustic pubs where bygone toilers refreshed themselves await discovery, while brightly painted craft and stone warehouses combine to create a feeling of stepping back into another era.

Indeed canals are probably our most hard-wearing and enduring legacy of the industrial revolution. Although their importance in transport terms has steadily declined since the war, some are still in everyday use for drainage, fire-fighting and industrial water supply, while many more are enjoying a renaissance for recreation by an increasing armada of pleasure-cruising enthusiasts, anglers and towpath ramblers.

Despite this, many people would be surprised to learn that there are more canals in the Black Country than in Venice. For example, the Birmingham

Canal Navigations, started by the engineer James Brindley in 1768 and improved on by Thomas Telford, who built a completely new line, is probably the most complex canal system in the world – certainly in Britain. It runs on three levels from Birmingham to Wolverhampton and Cannock and then back to Birmingham: a criss-cross of tunnels, by-passes, locks, bridges and aqueducts, 122 miles of it, cut over a 100-year period.

At the height of canal operations there was a route network of some 4,500 miles of navigable waterways carrying 30 million tons of freight a year. One of these was the Fossdyke from Torksey to Lincoln, built by the Romans probably for navigation as well as drainage. This apart, the first commercial canal in England was built at Exeter during the reign of Elizabeth I, to bypass a dam constructed on the orders of a Duchess of Devonshire in her efforts to prevent the merchants of Exeter from trading.

But development of the canal system proper really dates from the mid-eighteenth century. At this time the Duke of Bridgewater, crossed in love while living at his Hertfordshire mansion, retired to his Lancashire estate, where he built a canal to carry coal from his Worsley mine to Manchester. For centuries before this revolutionary innovation the coal had been slowly and expensively transported by pack horse.

Canal construction on the Continent had already been studied by the duke and he had the undoubted good fortune of having James Brindley, a millwright who could barely read or write, as his engineer. Brindley's engineering knowledge was entirely self-acquired but he tenaciously set himself to master the technique of canal building.

The duke almost suffered financial ruin in this first venture, which crossed the River Irwell on an aqueduct and later was carried deep into the mines. But his persistence paid off and the canal era was born, giving Brindley the opportunity to invent many devices that became standard canal practice, and with remarkable imagination to lay out the fundamental navigation plan for the whole country.

For about sixty years canal construction continued and initially meandered along land contours so as to avoid cuttings, embankments and locks. In a second phase the leading engineer, Thomas Telford, constructed canals along more direct routes, using the spoil from cuttings to build embankments.

Parochial politics resulted in early canals being conceived with purely local interests in mind, and consequently when longer journeys were undertaken the system suffered from a lack of dimensional uniformity. Apart from ship canals and main rivers, this resulted largely in two main types of inland waterway. Classification is broadly based on lock widths, but lengths also vary. Consequently some broad canals of the north have locks too short to take either broad or narrow boats from the south.

North of the River Trent most navigable waterways are classed as broad, with locks at least 12 ft wide, while narrow canals whose locks are 7 ft wide are found in a broad band from the south-east to the north-west of England. Operating on the narrow canals were the 70 ft long narrow boats (or monkey boats – but never barges). Usually working in pairs and initially hauled by horses, one boat had a diesel engine and the other (known as the butty) was towed. On wide waterways they operated side by side (breasted up) obviating the need for one person to steer each vessel.

In the heyday of canal operations it would appear that family boats with a cabin in which the boatman and his family lived were rare. Only later, when railway competition eroded traffic and revenue, were the boatmen forced by diminishing wages to give up their cottages, take their families aboard and become water gypsies.

Barges of widely varying dimensions and designs were built, but each vessel invariably conforms to the size permitted by locks in their working locality.

Canal mania was in full swing two centuries ago. Even the smallest town spawned companies anxious to plan and build canals; neither was there a shortage of willing investors to finance these ambitious proposals no matter how outlandish they were. Nevertheless, the resulting feats of civil engineering were prodigious not least for their ingenuity, imagination and sheer enormity of scale – reservoirs to maintain water at a constant level, aqueducts to carry canals across valleys, tunnels up to 4 miles long under hills, and sequences of locks to raise the boats from one level to another.

Coal and raw materials for industry were moved on a scale that would have been impossible by road at that time. In rural areas agricultural limestone, road and house building materials, fertilizer, grain and other bulk produce were transported by water, and passenger vessels carried farmers to market while high-speed craft provided the Intercity service of the day.

Indeed it was the advent of the railways that sounded the death knell of the canal system – faster, cheaper, more accessible. Improved roads contributed to the decline. Despite some modernization following nationalization and, more recently, restoration by some groups of enthusiasts, only around 2,000 miles of navigable waterways remain.

Nothing in this book, however, stands purely on its historical or even its nostalgic value; nothing has been included unless on re-reading it was found to be either entertaining, informative or thought-provoking. If the reader is in a serious mood and wishes to learn about some of the engineering feats associated with canal construction then 'Staircase to the South – The Story of Foxton' or 'Canal Inclined Planes of Shropshire' will probably entice. If on the other hand it is the people who fascinate, then the selection in the chapter entitled *Aristocrats to Tiller Girls* offers a wide diversity. Perhaps an antidote to sobriety is sought, in which case a mirthful remedy might be found in 'The Black Jack Mystery' or the antics of 'Five Girls and One Man . . . on a Boat'. Another possibility is a nostalgic yearning for yesteryear, recalled by 'The Great Frost of 1895', 'Honeymoon On the Canals in 1908', or 'Dad's Waterborne Army'. For the credulous there is the hair-raising tale of 'The Human Sacrifice', while 'Saturday Night Fever for Juliet's Ghost' is bound to induce a search for sanctuary whether it be in rationality or repose; and those of a more literary disposition will find solace in reflective contemplation of the poetic contributions.

I hope you will enjoy reading this anthology as much as I have enjoyed compiling it.

one

Tides of Joy

Two Centuries of a Water Highway Sponsored by Bradford Merchants

Riding their horses slowly and cautiously down the steep slope of Ivegate was a picturesque cavalcade of Lancashire and Yorkshire merchants, gentlemen, and yeomen resplendent in wigs and quaint hats, with heavy riding boots and colourful costumes showing beneath their riding cloaks. This was the scene in Bradford just two hundred years ago when nobility, gentry and clergy gathered at the Sign of the Sun Inn for the first meeting to sponsor the construction of the Leeds & Liverpool Canal.

The meeting to examine the proposal had been arranged for what in those days was considered the early hour of 10 a.m. and appears to have been successful in securing adequate financial backing from Bradford merchants and others. Among the list of subscribers was Mr John Day, mine host of the Sign of the Sun who donated one guinea, which doubtless represented only a small part of his profits from the sale of numerous draughts of punch, tankards of ale, bottles of port, and other liquid refreshment over which the merit and fortunes of the project had been discussed under his roof.

The idea of building a canal was prompted by the disgraceful condition of the roads which made transportation of merchandise at the time both tedious and costly. West Riding merchants were already able to use the River Aire from Leeds to the River Ouse to convey their products to the ports of the Humber and they shared the view with Lancashire colliery owners that they should have water communication both east and west.

Liverpool was rapidly rising into the first rank as a sea port although the population was given as only 34,000, but the slave trade was then at its zenith and Liverpool was the commercial and financial centre of the traffic. Support for the idea had also been expressed by newspapers of the day and in August 1764 one had gone so far as to point out that 'no season can be so proper for effecting works of this nature as times of peace when men and money can be not otherwise so well employed'.

1

Only six years elapsed before assent was given to an Act of Parliament for the construction of the canal

> which will open a short and easy communication between the several populous towns of Leeds, Bradford, Bingley, Keighley, Skipton . . . and the ports of Hull and Liverpool . . . which will be of great advantage not only to the trade carried on to and from the said ports but to many various and very valuable manufacturies which abound in most of the towns and places above mentioned.

Construction work started at both ends in the same year, 1770, and was completed in sections over a period of forty-six years. The result is the longest single canal in the country, 127 miles from Leeds to Liverpool, which rises to 487 ft above sea level to cross the Pennines. This rise necessitates forty-four locks on the Yorkshire side and forty-eight locks are required for the descent into Lancashire.

Among the problems that faced the engineer James Brindley, who planned the project, was raising the canal over a rapid change in the contour of the ground near Bingley where in less than 150 yards there is a total rise of 60 ft. His solution was the famous five-rise locks, which have been hailed as one of the seven wonders of the inland waterways. These locks lead direct from one to

An artist captures for posterity the scenic grandeur of the Five Rise Locks at Bingley, opened in 1774

the other so that the bottom gates of the first lock at high level are also the top gates of the second lock. Consequently, in the five locks there are only six sets of gates to pass through and five changes in water level.

The opening of this section of the canal, from Bingley eastwards, was greeted with almost lyrical enthusiasm by the *Leeds Intelligencer* when it reported:

> The noblest works of the kind that perhaps are not to be found in the same extent in the universe are exhibited viz:- a fivefold, a threefold, a twofold, and a single lock, making together a fall of 120 feet; a large aqueduct bridge of seven arches over the River Aire and an aqueduct and a large banking over the Shipley Valley. This joyful and much wished-for event was welcomed with ringing of Bingley bells, a band of music, the firing of guns by the neighbouring militia, the shouts of spectators, and all the marks of satisfaction that so important an acquisition merits.

Section by section, like Topsy, the canal 'just growed' and in addition to the carriage of goods, provided an opportunity for more comfortable passenger travel. Towards the end of the eighteenth century passengers were invited to take *The Packet*, a noted stagecoach from Bradford and Leeds to Bingley where they transferred to canal packet boats to proceed to 'Skipton, Liverpool and America'. This startling announcement conjures up visions of Bradford paupers emigrating to seek their fortune in the New World!

The advent of railways with their speedier transits precipitated the decline of canals such as the Leeds and Liverpool for commercial purposes. But it provides some of the most picturesque scenery in the north which provides a backcloth for modern pleasure-boating enthusiasts and patient anglers.

One Hundred and Fiftieth Anniversary of the Caledonian Canal, 1822–1972

Proposals to build a canal to link north and south Scotland were put forward early in the 1700s but nothing came of these until 1773 when James Watt on behalf of the Government surveyed the route.

Watt published his report in 1774 but nothing was done about the report, until 1801 when the Government asked Thomas Telford to investigate the causes for the high level of emigration from the Highlands at that time.

In his report he underlined the fact that the provision of suitable public works schemes such as the canal would not only bring immediate employment to the area but also increase the fishery and agricultural industry.

The final incentive for the construction of the canal came with the hope of safeguarding British shipping from attacks by French privateers. Telford estimated that a canal 20 ft deep would be cut from Corpach Basin in Beauly Firth near Inverness. He reckoned it would take seven years to complete at a cost of around £350,000.

In July 1803 an Act of Parliament received the Royal Assent granting the sum of £20,000 towards the cost of the project, and Thomas Telford was appointed principal engineer at £3 15s. per day plus travelling expenses. The consulting engineer was William Jessop, who estimated the cost of completing the canal at around £474,500. A further Act of Parliament of 1804 authorized an additional grant of £50,000 per annum towards construction costs.

Turf houses were built for the canal workmen and workshops were erected for blacksmiths, carpenters and other tradesmen. Wood for the project, principally fir and birch, was bought locally and food for the labourers was stored at Corpach. Even a herd of cows was established to give the canal workmen a fresh supply of milk daily. Initially 150 men including some Highlanders who had worked on another canal project in the south of Scotland were employed at the rate of $7\frac{1}{2}$d. a day. Any man who demanded more was not employed.

The construction work involved was more arduous, costly and tedious than had been anticipated. The number of labourers employed rose very quickly to over 900. However, most of these were local people and their attendance was intermittent as they put the potato harvesting and herring fishing and peat cutting seasons before their work on the canal.

Despite the difficulties, work proceeded and by 1809 three of the eight locks known today as 'Neptune's Staircase' near Fort William were completed. It was 1811, however, before the other five were completed.

Workmen at the east end of the canal at Clachnaharry had been having problems with constant flooding by sea water in the lock pits. Hand pumps were inadequate so these were replaced by a large chain pump worked by six horses, but the strain began to tell on the animals and one of the canal's 6 hp steam engines had to be brought into operation before work could proceed normally.

By 1812 less than half the canal had been finished and the expenditure had amounted to nearly £343,000.

There had been unexpected technical problems, legal problems and, as in modern times, rising costs of materials and labourers' wages. Even the cost of oatmeal to feed the workmen had doubled its price. By 1819 the canal had cost £700,000 and it was estimated that another £80,000 was needed to complete it.

As the year 1822 approached there were many public and private controversies on the usefulness of the canal and Telford had to defend the canal every inch of its way. The Loch Ness and eastern district was opened for

Overlooked by Highland peaks are the locks known as 'Neptune's Staircase' on the Crinan Canal

navigation in May 1818 to coasting vessels importing and exporting a variety of goods. One hundred and fifty voyages were made in the first summer.

In November 1820 Henry Ball ran a steam boat service, the *Stirling Castle*, which left Muirtown Locks at Inverness at 8 o'clock and arrived at Fort Augustus six hours later. The locks at the Corpach basin were in operation from 1819.

By 1822 criticism of the canal as a feasible economic venture had reached a peak. The project was being attacked from all sides including opposers in the Houses of Parliament, and in an effort to take some heat out of the controversy it was decided officially to open the canal in October 1822.

The *Inverness Courier* reported the opening of the canal: 'the Loch Ness steam yacht and another boat departed from the locks at Muirtown on their first voyage through the canal amidst the loud and enthusiastic cheering of a great concourse of people. . .'.

At Dochgarroch Lock the band of the Inverness Militia went aboard and as the party sailed down Loch Ness:

. . . the reverberation of the firing, repeated and prolonged by a thousand echoes from the surrounding hills, glens and rocks – the martial music –

the shouts of the highlanders – and the answering cheers of the party on board, produced an effect which will not soon be forgotten by those present.

The voyage was broken at Fort Augustus where, having been greeted by the whole population of the district, the voyagers spent the night.

The boats continued on the voyage at 6 a.m. the next day, reaching Corpach Basin late the same afternoon.

The termination of the voyage was marked by a grand salute from the Fort, whilst the inhabitants of Fort William demonstrated their joy by kindling a large bonfire. A plentiful supply of whisky, given by the gentlemen of Fort William, did not in the least tend to dampen the ardour of the populace. At half past 7 o'clock 67 gentlemen, the guests of Mr Grant sat down in the hall of the Mason's Lodge to a handsome and plentiful dinner.

After the official opening, criticism tended to die away and the canal was left to prove itself as a useful route between the north-eastern and south-western waters of Scotland.

Between May 1823 and May 1824, 844 vessels used the canal, 278 of these had passed from sea to sea. Three steamboats were operating between Glasgow and Inverness and at the end of 1825 the canal had been deepened to 15 ft throughout.

However, defects in the unfinished canal soon became apparent. The lack of towing paths alongside the lochs caused extensive delay to sailing craft when the wind was in the wrong quarter, and much of the middle section was suffering from the use of inferior stone and timber. Some £977,524 had been spent on construction work up to 1 January 1828 and though nearly 800 craft made passage the previous year, a deficit occurred on the year's working.

For a while as sail gave way to steam and the calms and the funnelling winds of the open waters of Loch Lochy and Loch Ness mattered less, things did improve. But with the loss of the Baltic timber trade due to the imposition of a 300 per cent duty, the main users were fishing vessels, coasters and passenger steamers.

There were several mishaps between 1834 and 1849. In 1834 after rain which had raised the level of Loch Ness by 2 ft in one night the Mucomir outlet of Loch Lochy was blocked and the water level in the loch rose to 3 ft above the top of Gairlochy lock gates.

In 1837 the north-west recess wall at the bottom lock at Fort Augustus gave way. In 1844 during repairs by the contractors Jackson and Bean of

Birmingham, Bean fell in the canal with his horse from an insecure bridge and was killed. January 1849 was stormy and there was serious flooding in Inverness. The canal bank was breached at Dochgarroch, at Aberchalder and in the reach between Aberchalder and Kytra. Flood water from Loch Ness poured through the breach at Dochgarroch until the water level in the loch was 6 ft above the regulating weir.

In 1837 the Board of Commissioners, worried about the increasing deficit, asked James Walker to report upon the condition and prospects of the canal. He estimated that it would cost nearly £130,000 to complete it as originally proposed, but the cost of abandonment would be at least as expensive. Repair work started in September 1843 and was completed nearly four years later. The improvements included deepening it to 17 ft throughout, the construction of an additional lock at Gairlochy and the provision of four steam tugs for towage purposes.

But revenue inevitably dropped as steam ships became bigger. In 1863 more than 15,000 passengers passed through the canal by steamer, but two years later the Perth–Inverness railway opened and inevitably the canal lost passengers to the age of speed.

In 1873 Queen Victoria journeyed through the canal in the passenger steamer *Gondolier*. The *Gondolier* was built in 1866 specially designed for service on the Caledonian Canal with comfortable accommodation for 622 passengers and 13 crew on her. She left the canal service in 1939 when she was taken by the Admiralty to Scapa Flow for scuttling.

John Davidson, who had been resident engineer of the Crinan Canal, was appointed engineer of the Caledonian Canal, and in 1888 he reported that 27½ of the 42 pairs of lock gates were made of cast iron with a sheathing of timber, while 12½ pairs were of timber only and two pairs were oak, larch and steel with a sheathing of pitch-pine. The cast iron gates were in an unsatisfactory state and the masonry of several locks had suffered from their excessive weight.

Davidson asked the Chancellor of the Exchequer for a grant of £20,000 so that all the lock gates on the canal could be replaced by new ones of oak and steel. He received the grant in instalments from 1890 to 1893, and by 1906 all the gates had been renewed.

By 1909 a Royal Commission dismissed the canal as antiquated. One year later more defects in the original masonry were revealed when Laggan Lock collapsed and banks at Corpach, Banavie and Fort Augustus crumbled.

However the canal was to prove its value in the two world wars when the Pentland Firth once more became dangerous because of enemy ships. During the First World War some 48,000 tons of mines and military stores had a safe passage from the Atlantic to the North Sea via the Caledonian Canal. During the war years there was no revenue because all the vessels using the canal had been brought officially under Admiralty control, but a Treasury loan of £20,000 was made during 1916 to 1919 which partly made up for the canal losses.

In 1920 management of the canal was transferred to the Ministry of Transport and in 1926 they closed the canal for nine weeks for a general repair of masonry and the eight locks at Banavie were thoroughly restored.

The centenary – 1922 – of the opening of the canal caused a comment from the *Glasgow Herald* that it was 'questionable whether the canal had ever justified the expense it entailed' and the Ministry of Transport refused to consider plans submitted for the reconstruction of the canal.

More trouble in 1929 when a herring drifter burst through two lock gates at Banavie, causing flooding damage and the closure of the canal for three months. All passenger services had ceased by 1939 and during the years of the Second World War the canal was again used for the transport of military goods and personnel.

The mechanization of the canal locks completed by British Waterways Board in 1968 has cut the time for the passage of a boat by around two hours.

The Chesterfield Canal, 1777–1977

Retford and Worksop do not really conjure up visions of the ideal locations to spend a holiday. But as they are both situated on the Chesterfield Canal, in parts one of the most idyllic of waterways, one could well be very wrong.

Access to the canal is via the River Trent at West Stockwith, 4½ miles north of Gainsborough and 1½ hours by water from Keadby lock which is the nearest canal outlet into the Trent downstream.

Adjacent to West Stockwith Lock is a large basin that gives safe moorings to many sea-going vessels. Here too, a marine repair and sales company offers facilities.

The canal is navigable as far as Worksop, a distance of 26 miles. The locks from West Stockwith to Retford are wide. Some locks have most peculiar names and one of them, perhaps the most unusual of them all, is Whitsunday Pie, located just before Retford, so called because a repair to this lock was completed on Whitsunday and a local farmer's wife baked a large pie to celebrate the event.

On the route there is one tunnel, Drakeholes, which is 154 yds in length and only partly lined as it cuts through solid rock. Many bridges cross the canal ranging from rustic stone bridges of character to concrete afterthoughts. One of the most fascinating is Old Man's Bridge on the Wiseton Estate; a stone structure with a man's head carved on each side in the centre of the span.

Drakeholes Basin is a haven of rural solitude for pleasure cruisers

The canal in many places is a typical James Brindley contour canal, twisting and turning on its route through and around villages, some of them well worth exploring.

The waterway is a haven for the naturalist. Swallows, the summer visitors, swoop over the water on warm evenings catching insects. The mute swans that glide majestically over the water complete any waterway scene. Of course the moorhens that are very common among British birds are there; liking dense vegetation these little black birds with red on their forehead and beak can be seen swimming from one set of cover to another, flashing their tails occasionally to show a patch of white. The kingfisher, usually seen as flashes of blue, frequents the waterway especially in areas with high banks in which it nests. Mallard, common on so many canals, can be seen in great numbers, with the most handsome drake adorned with a bottle green head, and magnificent plumage catching everyone's eye.

The heron when disturbed flies off with beating wings and trailing legs to return shortly to continue its stance, ready to pounce on to fish easily discernible in the clear water. Reed warblers, house martins, yellow wagtails and coot among others, help to make the ornithologists's lot a happy one.

The plant distribution along the canal banks is interesting with hedges of thorn and wild roses in places, along with honeysuckle, old man's beard and ivy. Flowering plants abound, the hairy willowherb with its many mauve pink flowers, and smaller plants like marsh marigold with golden flowers. The

9

Chesterfield Canal with so much to offer the naturalist is without doubt a beautiful canal with plenty to appeal.

The canal, like so many other waterways, was projected with the best of intentions. At a meeting in August 1769 at Worksop, James Brindley presented a scheme for the canal from Stockwith to Chesterfield via Worksop, Retford and Drakeholes Hill, estimated to cost £95,000.

The scheme was adopted and the route accepted with the landowners on the route endorsing their enthusiasm for the project by subscribing capital. Brindley was appointed the engineer on a salary of £300 a year, but stated that he could not give his full attention because of his many other commitments, and so his pupil John Varley was made Clerk of Works.

At a further meeting in June 1772 Brindley put forward his plans, first to complete the 2,895 yd tunnel in two years through the magnesium limestone ridge at Norwood, followed by a length of canal from the east of the tunnel to Shireoaks. He estimated that the canal would be completed in four years.

Work started on the tunnel. Meanwhile Brindley died and the committee left Varley in charge until Hugh Henshall was appointed engineer in March 1774. It was found that during the interim period Varley had failed to do his duty in the correct manner, passing work of inferior quality, and giving lucrative contracts to members of his family. Varley admitted the error of his ways and was made to enter a bond of £500 for the proper performance of his duties.

Financial problems arose and the proprietors suspended certain construction work until further cash was borrowed on individuals' personal security. During August 1774 contracts were issued for canal cutting from West Stockwith. In April 1776 the canal was opened from Stockwith to Killamarsh. Then shortage of money again became a serious problem, only resolved when £53,000 was borrowed from bankers at York and Nottingham. The influx of cash was sufficient to complete the canal and it was opened throughout in June 1977.

The tunnel at Norwood was opened on 9 May 1775, having taken less than four years to build. The opening was celebrated by the passage of 300 people, in boats, through the tunnel. On board one of the boats was a band, which performed during the voyage lasting one hour and one minute.

The opening of the canal on 4 June 1777 was marked by bringing a boat loaded with goods from West Stockwith to Chesterfield. The boat was met at the first lock by the proprietors, members of the committee and also by many local people. The boats moored up to the unfurling of flags, the firing of guns and the playing of a band. The goods were unloaded into wagons and these were hauled by the navigators to the town centre. Festivities followed including a banquet, bonfire, bell ringing and fireworks.

The expected traffic failed to materialize immediately and the liability of the loan bore heavily upon the finances of the company. Five years after the opening income was only £4,811, less than a third of what had been expected. Traffic eventually built up so that it was possible to pay the shareholders a 6 per cent dividend and the peak of traffic was reached in 1848. Early in 1840 the first cargo of Anston stone for the new Houses of Parliament was carried on the canal to West Stockwith for transhipment. Approximately 250,000 tons were dispatched.

With the coming of the Railway Age, a line was proposed in 1884 from Sheffield to Gainsborough, called the Sheffield and Lincolnshire Junction Railway, which would follow the canal line for part of its route, and was backed by the Sheffield, Ashton and Manchester Railway. To counter this proposal the proprietors of the Chesterfield Canal formed the Manchester and Lincoln Union Railway in 1845, intending to use the canal for parts of the line. The committees of the two railways formed a joint committee and agreed to future amalgamation.

Under the Act of 7 August 1846 the M&LUR was authorized to build the line from the Midland Railway at Staveley to the canal at Worksop, and also to amalgamate the railway and canals as the Manchester and Lincoln Union Railway and Chesterfield and Gainsborough Canal Company. Authorization was also given to amalgamate with the S&LJR. The canal lease was valued at £147,912 and the Canal Company was dissolved, the M&LUR leasing the canal in perpetuity.

The new body was not to dispose of any part of the canal, but to keep it in good order, preserve its water supplies and maintain just tolls. After amalgamation the M&LUR gave notice to the S&LJR to amalgamate. By this time the latter had been taken into the Manchester, Sheffield and Lincolnshire Railway. As a result of this the new Manchester and Lincolnshire Railway was amalgamated with the MS&LR on 9 July 1847.

At first the canal was improved and maintained and showed a resulting increase in revenue, and the Railway Company started to carry goods on the canal. A large proportion of the maintenance was repairs due to subsidence. The Company carried 7,811 tons out of 118,946 tons carried along the canal in 1854. In July 1863 it was decided to combine the canal with the railway for accounting and management purposes, resulting in the canal losing its independence completely.

Between 1871 and 1906 approximately £21,000 was spent on repairing Norwood Tunnel, including opening out a short length. Finally a roof collapse in 1908, by the Hartfill to Kiveton Park Road, caused the tunnel to be closed. This led to the cessation of most of the commercial traffic above Shireoaks; coal was carried from there until the end of the Second World War.

Between the two world wars the London and North Eastern Railway, which then owned the canal, continued to maintain it. The tidal lock at West

Stockwith was enlarged and repaired between 1923 and 1925. Attempts were made to cut and reduce the weeds, which have been a great problem in the canal, severely hindering navigation since its first appearance in 1852.

Two proposals were made to turn parts of the canal into roads (there is a proposal at present to use the canal line for a road between Chesterfield and Staveley). The last commercial traffic was bricks from Walkinham to Stockwith and this ceased in 1955. The canal then fell into disuse and became unnavigable. Since 1961 the canal has been gradually improved from Worksop to West Stockwith for pleasure cruising and now forms part of the British Waterways cruising network.

The Trent and Mersey Canal – 200 Years of Service, 1777–1977

Not only does 1977 witness the Silver Jubilee of our Queen, it also commemorates the two hundredth anniversary of the completion of the Trent and Mersey Canal. This canal is one of Britain's most historic waterways.

Its 93$^1/_2$ mile main line passing through Derbyshire, Staffordshire and Cheshire – links the River Trent at Shardlow (between Derby and Nottingham) with the Bridgewater Canal at Preston Brook (near Runcorn on Merseyside). On its route are the towns and cities of Burton-on-Trent, Stone, Berlaston, Stoke-on-Trent, Kidsgrove, Middlewich and Northwich.

In common with many schemes drawn up during the eighteenth century throughout the rapidly expanding Midlands and north, the pressing need was to provide a cheap and rapid means of transport by which merchandise could be moved from its source to its destination. Before the Industrial Revolution, the provision of an efficient means of transport was not such a crucial issue and the pack-horse or wagon was the usual form of conveyance.

If one reads the accounts of the early county historians, for example Sampson Erdeswick, the impression gained is that the geographical area covered by the North Staffordshire coalfield was devoid of any appreciable industry. It appears to have consisted of poor arable land and had few towns and villages worthy of note, in fact an area to be avoided by all but the traveller journeying through.

Dr Robert Plot, however, writing in the 1680s, does remark upon the growing pottery industry centred on Burslem. His observations show that the pottery trade was on the point of transition and about to expand to the demands not only of an élitist society but also the requirements of the industrial workers in the mills, mines and factories throughout the country during the late Georgian and Victorian eras.

At this time, even the best of roads were totally unsuitable for the bulk conveyance of goods. They were frequently the cause of costly breakages and perhaps, more importantly, often impassable during the winter and spring months.

Promoted by the famous potter, Josiah Wedgwood, and engineered by James Brindley, the original purpose of building a canal was to bring into North Staffordshire the raw materials for the growing pottery industry and to transport to Liverpool finished wares. This soon lived up to its original title of 'The Grand Trunk' and became the backbone of the fast expanding north Midland canal network.

Brindley surveyed the proposed 'cut' in 1758 at the request of Earl Gower and Lord Anson. The original plan was, however, abandoned mainly because of lack of funds, but the demands of the growing industries of North Staffordshire revived the initial interest and only eight years later, after much hard thinking, and speculation, it was decided, probably as a result of the success of the Duke of Bridgewater's canal from Worsley to Manchester, to resurrect the scheme.

In 1765 an association was formed to obtain the necessary parliamentary powers to construct the canal and Josiah Wedgwood spent the next year issuing pamphlets explaining the advantages of the scheme and soliciting help.

The Act of Parliament for the Trent and Mersey was passed on 14 May 1766 and a committee was formed to carry out the work. Josiah, who had subscribed £1,000 in shares towards the cost of the scheme, was elected Honorary Treasurer and offered security of £10,000.

On 26 July 1766 he cut the first sod at Brownhills, between Burslem and Tunstall, in front of a large crowd. It is recorded that an ox was roasted to commemorate the occasion.

The canal was not fully opened until eleven years later, in May 1777, mainly because of time needed to drive the 2,879 yd Harecastle Tunnel – one of the wonders of its time. Because of subsidence of the original tunnel, a parallel bore was driven through Harecastle Hill by Thomas Telford between 1824 and 1827.

The opening of the Trent and Mersey Canal represented a great engineering triumph for Brindley – although he never saw its completion as he died in September 1772. It passed through the Wedgwood estate at Etruria and a branch was brought to the factory itself.

In a letter to R.L. Edgeworth on 13 February 1786, Wedgwood remarks about the cost of the venture: 'I cannot give you any satisfactory account of the price of cutting our canal per mile. The whole length of the canal is 94 miles and it has cost to complete it near £300,000 but I suppose the mere cutting of a mile of our canal would not cost more than £700 or £800.'

However, the reduction in transportation costs more than compensated for the initial outlay. The cost of transport was effectively reduced from 10d. to 1³/₄d. per mile per ton for material.

An amusing account of Wedgwood's 'close link' with the canal was recorded in a book by Henry Wedgwood *Romance of Staffordshire* when he writes about Francis Wedgwood (third son of Josiah Wedgwood II).

During a long icy winter when the canal was frozen over Mr Wedgwood:

> . . . took a short cut from his hall to the works by crossing over the icy bound canal instead of going round to the bridge at a little distance. This he did for days together, taking it as a matter of course, as though the convenient cut was going to last for ever, and the ice was never going to change to water.
>
> One morning a little mildness was observed in the weather and there was every sign of a break up. So mustering up courage the ice boat released from its frozen position, and with the aid of about 15 horses and 30 or 40 men, made its way along the canal. Mr Wedgwood unaware of this fact, and the change which had taken place, came gaily on, selecting as usual the near cut over the canal. But stepping upon the ice as he imagined, he stepped up to the middle in the water, and thus for a second time that morning took a cold bath.

Some of the major engineering works on the Trent and Mersey Canal include three tunnels; at Preston Brook, Barnton and Saltersford, and a long aqueduct over the River Dove near Burton-on-Trent. Forty locks raise the canal 316 ft from Derwent Mouth, Shardlow to the summit level at Harecastle, and it descends 326 ft via thirty-six locks to Preston Brook. Many of the canal's minor structures date from its original construction and are, of course, aesthetically pleasing and of considerable historical interest.

Of the canal companies operating throughout Staffordshire, the Trent and Mersey was the second largest carrier of freight, being second only in importance to those concerns controlled by the Birmingham Canal Navigations. Freight returns from 1846–68 give some idea of the extent to which goods were being transported via local inland waterways. During this period, 1,341,6212 tons (1848), 1,363,384 (1858) and 1,494,525 (1868) tons respectively had been carried by the company. In addition to coal, goods included raw materials for the pottery trade such as china clay, bones, borax, cobalt, and frits. Finished ceramic products, timber, grain and South Staffordshire iron were also transported on this canal.

Commercial carrying is now confined to the short haul of ware between two canalside potteries in Stoke and the sale of house coal by narrow boat.

Designated a cruising waterway under the 1968 Transport Act, the canal's major uses are now for pleasure craft, angling, water supply, and land drainage. The Trent and Mersey has benefited from the rapidly increasing pastime of canal cruising and there are now considerable numbers of boats privately-owned and holiday-hire craft, both based on and using the waterway.

The association of Wedgwood and the Trent and Mersey Canal continues to the present day, as the waterway runs alongside the Barlaston factory and through part of the Wedgwood Estate. And it is appropriate that the 1977 bicentenary of the completion of the canal should be celebrated at a rally organized by the Trent and Mersey Canal Society on Wedgwood land alongside the canal. As co-sponsors Wedgwood Limited provided special facilities for the event.

At 3.15 p.m. on Saturday 28 May 1977 the firing of a siege cannon, mounted in a canalside field in the Wedgwood estate, officially marked the beginning of the bicentenary celebrations.

The Lord Lieutenant of Staffordshire, Sir Arthur Bryan, who is also Chairman of Wedgwood, carried out this ceremony – a re-enactment of the cannon firing which celebrated the opening of the Stoke-on-Trent section of the canal over two centuries ago.

Yorkshire Ouse – River of Destiny

An official ceremony took place in York in April 1990 to commemorate the transfer of the River Ouse Navigation from York City Council to British Waterways in October 1989.

The navigation is 41½ miles in length stretching from Widdington Ings, approximately 10 miles north of York, to a point 100 yds downstream of Goole railway bridge. British Waterways now control navigation from Ripon to Goole, with access to their northern network at Selby via the Selby Canal.

Unlike most rivers the Yorkshire Ouse has no mountain source. It is born of the union of the Ure with an insignificant stream called Ouse Gill Beck, and does not begin its journey, as is often erroneously suggested, at the junction of the Ure and Swale further north.

The Yorkshire Ouse has been used for centuries as a navigable river, most spectacularly by the Vikings in AD 886 when laying siege to capture the City of Eboracum, named by the Romans, and renaming it Yorvik from which the present name of York has been derived.

Conservancy of the river, first established as long ago as 1805, was confirmed by charters of Edward IV in 1462, which vested it in the hands of the Lord Mayor, Aldermen and Recorders of the City of York.

At this time the river was tidal throughout its length – the tide flowing up to 4 ft at Ouse Bridge in York, and consequently small sailing vessels were able to link the city by direct water connection to the coast and London.

That the Ouse continues in its present channel is purely fortuitous, for around 1616, in the reign of James I, a bold scheme was put forward to engineer a gigantic tidal canal of about 25 miles in almost a direct line from Fulford Beck, south or York, to Blacktoft on the Humber.

As always finance was scarce and York Corporation sought support from the King when he visited the city.

Arriving at Ouse Bridge he was welcomed by a brief charade composed by a local rhymester. This was produced 'to declare the shallowness of the River of Ouse', and in one memorable line, the 'tired river' who was the chief speaker complains, 'I scarce have means to ebbe or power to flow.'

The plea seemed to have touched the royal sympathies and James I encouraged the Corporation to promote the necessary Act of Parliament. Tenacious almost to the point of desperation they persisted, but their efforts never came to fruition, and the old Ouse was left to its own devices apart from some dredging near the city.

Navigation of the Ouse, which varies in width from over 1,500 ft at Trent Falls, to about 200 ft at York, and has thirty bends of less than 100 ft radius between the city and the Humber, was always difficult. In this section the tides are by no means insignificant, flooding in with a fierce rush possibly unequalled by any other river in England.

The flood tide averages about 6 knots, bringing about 17 ft of water at Goole and 10 ft at Naburn; and this after much of the river's tidal flow has been swallowed by the Humber after the draining of Hatfield Chase by Dutch engineer Cornelius Vermuyden.

Acts of Parliament in 1727 and 1732 reorganized the Trustees of the Ouse (henceforth a committee of York City Council) and enabled them to levy realistic tolls.

These ranged from 2s. 6d. (13½p.) for the conveyance of a ton of groceries or wine, to 6d. (2½p.) for such items as salt or corn. From the complaints in the Trustees' well-preserved leather-bound minute books, it is clear that many found a means to evade such payment.

Despite these practices toll receipts did increase with a result that the Trustees were able to get themselves a £10,000 lock at Naburn some 5 miles below York.

Opened in 1757 with a toll of 1s. 2d. (6p.) levied on every vessel passing through, the lock was hailed as a great stride towards boosting river navigation for commerce to York.

With an eye on future prospects, Linton Lock Commissioners were

Standing about 12 ft high, this stone obelisk is situated in the grounds of a former workhouse at Great Ouseburn. Ravaged by wind and rain, it bears four inscriptions: 'Ouse River Head, Ouse Gill Spring Ft, York 13 miles, Boroughbridge 4 miles'

empowered by Parliament in 1767 to improve the upper reaches of the Ouse and part of the River Ure. Subsequently they built locks at Linton-on-Ouse and Boroughbridge.

For almost a century the Ouse was probably the most important means of transport possessed by towns like Selby and York. An estimate for 1835 reveals that 93,000 tons of coal, 40,000 tons of stone and 9,000 tons of general merchandise were carried annually on the river. And the number of travellers who ventured by water was stated to be in excess of 20,000 each year!

Amid great local interest the iron paddle steamer *Arrow* made her maiden voyage on 16 March 1835 and after the completion of a second steamer called *Ebor*, the *York Herald* was even speculating on a direct steamer connection with France, though nothing so exotic resulted.

However there were soon regular steam services to Goole and by 1838 the speedy *City of York* was plying between the county town and Hull.

But someone had to pay the price of progress. Smoke nuisance sometimes arose, and on one occasion the Archbishop of York was moved to write to the Trustees requesting them to ensure that steamers' furnaces were not stoked when the vessels were passing his palace at Bishopthorpe.

Sensing impending problems with the advent of railways, in 1834 the Trustees had, on the recommendation of the famous Thomas Telford hired Thomas Rhodes, 'a very skilful mechanic', to report on the condition of the river.

He found the Ouse 'well calculated to carry on trade to an almost unlimited extent, were it not for the shoals and obstacles', which impeded navigation and often left larger boats high and dry for days on end.

Many portions of the river bank he found to be 'in a state of nature' reflecting neglect of maintenance and resulting in a poor towing path as well as an increase of shoals on the river bed.

The answer, suggested Rhodes, was a £33,000 scheme of improvements, which included a new lock at Naburn. The heaviest task was 'the removal of the great shoal at Acaster Selby', which had grown to some 2¼ miles long, and had been the undoing of many an unlucky keel or barge.

The new, bigger lock at Naburn was formally opened amidst great rejoicing by Prince Albert Victor on 22 July 1888, when all vessels carrying 200 tons or more were allowed to pass through free of tolls all day.

The *Wild Rose* carrying a cargo of 720 quarters of wheat – the largest consignment that had ever passed up to York until then – was the first vessel to be piloted through the lock.

Trade soon improved remarkably, but the inexorable pressure of competing railways had its inevitable effect. Nevertheless, in 1979 some 25,000 tons of cargo in 160 barges passed through the locks as did 1,400 pleasure craft, which confirms that the enterprise was not in vain.

In the same year over 400 ships and nearly 300 barges landed 270,000 tons of merchandise at Selby – 65 miles from the sea – in addition to cargoes landed at Howden Dyke wharves and elsewhere on the river banks.

In addition to York, the river also boasts many treasures that have always attracted visitors – including unwelcome ones like Harald Hardrada with his invading force of 500 ships bearing a horde of marauding Norsemen, who sailed up and ransacked the city.

Cawood Castle, home of Cardinal Wolsey, was in 1465 the setting of the biggest banquet ever held in England; Drax electricity generating station boasts the tallest chimney in the country (859 ft high); Selby's pride is its ancient Abbey and new super coalfield [1991]; and going down river the £10 million concrete bridge which lifts the M62 over the river at Howden is a fitting overture to Goole.

two

Beyond the Locks

An Inland Voyage

I am feeling rather proud of my veteran canal boat, *Christine*. She was built in 1915 or 1916 and must have borne thousands of tons of cargo before she came into my hands just after the war, when I converted her into an inland cruiser. Now she had carried me over 250 miles of canal and river and through 210 locks, in twelve days and with unfailing reliability.

As in 1950, the Docks and Inland Waterways Executive granted a concession of half rate travel for the purpose of attending the Inland Waterways Association rally of boats, this year organized by the Midlands Branch on the Avon at Tewkesbury.

I decided to take advantage of this generosity to add to my small store of canal knowledge by covering the greatest possible distance in the time at my disposal.

The route I planned took in parts of the Grand Union, Stratford-upon-Avon and Birmingham and Worcester Canals, the Severn and Avon, the Worcestershire and Staffordshire, Trent and Mersey, Coventry, Oxford, and once more back into the Grand Union Canal.

Such a route could not fail to offer an intense variety of interest, but it demanded twelve or fourteen hours of travel nearly every day, and inevitably, the sacrifice of that rare tranquillity which is the reward of more leisurely waterway journeying. On the other hand, it is doubtful whether travel by any other means could have afforded so balanced a picture of the agriculture, architecture, transport, mining and industry which have shaped the development of England.

Although we voyaged in a big circle enclosing the Black Country and Birmingham, and indeed often on their very fringes, the overwhelming impression was of the honest, natural, beauty of the Midland shires. There was much evidence of the work of our engineering and industrial pioneers, and in spite of the many drab views presented, it was not possible to forget that the courage and foresight of those men have put our country in the forefront of technical ability.

At the very commencement of our journey we were faced, in sheeting rain, with the 2½ hour grind up Hatton locks – twenty-one of them. Not far above Hatton Top and in kinder weather we entered the top portion of the Stratford-upon-Avon Canal which has an evil reputation among amateur inland navigators. The first few miles of this waterway were so charming that one is beguiled into thinking that its bad name is underserved.

Disenchantment is swift as one comes into the outskirts of Birmingham. More hours were spent than miles covered in negotiating the upper extremity of the canal. The depth of water would have been inadequate to a punt, and under every bridge was a practically impassable bar of rubbish. In sober truth, more than half-an-hour's back-breaking struggle with shafts and lines was necessary to get under each of several bridges. Our propeller was constantly fouled with rubbish, and when we had removed a good sized coconut mat from its blades, it promptly picked up a jacket and a bicycle tyre. I also retrieved a bicycle, complete except for tyres, saddle and bell.

When I was on the point of desperation, we at last reached a point which the authorities had dredged, and in fairness it must be said that they are dredging as fast as possible. After this, our day's troubles were ended and without further delay we entered the Birmingham and Worcester Canal at King's Norton.

It was on this canal that *Christine* passed through the longest canal tunnel I personally have experienced. It is 1¼ miles long and was bored in the eighteenth century. I was humbled with respect for the men who carried out a task of such magnitude without the aid of bulldozers and earth moving machines which are commonplace today.

The Birmingham and Worcester is also remarkable for the greatest concentration of locks in one flight in Great Britain – thirty at Tardebigge near Bromsgrove.

On the third night out from Warwick, *Christine* lay moored at Worcester, a full moon bringing magic to this broad sheet of water on the threshold of the deep River Severn.

Christine delighted me with her pace in the deep broad river, where she bowled me downstream to Tewkesbury with a fine wave at her bows.

In contrast to the Market Harborough Rally last year, the attending boats did not remain moored throughout the week, but moved in convoy up the River Avon to Pershore. After the rather dull Severn, the lower Avon is a perfectly lovely river, and great credit is due to the Lower Avon Navigation Trust who are busily engaged in improving the Navigation.

In order to maintain our schedule, it was necessary to leave Pershore very early indeed to reach Stourport-on-Severn the same day. Curiously, I have no trouble at all in overcoming my reluctance to get out of bed when I am boating, and on that particular day, virtue was richly rewarded. The loveliness of the countryside was quite unearthly as the last stars faded and moonlight changed into dawn. The memory of it will be with me long after I have ceased to bother about the trivialities of day-to-day life. Such an experience restores one's sense of proportion.

In spite of our early start, we reached Stourport fifteen minutes too late to get through the locks by which the Staffordshire and Worcestershire Canal leaves the Severn and perforce we spent the night in that interesting but dismal town.

Stourport was created by the canal, when the pioneer Brindley linked Severn with Mersey and Trent. It is almost a little Venice, with its wide basins, and connecting canals, but, alas, a shabby Venice, for the water traffic from the Midlands, which once brought vigorous activity and prosperity, has now vanished, and the warehouses are quietly decaying.

My somewhat sorrowful impressions of the place were largely dispelled in an inn that night where I fell into conversation with a retired canal boater, who taught me much with his rich reminiscences and paid me the compliment of a lifetime when he called me 'a real Englishman out to find the best in life'. He also gave me a handsome bag of beans from his garden.

Christine worked her round-about return to Warwick through Kidderminster, past Wolverhampton, nearly to Stafford; through dreary Fazeley on the Watling Street near Tamworth and the coalfields at Pooley Hall and Bedworth; in a grey dawn drizzle through Hawkesbury junction, near Coventry, sombre, but not depressing because of its activity and colourful vitality.

A call was made at the little canal boatyard at Braunston where *Christine* was bought, and where we chatted with the shy Frank Nurser, who is a master craftsman and builds wooden boats. He is also one of the very few genuine painters of traditional canal boat decorations, which is England's sole surviving folk art.

It is impossible to complete such a journey with one's eyes open without a sense of amazement that so fine a transport system is not more fully used in these days of over-crowded roads and railways which cannot cope with their burdens.

My worst enemy would never call me a believer in nationalization. Nevertheless, there is abundant evidence that the Docks and Inland Waterways Executive are seriously tackling the problem of restoring the canals to proper use. I saw many dredgers at work, including one in that infamous stretch of canal passing through Leamington. Privately operated fleets of boats working over a network of state maintained waterways could very subsequently reduce transport costs and alleviate the congestion on the roads and railways.

D.R.M. ADAMS

Five Girls and One Man . . . On a Boat

Such a lot of things happened: the time when I fell in; the antics of the horses; getting stuck on a mudbank; the nervous heron; late-night pub crawl. . . .

It all began on Saturday 6 May 1961 at Gas Street Basin, Birmingham, a salubrious setting for the start of our six-day trip on the *Water Vixen*, a 4/6 berth luxury cruiser.

The crew were Eve Gerry and Hazel Chessborough, Clerks, Accounts department; Yvonne Thompson, secretary to the Divisional Traffic Officer; Molly Sizmur, Machine Operator Supervisor (who stayed only three days); Joe Swain, Auditor for the SE and SW Divisions; and yours truly, Josephine 'Jo' Coles (Secretary to SE Divisional Accountant, Watford).

We set sail – or is it 'cast off'? – about ten in the morning, on what seemed to be a promising day – for rain! Soon, with the busy life of Birmingham behind us, we were bound for greener pastures. We stopped for an hour at Lifford for a supply of tins and bottles to last us for the week (in actual fact we ran out in two days) and we all had wonderful ideas about cooking spaghetti and curry and other delicacies with similar nutritive values.

Before lunch we reached King's Norton Junction, where we left the Worcester and Birmingham Canal and went along the Stratford-on-Avon Canal.

All Saturday morning we spent our time getting to know the 'blunt end' from the 'sharp end', and making up bunks and unpacking clothes and trying to learn the numerous nautical terms.

We had already begun our great adventure when the shout was raised for 'all hands on deck.' We were stuck already! We had been passing through a stop-lock (shaped just like a guillotine) which gave us no spare room, when one of our fenders jammed between the stop-lock wall and the boat.

For half an hour, in pouring rain, we struggled with boat hooks. Sheer brute strength and much puffing and panting. Finally we pulled the wretched thing out! A mile later, catastrophe number two occurred – we had no padlock key for opening the lock on the swing bridge. So we tossed up as to who should sprint back to get it.

Then we took on board two very keen enthusiasts – boys (aged about nine). But unfortunately one of the little blighters fell in the water. We dried him out but did not wait to hear what his mother had to say!

The Stratford-on-Avon Canal passes through some very beautiful English countryside, but the drawbridges being used very infrequently could do with a spot of oil occasionally. Once you have pulled drawbridges up it's just as awkward to push them down again. We came across a tough one. Heavier members of the crew (no names!) had to sit on the balance beams to help raise the bridge!

That afternoon we all had a go at steering. And with the help of the wind we managed to steer ourselves into a few awkward situations.

Then – great excitement – our first lock! But only Skipper Joe knew how. He remained cool, calm and collected but frightened us poor girls on the first day with such terms as 'paddles up' and 'paddles down' and 'lock empty' and 'lock full'.

After working paddles on the next twenty locks – the toughest we met on the whole trip – we were broken in thoroughly and were thus surprised later at the ease with which we could operate the Grand Union lock paddles. Our task was certainly made easier by a few willing males who insisted on doing all the hard work! We decided it would be a good idea to save our strength for the formidable Hatton Flight.

The locks on the Stratford-on-Avon Canal are almost the exact width of the *Water Vixen* with about an inch to spare on each side, so aiming your sharp end at the lock entrance is quite an art.

Had my hobby been botany, I should have had a wonderful collection on this trip. The inner lock walls on this particular canal are thick with tiny plants and flowers. And when the water is reduced in the lock these various plants change colour. I can't imagine how the flowers manage to grow when they are constantly being covered with water and knocked by barges passing through. Weeds and plants grow in the crevices of the lock gates, and where the wood has been cracked by other inexperienced boatmen. We even saw a bird's nest in one of them.

We were all very upset when we overturned a moorhen's nest with the wash from our boat and the eggs were left bobbing up and down in the water behind us – our saddest moment.

At the end of thirteen locks we were beginning to feel a little tired so decided to moor the boat at the tail of Lock 4, Lapworth, for the night. We spent the evening happily at The Boot inn.

On that first day we covered 17 miles. We tied up, turned in, and slept soundly in our bunks.

The next morning, Sunday, we were roused by the sun and by a few unpopular members of the party who were early risers. And after a good breakfast we left Lapworth about nine.

After a peaceful trip to Kingswood, the junction of the Stratford-on-Avon Canal and the Grand Union Canal, we navigated the corner with too wide a sweep and got stuck on a mud bank. Several boatmen chuckled at our antics for half an hour!

We had to study our first Grand Union lock for minutes before discovering how to work it. These locks are much larger and will take two boats at a time. They have great big gates which move with the utmost ease for their size, and the water is let in, or out, at a much faster rate. In fact, it is only really necessary and much safer for the novice to open one set of paddles, unless you have enough men to hold the boat firm.

The steerer has no control whatsoever over the boat at this stage and no amount of reversing will alter the course of the craft while the water is rushing into the lock. It was quite a relief to operate the paddles on these locks after our previous experiences.

We reached the middle bridge of the Hatton Flight just before lunch, and decided that we would need a little sustenance as the locks ahead were all against us. After lunch the sky cleared and we had no more rain that day. When we had completed the last of the twenty-one locks we went on to Leamington for tea, mooring the boat near Radford Locks for the night.

We completed thirty locks and about 13½ miles on that day and considered we should have a rewarding glass of beer for our efforts. We spent the evening at The Lion inn, Radford Semele, where one lucky member of the crew won £1 which she generously used for a round of drinks and packets of cheese-and-onion crisps.

The next day – Monday – dawned bright and fair and remained dry throughout.

We left Radford at 9.30 a.m. sharp with hearts a good deal lighter than is usual for Monday mornings! We had a wonderful cruise along the Grand Union Canal and got quite used to the locks.

We took a keen interest in the numerous types of waterfowl – moorhens, mallard, drakes and ducks with their families in tow, and during the week we saw, in all, four swans' nests. Swans, in their efforts to defend their nests and cygnets, would raise their wings aggressively, so we usually slowed the craft right down until they moved out of our path.

We reached Long Itchington, the end of our trail along the Grand Union, before noon.

At this point, one over-eager member of the crew (female, of course), in her efforts to moor the boat from the blunt end (hereafter called 'aft' or 'stern') leapt for the boat with her mooring rope dangling. Alas, she slipped, went under and came up covered in mud and slime; she disappeared again and re-emerged looking cleaner.

The rest of the crew showed their appreciation of this action by laughing like blazes. Meantime, our boat swung into midstream, with stern dangerously near the opposite bank.

Once again, to the rescue came Skipper Joe (what would we have done without him?) bringing us all to our senses with 'You're a D . . . rotten crew! I'm real mad at you now!'

At this, we all got busy moving the boat back to its mooring and proceeded

The crew of *Water Vixen*, who started from Birmingham and returned to Wolverhampton after travelling 100 miles and working 109 locks on the Grand Union Canal and Worcester and Birmingham canals. On the boat, left to right: Josephine ('Jo') Coles, Hazel Cheeseborough, Yvonne Thompson, Eve Gerry. Joe Swain went along to keep the wolves from the door. Molly Sizmur stayed with the party for only three days

to dry out the nearly drowned lady and to mend the frayed nerves of our skipper.

After a thirsty shopping and postcard sending expedition, we all popped into the Two Boats inn for a quick one or three and returned for lunch at two o'clock.

We returned up the Grand Union the same way we had come and got stuck for twenty minutes on the bank near a lock. The lock-keeper who helped us, grinned and said that the previous week a boat had been stuck there for two days. To think – somebody worse than us!

At one of the locks someone shouted, 'Look out, there's an eel.'

Joe pulled it out of the water. We all studied it very carefully and decided – democratically three to two – that it was an adder. We hastily threw it into the long grass with a boat-hook.

After a late meal that evening, just before mooring, two horses in a field – a stallion and a mare – ran down to inspect us. They cantered along beside our boat for quite a distance. The mare, being the shyer of the two, followed her husband all the time, and we left them looking at us over a five-barred gate. Their curiosity was really quite puzzling.

We moored *Water Vixen* at the foot of the Hatton Flight fairly late and as we did not feel inclined to walk the 5 miles into Warwick (and 5 back), we spent the evening discussing our eventful day going through twenty-two locks, covering 14$\frac{1}{2}$ miles. Then to bunks – and shut eye.

The next day – Tuesday – we were pleased to learn from our early morning scout that the locks were ready for us to proceed. We passed the *Water Rambler* moored just above Hatton Bottom Lock, but we saw no signs of life so early.

We got through the Hatton Locks in less than two hours, with the help, I might add, of a friendly lock-keeper who opened at least a dozen paddles for us.

Halfway up the Hatton Flight we had another 'man overboard', complete with windlass, in the middle of one of the pounds in 12 ft of water. Luckily, she was a good swimmer. Once more a good laugh was had by all. (Aren't we an 'orrible lot!)

We returned to Hatton Workshop and with the help of a little feminine charm were given a new windlass. We continued to Rowington Green and there shopped. We made good friends with another publican who gazed at Skipper Joe with admiring eyes for taking on such a crew for six days!

We lunched late as our attentions were distracted by two stowaways we acquired – a mongrel and a scruffy-looking cairn terrier. A bachelor swan and two bachelor drakes arrived shortly afterwards to share the food we had to offer.

We were sorry to leave them all behind, but we had no time to lose and were soon cruising along the Stratford-on-Avon canal again.

We were quite disgusted to read a notice at the first lock which said, 'All locks on this canal must be left empty. By order!' Many a nautical word was used to help us work the tough paddles on these locks and the lock-keeper in charge had the cheek to say he liked them as they were so easy!

We moored at Lapworth and sadly waved goodbye to one of our party who had to return home. We bought a few odds and ends and sent a few more postcards, then returned to the *Water Vixen.*

We moored below Lock 10 at Lapworth for the night, paying another visit to The Boot inn, where we were warmly received.

In good weather we did thirty-three locks that day, but only 8 miles.

Fairly early – Wednesday – we left Lapworth with the prospect of a beautiful day ahead of us, completing the last eight locks of this flight, with some assistance from another lock-keeper.

We reached Hockley Heath at noon to shop for lunch but proceeded to a more picturesque part of the canal to moor. The rest of the day was 'lock-free' so we sunbathed on the top of the boat.

We reached King's Norton Junction at about five o'clock and from then on sailed the Worcester and Birmingham Canal, towards Tardebigge, near Bromsgrove.

We all marvelled at the long West Hill (King's Norton) tunnel – 2,726 yd, and took a long twenty-five minutes to get through.

At the entrance to tunnels notices said 'No Canoes Are Allowed', 'All Boats Must keep to the Right' and 'Beware of Pleasure Craft'. I don't know what they think crafty pleasure cruisers get up to in tunnels! Anyway, it was very exciting and quite an experience. We also travelled through two shorter tunnels of 613 and 580 yds on this canal.

We tied up at New Wharf, Tardebigge, for the night. What a lovely part of England this is – rolling hills and green valleys, stretching as far as the eye can see. We had a brisk walk to The George inn through the fruitfields (with the sound of two poor railway engines puffing and blowing their way up the 2-mile-long Lickey incline in the background) returning to our beds well after 'closing time'. We completed 18 miles and eight locks that day.

Came Thursday: we began early as we had quite a distance to travel before nightfall. The sun was again shining but with a new warmth. We retracted our steps (or should I say 'wash'?) through the three tunnels, back towards Birmingham.

We saw a heron, but it was too nervous to stay still long enough for us to have a good look.

We had lunch alongside Cadbury's factory. And at mid-afternoon, the *Water Vixen* reached Gas Street, Birmingham, for fuel and water.

We left Birmingham at about 4.30 p.m. and continued through the Black Country, along the Birmingham Canal to Wolverhampton; and though the scenery could not be called picturesque, it was very interesting to see where some of our prosperity comes from!

This is a wonderfully constructed canal, very broad and deep. At intervals along the banks private arms connect small basins for the convenience of the many large industrial concerns there. But in these days the factories don't seem to use them as much as they did in the past.

We approached our last three locks with heavy hearts intending to take as long as we could about operating them. The paddles on these gates were so well oiled that they needed little effort.

We had tea whilst mooring.

At about the same time, workers from the factories going home along the towpath gave us many an envying glance. We realized just how fortunate we were to be having such a trip, and that we had a few green fields to go home to.

The factories got bigger as we neared our destination and the sky darker with the oily fumes. We reached the British Waterways depot at Wolverhampton at about eight in the evening, the end of the trip.

To cheer us, Skipper Joe promised us a short conducted tour of Wolverhampton with a little liquid refreshment for added interest. The venue was the Blue Ball inn. And we topped up the evening nicely with fish and chips – in newspaper of course!

We felt we'd earned it after 27 miles of canal and three locks.

Came Friday – the last day. All the crew rose at 6 a.m. to clear up the debris and pack clothes.

We had been very enthusiastic about cleaning the boat, but the job wasn't too easy; the top of the boat was quite dirty and a member of the party in exasperation threw not one, but two, buckets of water over the roof. Remaining perfectly calm, as usual, Skipper Joe, who was amidships packing his case, said 'I say, my suit's a little wet!' and left us to fend for ourselves for the few remaining hours before seven o'clock. He returned still our smiling Skipper Joe, his sleeves still damp and some of his clothes wet in his case.

What a man! We all salute him for his courage and patience. We thank him, too, for helping to make our trip a never-to-be-forgotten one. And – sh! – girls, he's still off the hook; you know – a bachelor!

JOSEPHINE (JO) COLES

Honeymoon on the Canals in 1908

When John Fox married Olive Sharp in 1908 in the heyday of gaslight and hansom cabs, bacon was 6d. a pound and small boys read Sexton Blake while their parents enjoyed Little Tich in the Edwardian Music Halls.

Both of them, always keen on the water, decided on a honeymoon afloat, amid the quiet of the countryside – and the independence of their punt such as was used in the double punting championship.

With a width of only 2 ft and a length of 30, it was decked at both ends to a length of about 3 ft leaving plenty of room between for the two passengers and a considerable amount of luggage.

It was a five week trip. The couple covered about 340 miles, on the River Thames from Lechlade to Laleham and on canals now in the British Waterways network.

The punt had two green canvas covers, one to cover the luggage and make the craft shipshape; the other could be rigged on iron hoops overall for night camping. The weather was absolutely 'flaming June and July', with only two days of rain in six weeks which included a week's interlude in North Wales.

How did the young and vigorous John get the punt along? By various means. Generally with the punting pole; sometimes with a paddle. But on some stretches, such as the Oxford–Napton Canal where poling was not allowed, he used a tow-rope and towed the little craft along while his wife steered.

On the hottest day of that scorching summer – a Sunday – John Fox towed his punt for 19 miles and worked thirty-two locks himself. Don't the young love punishment?

Their journey started on the River Thames, at Marlow; after spending two nights at Streatley with friends they continued up the river to Oxford. At Shipton-on-Cherwell they camped; and John recollects that the nightingale sang throughout the night.

Later they went through Banbury on the Oxford Canal to Warwick, passing over the Great Western and Avon Aqueducts which cross the Paddington to Birmingham railway and the River Avon respectively.

There with the aid of a friendly stranger they carried their punt and baggage across a field to the River Avon. All the locks between Warwick and Stratford-on-Avon were out of use. So John and his wife had to unload the luggage and drag the punt over the weir each time.

'At Stratford-on-Avon,' says John, 'we created much excitement among the onlookers. People ran down to the waterside to see us and our little boat. They had never seen anything quite like it before!'

At Tewkesbury where the River Avon joins the River Severn, the lock was large enough to hold about twenty narrow boats; and a number of dumb boats were strung together behind a steam tug. John asked the boatman of the last of them whether he could tie up to his craft and be towed to Gloucester. The boatman cheerfully agreed and so on that part of the journey, hardly suitable for such a frail and heavily laden craft, the 15 mile journey from Tewkesbury to Gloucester was done in idleness and comfort.

The punt must have made a fine sight at the end of a string of about twenty dumb boats gliding along the River Severn in the summer sunshine.

It was tea-time when they got to Gloucester, and the honeymooners said farewell to the friendly boatman and his family, then travelled along the Gloucester and Sharpness Canal for about 7 miles to Wallbridge.

They tied up for the night to punt poles fore and aft and hoped for the best. But it was only a short night, for at four in the morning they both awoke, to the sound of a booming siren. The dazed honeymooners peeped from under the green canvas and saw a great ocean-going vessel looming up. John shouted to the captain whom he saw on the bridge, asking whether he was afraid the punt would sink his ship. The captain bawled back, 'Don't worry about that, young man, my wash may well sink you.' By skilful management of both vessels all was well.

That day they reached Stroud near Gloucester and went along to the Thames and Severn Canal office to book a water passage to Lechlade where the canal joins the Thames. They had a delightful trip, climbing up the Golden Valley into the lovely Cotswold country. All told, there were twenty locks on this stretch to be worked.

At the Sapperton tunnel, which was over 2 miles long, water was exceptionally low, with barely more than 7 in of depth, and the punt was

As early as 1766 the Duke of Bridgewater was offering passenger travel for 1*d* a mile and within four years the service on the Bridgwater Canal was returning a profit of £100 a year, which by the turn of the century had rocketed to £4,787. The Packet House at Worsley with its fine stone steps down to the canal is an attractive reminder of the beginnings of packet boat travel drawing 6 in. The canal bottom was still breaking and after somewhat anxious discussion it was decided to go ahead.

The low roof and the muddy bottom made poling impossible, so John paddled as best he could.

Before entering the tunnel, they had been warned that half-way through there was a serious leak in the roof; water simply showered down. And John recalls, 'How glad I was that I took an umbrella; it was just enough to protect us both from a severe soaking.' It was an eerie feeling in the middle with a mile from either end, to see two tiny specks of light from the outer world.

A few hundred yards beyond the tunnel, the canal bed was dry and there was nothing for it but to spend the night there. The next morning a kindly local farmer came with a farm wagon which carried the punt and luggage through fields until water was found again.

They finally got to Henley-on-Thames in time for the first Olympic Regatta ever held in England. A final lap on the Thames took the young couple to their home at Laleham, a few miles from Staines.

His grandfather, also called John Fox, had been an intrepid traveller and kept a diary of his travels from 1800 to 1880.

In the year following Queen Victoria's coronation, 1839, John Fox travelled by boat from Preston to Kendal on the Lancaster Canal.

His diary reads:

21 September . . . Rose at six – breakfast – came outside three-horse coach to Manchester . . . Streets of good red brick houses within three miles of Manchester; many buildings in a place to be called Victoria Park . . . From here to Preston saw many new factories building. What is it to come to? Heard of a passage boat (at Preston) by Lancaster Canal to Kendal. . . .

And now I made the most delightful journey that ever I made in my life, starting about half-past one in the afternoon. The day was most beautiful. The boat was 72 feet long and just wide enough for two persons to sit opposite each other. It will hold about 70. Unladen it draws, I think, three inches of water. The head comes to the sharpest point from which 10 feet downwards, open, covered with tarpaulin, is the luggage; then eight feet open for a boatman and about six passengers can sit in the open air. From this point the boat is covered with a hoop shaped covering, watertight, and divided into three compartments – the first, fare 6s. – the middle a small sort of steward's room – the aft cabin fare 4s. The thing looked like a canoe.

It ran into a covered dock. The passengers from the north disembarked and we entered. I took a seat in the open air at the head. . . . The canal along which we went was beautiful as a stream, winding in and out constantly, then sometimes a wide prospect, sometimes between green fields wooded, then under little groves.

We passed beneath 160 grey stone bridges nor came to a lock till we had gone 40 miles: then there were several together for half-a-mile and then no more. Lancaster was rather more than half way, being 30 miles. . . .

As the sun set the full moon rose. Our boat rushed along at the rate of nine miles an hour with a smoothness incredible. Two horses, one before the other, towed us, and they were changed every four miles, not half-a-minute being taken to change. We had but two postillions for the whole way – one, a boy of 19, to Lancaster from which he had but just returned so that he rode 60 miles post without stopping. I never did enjoy a journey as I did this. It was like a journey in a dream or in an eastern tale – water, weather, scenery, motion – all was most beautiful. We were at Kendal before 9 o'clock.

Two Nice Ladies Went Astray

It happened at Banbury Locks, on the Shropshire Union Canal, about a dozen or so miles outside Chester, one day in the middle of October 1962.

Motoring home through Cheshire we stopped the car as we passed the locks, just to see if there was anything doing. There was. One of the Water Baby class hire-cruisers was coming up from the south, and heading in the direction of Chester. This tiny little two-berther, with her outboard engine, was 'manned' by two ladies.

The usual knot of bystanders gathered around, and gallantly pushed and heaved to open the gates to let the little craft into the top lock, but when they came to open the paddles to lower the water level, first one paddle refused to budge, and then the other.

That was where we came in. It was a bit tricky; some driftwood or something had stuck in each paddle hole, and at first neither of them would budge. But after just enough time had elapsed for my son and me to get ourselves into a beautiful mess from the commendably well oiled gearing, one of the paddles condescended to open a fraction and the water level began to drop.

It was a beastly slow business, but, well content with the results of our efforts, we let matters take their course, and chatted meanwhile with the crew of the boat. The two ladies, we gathered, had started out from Middlewich some hours earlier, at the beginning of a week's cruise, and conversation centred round the boat itself, and how they liked the life afloat. They were newcomers to canal cruising, and were anxious to learn.

Below the pair of locks were two other boats waiting their turn to enter, and ascend in the opposite direction. Eventually, the top lock emptied, but it seemed to take half the afternoon, and our adopted craft moved into lock No. 2, and after that there was no further trouble with paddles. In next to no time after that, we opened the bottom gates and let them out, while the waiting boats changed places with them and began to rise – out of this story.

The little boat drifted away from us as the lady-in-charge prepared to start up the outboard engine. Being warm after its run from Middlewich, the engine should have fired at once, but it did not, and I thought I knew the reason why. The lady pulled, and pulled, on the starter cord, but the engine would not have it. Now these are good little engines, well maintained, and I began to feel just a little embarrassed when a crowd collected on the road bridge above and much fruity advice began to shower down on the still waters below. The lady concerned (she was becoming very concerned by now), redoubled her efforts with the apparently obstinate motor to the accompaniment of 'Give it a tickle, Miss', 'Stick it, you're doing fine', 'Like a tow?' and other such gems of oratory.

Then a police patrol car drew up, and one of the officers, with mock severity, demanded with a wink to know whether they had 'got a licence for that thing'.

By this time the boat had drifted from the opposite bank to nearer where we stood on the towpath, and I was able to catch a glimpse of the engine control settings. As unobtrusively as I could, I indicated that perhaps . . . if she released the choke . . . ? That did it, the engine exploded into life at once, and with a jerk as the clutch went in, the boat began to disappear under the bridge with some dispatch. Just before it vanished I spotted the *other* lady with a book in her hand, and the book had a very familiar blue cover. Heavens, no! Not after all that! 'Where are you heading for?' I called after them. 'Llangollen' came the answer down wind, and my worst fears were realized.

Our two ladies were now on their way to Chester. They must have taken the wrong turning out of the Middlewich branch, at Barbridge Junction; and we were left to hope that they would relish their involuntary visit to Chester as much as they would undoubtedly have enjoyed a Llangollen trip. Unless, of course, they had further adventures at the next lock. We never did find out.

G.H. PURSELL

Summer Cruise

It was a chance remark that turned a wistful idea into a dream come true. Besides what self-respecting male would allow his wife the use of their boat for six weeks, while he slaved away in his office, cooked his own meals at home, and spent his evenings catching up with the housework and gardening? But happily my husband did, while I cruised around the countryside in the summer of 1975 with our baby daughter, Emma, two dogs, a guinea pig, and my seventeen-year-old student sister, Wendy, as crew.

The weather was perfect as we waved goodbye at the top of Foxton Locks on the Grand Union Canal. My smile was radiant, but my heart was sinking! In front of me was 45 ft of newly built narrow boat, traditionally painted red and green in Fellows, Morton and Clayton style. I felt like Columbus, about to discover the canals and rivers of England for the first time.

After a few lock-free miles and feeling full of confidence, we entered Husbands Bosworth Tunnel. The engine noise vibrated through my head, and I hoped fervently that we would not meet an oncoming boat. We had slowed the engine down to tickover on entering the tunnel, in order that we would have full control of the boat's movements. The dogs were tied up and the baby played happily and safely inside, a gate obstructing her passage to the deck.

It may have been imagination but I am sure my heart missed a beat when I saw a beam of light filled the speck ahead which had been the end of the tunnel. We crept slowly forward, the oncoming light growing steadily larger, until the two boats met. They slid past each other, but my concentration was intense. If this was only the beginning, what was the rest of the journey going to be like? I couldn't for a moment, at that time, imagine the canals as a place to relax, the nervous tension was too great!

We moored at Welford, at the end of the short but attractive arm off the summit level. We must have checked our stakes and ropes half-a-dozen times that first night, and I think we used every knot we knew at least three times over to make sure we were secure.

By midday of our first full day alone we had committed a major error. Forgetting the dire warnings surrounding the gathering of bulrushes, we carefully eased the boat bow first into a profusely growing patch, taking considerable care not to obstruct the channel. It was then that we realized the full implications of our foolish errand.

The boat was well and truly wedged on the soft mud. Despite our efforts, poling and reversing, there was nothing we could do to move the boat forwards, backwards, or sideways. It took us exactly twenty minutes to admit defeat, and a further twenty before a passing boat pulled us free.

From the Grand Union Canal we travelled west, joining the popular and attractive Oxford Canal, and so on to the River Thames. We took extra safety precautions for our passage on the river. An anchor was placed on the front of the boat attached to a strong chain in case of emergency, and ropes were tied to the two lifebuoys placed on top.

Compared to the canals the River Thames is like a motorway. For though we passed some beautiful towns and villages, admired riverside houses, and looked

Val Oxley finds a peaceful mooring outside the Rose Revived Inn at Newbridge on the River Thames

longingly at cool waterside pubs, they all appeared slightly remote, aloof and unobtainable. We were thankful to escape to the solitude of the River Wey, and spent two peaceful days exploring and discovering this delightful waterway.

The Wey, owned and run by the National Trust, has remained quiet and undisturbed, though it supports an active boatyard at Godalming.

It was early morning when we left the River Thames at Brentford, and proceeded along the southern part of the Grand Union Canal. We had not gone very far when we caught sight of a calf struggling in the water, and calling distressingly. We knew we had not the strength to assist the animal ourselves, but after half an hour of watching and waiting we heard a welcome sound of a boat engine, and the narrow boat *Columba* came into view. The crew were anxious to make the tide at Brentford, but agreed to help rescue the calf. After some minutes of struggling with ropes, nettles, and briars, our task was accomplished, and, with a thankful moo the beast bounded away and we continued on our journey.

Struggling through low pounds, an evening meal by candlelight with good friends at Stoke Bruerne highlighted the remainder of our journey along the southern Grand Union, which we agreed was the most exhausting part of our journey.

We negotiated the Hatton Flight of twenty-one locks during the heat of one afternoon, arriving at the top at five o'clock and having to continue till seven as we were unable to find a spot where we could moor near to the bank. Low water levels hampered our journey the next day also, causing us to stick twice on the soft mud. By this stage we had learnt the judicial use of the engine and long shaft to extricate us from the bottom.

Routine at the locks was simple and effective. Feeling ultimately responsible for the boat, I usually steered. On arrival at the lock, Wendy alighted with the front rope, tying it quickly to a bollard, using a round turn and two half hitches. She then similarly secured the back rope. I stepped off with the push-chair and then with Emma. Wendy proceeded with the operation of the lock while I looked after the handling of the boat, assisted each other where we could, and as was necessary.

The push-chair, with Emma strapped safely inside, was placed at a safe distance from the lockside, yet where the baby could see all that was going on. In this fashion we proceeded through most of the locks on our journey.

Although we had decided on a leisurely cruise down the Stratford Canal, again water levels planned our passage for us, and a five-hour stoppage on the Wilmcote flight introduced us to numerous other waterway users. It is incredible how many solutions to the problem of an empty pound are considered by self-appointed 'canal engineers'. While overgrown boy scouts acted as runner carrying messages of devastation, each more terrifying than the one before, groups of men surveyed the situation, knowingly wagging their heads together. We settled down for the afternoon, brewed numerous cups of tea, drank as many pints of beer with our new found friends, and contented Emma with an endless stream of playmates from other boats.

It was half past nine and dusk when we eventually entered Stratford Basin, and ten o'clock when we tied up for the night on the banks of the River Avon.

We had been eagerly looking forward to our trip down the River Avon, and we were delighted that the rumours of its beauty had not been exaggerated. The sparkling water and tree-lined banks enhanced the landscape for many miles. We always took the precaution of mooring facing upstream on rivers.

Leaving the River Avon at Tewkesbury, we joined the River Severn to Worcester, where we turned into the Worcester and Birmingham Canal. We spent three hours locking up the Tardebigge flight, aided by a group of lively boys and girls aboard a camping boat belonging to Stroudwater Carriers Limited.

It is normally more than a little disconcerting to find your way barred by a fallen tree, but when the evening is drawing in, the baby needs feeding, and you cannot moor up because of the low water levels, a fallen tree makes one inwardly groan. In our case the tree had fallen just before the entrance to West Hill Tunnel. It was a tall slender ash and had crashed to the ground some twenty minutes before our arrival.

Groups of people standing round issuing instructions to a man perched in the middle of the trunk, told us that an operation was in hand, and that our views on tree removal would not be required at this stage. We could do nothing but sit and wait, so we popped the kettle on and prepared Emma for bed.

Eventually our help was sought and we came to the rescue as a form of a tug, pulling sawn-off pieces of the tree away from the channel. Our mission completed we set off through the tunnel some two hours later, and moored for the night in darkness, but in the company of our friends on the camping boat.

We cruised through Birmingham next day in pouring rain. Cheery calls from factory workers enlightened the grim, grey journey. We replenished our food stocks at Farmers Bridge Junction, and also visited the British Waterways Board shop, where we eyed the beautiful painted ware, and brass work, but left with only a couple of postcards.

This area of the Birmingham Canal Navigations is certainly well worth a visit, for it has been completely restored by the British Waterways Board and the City Council. A pub and a housing scheme have been carefully incorporated and blended into the surrounds of the canal. It is strange that other councils have not been actively encouraged by the success of the venture to conduct a similar exercise themselves.

From Farmers Bridge we continued down the Birmingham and Fazeley Canal to Fazeley. Here we joined the Coventry Canal, and had not cruised very far before we discovered that the engine was only running at tickover, and we later discovered that the throttle cable had broken, causing a day's delay while a new one was sought and fitted. We made one last detour before returning home, along the lovely and peaceful Ashby Canal. A family favourite, the Ashby Canal is a haven of wildness and solitude and we spent some time visiting the quiet Leicestershire villages nestling near its banks.

Finally returning along the River Soar, and eventually mooring at the Derby Motor Boat Club, we reflected on our experiences and journeys. The places we had visited, the people we had met, coupled with the incidents and outings, combined to make this an unforgettable holiday, and to my husband's dismay, one we should love to repeat!

VAL OXLEY

Inland Cruising Sixty Years Ago

Long before the present era of amenity waterways, a few people had discovered the pleasure of cruising on canals. Some of them wrote books about their experiences; one of the most interesting is *My Holidays on Inland Waterways* by P. Bonthron, published by Thomas Marby and Company.

It was published in 1916 and went into at least three editions – it was, perhaps, pleasantly escapist reading for those whose duty took them to the battlefields of the period. Many of his cruises evidently took place several years prior to publication, and waterways seen through Bonthron's eyes make an interesting comparison with those of today.

So does the man himself. He must have been the original canal hustler. His ambition seems to have been to cruise as far as possible in the day, and to keep going for as long as possible. It is significant that he was a pioneer of motor boats, although he also used sculling skiffs.

As a young man, he and two friends took a skiff from Thames Ditton to Windsor and back in a day, 45 miles or so, non-stop in twelve hours. Also on one of the motor cruises described in the book he travels in one day from Hockley Heath (Stratford Canal) to Napton (Oxford Canal); 25 miles and sixty-six locks, which he considers a record. In those days, of course, all the locks on that section were narrow.

Naturally, this sort of thing meant some late-evening arrivals, yet he seems never to have failed to find overnight accommodation for his party, even if he had to raise an innkeeper from his bed. None of the boats he describes had sleeping accommodation.

Part of the secret of swift travel was the size of his party; on the skiff at least three to scull and one to steer, changing over every three-quarters of an hour or so, and on the motor boat usually three plus two paid hands. Where locks were frequent he took on an extra hand.

P. Bonthron and friends going down the Oxford Canal

On other occasions one of the paid hands doubled as chauffeur of his motor car. To cruise the Leicester section of the Grand Junction (as it was at that period) Bonthron was driven from a Daventry hotel to Norton Junction, from which point he and his party walked along the towpath as far as the top of Watford Lock. There they found a hired skiff which had been ordered and set out in it. Meanwhile the chauffeur had been sent to take the motor car round to North Kilworth, 16 miles ahead, from where he was expected to set out on foot, back along the towpath, to meet, rejoin and help with the boat. This sort of operation went on as far as the Trent.

Bonthron's motor boat was *Balgonie*, a timber hulled launch with straight stem and counter stern, 27 ft long, 6 ft 3 in beam and drawing 2 ft 9 in aft. To protect her elegant hull on canals, tarpaulins were draped from her gunwales, which gave her a curious appearance. Amidships was a 6 hp Daimler engine protected by a glass-topped wooden case after the manner of steam launches of the time. Although other motor boats were to be seen on rivers, such as part of the Great Ouse and the Cam, and no doubt on the Thames, *Balgonie* was the first motor boat to appear on part of the canal system.

Where for one reason or another – weed, shallowness or inaccessibility – Bonthron could not go in his motor boat, he used a skiff, *Three Men In A Boat*-style. On the Scottish canals, Union, Forth and Clyde, and Caledonian he used a gig – a slightly larger vessel, I believe, though even so he concluded that it was so small that it had been foolhardy to use it on the lochs of the Caledonian Canal.

Skiffs could be, and were, sculled, paddled or towed from the bank by man or horse. They could also, as is now generally forgotten, be sailed, when the wind was favourable, and Bonthron covered many miles of inland waterways under sail. Even then, though, there were clearly places where such things were unfamiliar; approaching Linlithgow on the Union Canal under sail through the gloaming – another of the late-evening arrivals – he met a horse towing a barge. The horse became restless at the sight of this 'apparently phantom ship', turned and bolted!

Skiffs and gigs were not, however, the only vessels to move by sail on the canals. Rounding a bend on the Fossdyke he encountered four keels, close together and with main and top square sails set. With such a rig they looked like a miniature armada.

Another advantage of the skiffs, which present-day craft lack, was the ease with which they could be sent to the start of the cruise by rail, or returned similarly at the end of one. Nowhere does Bonthron refer to a straightforward out-and-back cruise, and even with the motor boat he contrived round trips as far as possible. Salter Brothers of Oxford would in those days despatch hired skiffs to any part of the country and Bonthron had skiffs, either his own or hired, delivered by rail to (among other places) Basingstoke, Bristol, Hay (for an adventurous descent of the Wye), and Stratford (for descent of the Avon which, as far as Evesham, was equally adventurous, the navigation works then being derelict). He even went down the Nene from Northampton to Sutton Bridge and then had the boat sent 30 miles by rail to Boston to continue along the Witham and Fossdyke.

He had hoped to use the motor boat on both the Basingstoke and Kennet and Avon canals. That he did not do so was due to weed, on both canals, to shallowness of the top pounds of the Kennet and Avon, and to some of the locks being out of order on the Basingstoke. This showed up another advantage of the skiff; it could be carried around obstructions.

Weed, he had been told, would be a problem on the Thames above Oxford too. He therefore hired a horse and man to accompany *Balgonie* along the bank, in case the boat became immobilized. As things turned out they were not needed, but activities of horse and rider caused amusement, disappearing to seek short cuts and then reappearing at a lumbering gallop.

It was fortunate, though, that he re-engaged horse and man to accompany the boat along the Thames and Severn Canal. There the weed was so bad that the horse became essential. Even in Sapperton Tunnel patches of weed were bad enough for him to stop the engine and work the boat through by boathooks and a wire running along the side. This took one hour and thirty-five minutes. The following day he had another late-evening trip; delayed at Saul Junction for three hours by a misunderstanding over a lock pass, he nevertheless set out for Worcester in the late afternoon – and arrived, by the light of the moon, at midnight.

On another trip on the Severn – by daylight – he remarks on the lack of traffic; until, near Upton, he met a tug towing no less than seventeen canal boats. On yet another occasion he came down, by skiff, from Shrewsbury to Worcester, encountering rapids on the way and having the river to himself as far as Stourport where he found boats, houseboats and motor boats. On the way, though, he had talked with inhabitants of Ironbridge who remembered barges of 60 tons burthen trading to that town.

Similarly at Pallingham on the River Arun he met an old boatman who, when young, had travelled through the Wey and Arun canal, closed in 1868.

On the Great Ouse he found that the first nine locks downstream from Bedford had been reopened for pleasure boating, but that those further downstream were closed – the reverse of the situation in recent years, though the Great Ouse Restoration Society is now achieving results in its long campaign for full restoration. His comments on the Grantham Canal are interesting too, in view of current interest in restoring that waterway. Bonthron found it in good condition, and its scenery remarkably beautiful. There were

One of the original ominous notices now preserved in the Waterways Museum at Stoke Bruerne

no motor boats but he met a barge drawn by two horses in which a *chief* of the owning railway company was making a tour of inspection.

His entry to the River Stort was interesting, too, in his own words:

> At the first lock on the River Stort the eye meets a formidably worded old notice board, which reads as follows:- 'Punishment for tampering with these works is penal servitude. By Order', and further on our journey a similar intimation is observed, but instead of penal servitude, the punishment is 'transportation'.
>
> This notice struck terror into the heart of the crew, and altogether it had a salutary effect, and glad we were to get free from the clutches of the law, and this Merrie England, too, in the 20th century.

To which there is little to add, except that the transportation notice survives in Stoke Bruerne museum.

P.J.G. RANSOM

three

Of Castings, Chocolate and Conjugal Bliss

Severn Merchant Adventurer

The harvest has been gathered in, and in the south-west the facilities at Diglis Wharf, Worcester, have played their part.

It has been a wet season, conditions far from good, but farmers take every advantage of dry spells between the storms to cut, thrash and bag the grain in the fields, often using combine harvesters. These machines, although they ease the burden on the farms, create problems of their own elsewhere. Sack contractors have to ensure a rapid turn-round of sacks; points for the receipt and storage of large tonnages during the peak harvest period have to be arranged and transport fixed from the farm to store and later from store to mills at the ports. This is where the service of the Executive provides a link between farmsteads in the lovely Worcestershire countryside and the mills in the Bristol Channel.

Diglis Wharf has a fine transit shed where the grain is received in large quantities from the farms. Modern appliances, which include belt conveyors to carry the grain to pile from hoppers into which it has been tipped from sacks off the lorries, and a suction plant for loading from shed to craft alongside, enable the large tonnages to be dealt with quickly. At the height of the season, the intake often exceeds 200 tons a day. Distribution must be regularly maintained to avoid congestion at the shed and this is carried out by Executive craft.

One of the early orders this season [1950] called for delivery of about 125 tons to a mill situated in the Executive's docks at Swansea. This provided a most interesting freight from a Midland waterhead to an important Bristol Channel port of the Executive. The *Severn Merchant*, one of the Executive's motor vessels, was briefed for the load and left Worcester on an August Friday. Delivery was required at the mill on Monday and as the craft was needed to deal with another cargo at Avonmouth on Tuesday, a quick passage was necessary.

In view of the interest of this movement, and the fact that small craft such as the *Severn Merchant*, do not regularly trade to Swansea, a member of the inside staff travelled with her, to obtain some experience of the conditions involved. A few jottings from his notes are given below.

We left Gloucester promptly at 8 p.m. on Sunday morning. Weather prospects were not good for the long trip before us but there was every confidence in the ability of the Master and his crew. The Master, Captain J. Herbert, was brought up in sail and apart from telling many an interesting yarn of his early days afloat, he does know how to grapple with weather and rough seas. Mr G. Dunn, the Engineer, has also had a long experience on the long trip. With the Mate, Mr C. Gale, this made as good a crew as any sailing in the Bristol Channel.

Sharpness was reached at 11 a.m. and we were locked down ready to sail at 11.45, an hour and a half before high water. Weather conditions had deteriorated, and our Harbour master, in wishing us 'bon voyage,' suggested with a smile that we were for a ducking. Outside the piers, an Executive tug, with two lighters loaded with feeding stuffs, waited to enter. A little further down channel, we passed the SS *Maywood*, heavily loaded with timber, completing her voyage from Bordeaux to Sharpness.

The Master took his course down the well-marked channel to King Road off Avonmouth, during which time we enjoyed an excellently cooked dinner, marred only by the Mate asking if the passenger was a good sailor! Off King Road the clouds were extremely heavy, visibility was poor, a freshening southerly wind caused a nasty chop and the rain simply emptied down. However on we go, keeping a careful watch for the marker buoy to set us on the right course. Portishead is passed on our port side and a little further on we see the *Togo*, which went ashore in heavy weather at Redcliffe Bay last winter. Past Walton Bay where the *Ino* is lying at anchor waiting to proceed to Bristol on the midnight tide. The sea has now got up and after the thrill of seeing the rather bluff bows hitting a wave and cascading a great volume of white foam in all directions, we see the bows plough under the heavy green seas, allowing the waves to roll back along the decks to splash against the wheel house.

Visibility is still very bad but we manage to pick up the market buoys until we round the English and Welsh Grounds Lightship where the course takes us across channel, leaving the Steep and Flat Holmes on our port quarter. It was here that we encountered heavy beam seas and we started to roll so much that the cups from which we had just enjoyed a welcome drink of tea were scattered in all directions. However, we plough on, the skipper neatly turning the wheel to keep the craft with her head to the seas. At the time we had a fair wind and the next order was 'Up with the sail', and despite a good wetting the crew soon had a mainsail set, which not only improved progress but also kept the ship more steady.

The entrance to Cardiff Docks was left on our starboard quarter, Sully was passed and Barry Docks came into view. Several ships were seen making their way up and down the channel, but the beach at Barry Island, normally filled with holiday makers, was deserted. The weather was still atrocious. As the channel opened out below Barry, the waves were longer and more regular, so that our movement became a long steady undulation which was an improvement on the spirited high kicking as we crossed the Channel.

At the Nash, with its tall cliff surmounted by the lighthouse, the Captain had to decide whether the weather was suitable to proceed into the wider waters and if so, which would be the most suitable course. We had three alternatives; to run down under the Devon coast, taking advantage of shelter from the wind blowing offshore and rounding the Scarweather Lightship or cut across the channel into Swansea Bay; to take the recognized channel, or to hug the Welsh coast where we should get some protection from the seas. The Captain decided to go ahead on the latter course, but unfortunately the weather had delayed us and we soon had the turn of the tide to contend with. This was disappointing, for we had hoped to be much nearer Swansea before having to punch against the incoming tide.

Progress became much slower, the Welsh coast was still overcast with heavy clouds, but in sharp contrast on the other side of the Channel, Porlock and Countisbury Hills were thrown into relief by sunshine which persisted for the next two hours. We had time to watch this lovely part of Devon as we were an unconscionable time in moving ahead. The tide brought on a nasty chop; the Captain felt we were too near the shore for safety (the passenger silently disagreed) and we diverted to the outside course. The wind had stiffened and the crew had to perform feats of acrobatics to take in the sail as the little craft was tossed about. The coastal scenery changed very, very slowly and from time to time, despite the skipper's vigilance in keeping her head to the seas, we took a beam sea on the deck. It was on one of these occasions that the passenger caused the crew their one fright of the trip. Dusk had come on early, no other ship was in sight, when right in the middle of a heavy roll, the blast of a ship's siren deafened our ears. The crew, to a man, jumped and stared ahead and astern with unbelieving eyes, until they realized the passenger had clutched the lanyard of the whistle as the first thing available at a lurching moment.

As the evening closed in, lights appeared on the shore. The flash from the Scarweather Lightship is seen to port and the Mumbles Light ahead on the port bow. It is now time to change our westerly course and to bear north-west across the bay. This meant more beam seas, but by skilful manoeuvring, the Captain eased her round very gently, for every time the compass points to the right course, we hit seas and get a heavy shaking. Swansea lights are now sought and found, the pier lights are seen dead ahead. At 10 p.m. we round the pier and feel with relief that we are in calm water. We move forward to the lock entrance where our dock colleagues of the Executive give every facility to lock through to our berth without delay.

An eventful trip over, the *Severn Merchant* discharged her cargo on Monday morning, sailed and arrived at Avonmouth that evening, ready to load next morning. Right on schedule!

H.A. ROBERTS

Charlie and his Chocolate Boat

One look at Charlie Atkins and you know where you are. The thousand-wrinkled, leathery face, tanned by a life in the open; the massive frame; the powerful hands, black and horny; the weather-worn clothcap, cocked over one ear; heavy jacket with the smell of diesel fumes and a thousand rains – Charlie of the Canal, of the Black Country. He goes with coal, steel, scrap iron, with gravel, chemicals and giant tubes. And also with chocolate.

For Charlie and his blue and yellow canal barge, the *Clematis*, have now been calling for many months at Knighton, where Cadbury's have a factory for making chocolate crumbs. In the afternoon Charlie loads bags upon bags of the costly stuff onto the barge and in the evening he has reached Wheaton Ashton. There he ties the boat up for the night. Next morning at five he is up and on his way again, steering his lonely boat on the misty waterway, to Bournville.

It is a long way to Birmingham, a good fifteen hours. No eight-hour day for Charlie and the *Clematis* because they're waiting at Cadbury's for his cargo of chocolate crumbs, to turn them into smooth, melting-in-the-mouth bars.

Charlie was born on a canal boat, as his father and grandfather were. His father's barge, pulled by a horse then, had tied up at Newport in Shropshire for that happy event fifty-odd years ago and so Newport is his official birthplace. It wouldn't do to have on a birth certificate: Born Shropshire Union Canal; coal barge on board thereof.

He grew up on the tiny floating house, not knowing the boys and games of the back streets, for his streets were the canals and he learned to know every yard of them.

Charlie Atkins, aged seventy, on the very top of the Anderton Lift, where all the wheels and cogs are located

When the boat stopped somewhere for a day or two, at Chester or Wolverhampton perhaps, he would be pushed off to school for a quick haphazard dose of learning and that was all the schooling he had.

You wouldn't notice when he's talking to you. His vocabulary is as good as if he had had the usual trimmings of education. His opinions on the affairs of the world are sound, his manners are gentle and free of coarseness. Perhaps it's not a bad school, a barge, if it can make a man like Charlie.

I got on Charlie's boat at the British Waterways Board Depot in Wolverhampton. The 70 ft long narrow boat *Clematis* was not exactly an inviting prospect on a squally, blustering, rainswept afternoon.

Charlie emerged smiling from under the tarpaulins which covered his cargo and got one cylinder of his 15 hp diesel engine stuttering and spluttering. Slowly, skilfully, he edged the unbelievably long boat into the 'open water'. At once the wind caught us and slapped our faces and the smoke of the engine and of the coal stove in the cabin wrapped us up. What goes as the skipper's bridge is only a tiny foothold above the entrance to the cabin, at the very end of the boat.

There stands Charlie, the small of his back wedged against the steering, his hands incessantly fiddling the controls. There is no room for passengers on the fully laden boat and I have to balance on the ledge next to him.

Narrow boats are off-loaded at Cadbury's Knighton factory wharf, 1925

There is of course the cabin, a cosy sardine-tin with a beautiful black stove, named *Signora*, and also a bench, a built-in bed, a table and a cupboard. The boat has no lavatory and no water tap. It couldn't be more austere. Yet in such a cabin, Charlie and his family and generations of canal boatmen grew up.

The engine settled down to a steady rhumba rhythm and spat the smoke into our faces and lungs. The sky hung down sulkily, spraying us with heavy pellets of rain.

On both sides of us rose in all the majesty of breathtaking ugliness the chimneys and furnaces, cranes and gas holders and retorts, the mountains of coal and slag and tangled scrap . . . citadels of industry, erupting steam and smoke and belching fire, hissing and clattering and glowing.

If you want to hear the hammering of the great heart of the Midlands, of the Black Country, if you want to feel the greatness of man's ingenuity and the grandeur of industry, a journey on this stretch of waterways will give it to you. Coal barges passed us. Their skippers exchanged greetings with Charlie.

'Traffic now is nothing to what it used to be twenty, thirty years ago,' he said. 'The canals were crowded then. Mind you, conditions are better now since nationalization. And it's a healthy job.'

We entered a tunnel. The echo of the engine bounced off the smooth wet bricks. When we emerged again in the open, a gust of wind almost blew me off my precarious foothold, Charlie smiled. 'It's lovely in summer, it really is.'

He is one of those rare men who love their jobs. It is not particularly well paid considering the responsibility, the value of the cargo, the long hours, the exposure to all weathers, the lack of amenities. You also have to be tough, handling the loads, the heavy boat, the innumerable locks (twenty-one alone at Wolverhampton, over fifty at other places, often iced up in winter). Charlie loves it.

He chuckles. 'My sister's lad, one day, he says, "Do boatmen ever wash?" So I got him to come with me for a fortnight. At the end of it he was as black from the wind and rain and sun as me. He enjoyed that.'

'Navigating the narrow sharp bends and the hundreds of bridges with a 70 foot long barge requires supreme skill. Many stretches of the canal bank have fallen in and the water is often strewn with obstructions. Some foul the propeller of the boat. It's a very slow journey at 4 miles an hour, often less, but eventually you get there. Usually, when I get somewhere before night break, I go to the pictures. Or listen to the radio. Don't like to leave the boat. We're responsible for any damage to the load.'

The hours dragged on. The clouds dropped, pouring angry showers over us. The light was fading quickly now. Factory windows lit up, throwing a crazy pattern on the water and creating patches of bottomless darkness. Weird hazy islands suddenly loomed out of the water. Locks changed to dangerous pits. Bridges and walls closed upon us. My face, battered by wind and rain, felt like a stiff mask. My fingers and feet were numb.

Cadbury's waterside wharf at Bournville, 1911

But Charlie stood sturdily on the same few square inches from which he had not moved for six hours, except when he attended to the locks. He could have stopped, stretched his legs and back, brewed a cup of tea on the homely *Signora*. But he wanted to get to Bournville the same night so he could unload first thing next morning and be off to Knighton again for some more chocolate crumbs.

'You know something? With all the chocolate I've taken to Bournville, I've never been inside Cadbury's. I have never seen what they do to the crumbs.'

We squeezed out of the tunnel, under Broad Street, in the centre of Birmingham. The moon had broken a window in the night sky and scattered splinters of pale light on the canal.

'Another two hours and we're there,' said Charlie. 'What's the matter? You want to get off? Got enough? Alright. See you again, eh? In summer?' The *Clematis* droned away, a huge black pencil drawing a black line on the water, slowly merging with the night.

ANDRE DRUCKER

A Barge-load of Elvers

At Sharpness Dock there is a British Waterways Board notice which could be unique. It reads: 'NO ELVERING'.

Though the tidal basin may not be a suitable place, elvering goes on along the River Severn from Sharpness to Tewkesbury. It can be profitable and, like burgling is mostly done stealthily at night. It is, however, legitimate and traditional in Gloucestershire: it is the catching of baby eels, the only fish fry which may legally be taken as food.

Elvers come up the Severn estuary in spring and are scooped out by the millions. In Gloucestershire they are considered a great delicacy and the first feed of elvers, like the first bunch of daffodils, is as welcome as the spring itself.

To most outsiders a plateful of these worm-like fish, little black eyes and all, has little appeal, but at Frampton-on-Severn, a village alongside the Gloucester and Sharpness Canal, they make a great thing of elver eating. Each year there is a speed trial and the record for swallowing a pound of cooked elvers is forty-three seconds.

Elvers have been taken from the Severn for centuries for local consumption but in recent times they have become part of the export trade. They are in demand for stocking rivers with no natural supply. They are also served in famous European restaurants – in Madrid for example, where the price of cooked elvers in your mouth would take your breath away.

Around Gloucester there are several places where elvermen sell their catches for the markets. The most interesting of these elver stations, and the only one of its kind in the world, lies alongside Baker's Quay at the head of the Gloucester and Sharpness Canal. It is a converted dumb barge, the 80 ft former grain-carrier *Frenchay* which used to work out of Avonmouth. Two years ago Bristol Channel Fisheries bought *Frenchay* and towed her to Sharpness.

Here, in the old timber pools alongside the canal, the wooden floorboards were ripped out and lightweight concrete poured in to make a smooth and easily-washed-down bilge. An upper deck framework was fitted with plastic tanks fixed on both levels. A pumping system for overside abstraction and return was installed, with splash delivery into the tank to give aeration for the elvers swimming about.

The virtue of a floating station is that elvers can be sustained in water natural to them, and are therefore more likely to survive. The *Frenchay* takes canal water, most of which is lifted from the Severn by the pumping station in Gloucester Basin.

The barge conversion was an expensive investment and, as bad luck would have it, the first operational year was a poor one for elvers. In 1976 most of them ended up in the rivers of north-west France, presumably because of a quirk in the current which carries them to the shores of Western Europe.

Elvers are spawned in the Sargasso Sea and spend three years as larvae, drifting along the great loop of the Gulf Stream. Over the Continental Shelf they turn into wriggling translucent baby eels, 2 or 3 in long, and when the temperature is right they swim up the estuaries.

They use flood tides to help them in the last lap of their astonishing 2,000 mile journey and, luckily for them, the Severn has a fast flood stream in the estuary and a useful bore further up. When the tide ebbs they seek the slackest water and bide their time.

Most of the elvering goes on during the half-dozen periods of high tides between March and May. Night tides are favoured for a variety of reasons, some of them none-too-convincing, but it is a fact that most elvers are caught in the dark.

The Severn bore seems to concentrate the elvers into batches which travel the 30-odd river miles between Sharpness and Tewkesbury, each tide sweeping them a few miles further. The best time to fish is about an hour after the passage of the bore, when the tide begins to ebb and the elvers swim to the slacker water near the banks. The experienced elverman follows the batches up river, choosing his spot well, waits for the ebb and then slides in his scoopnet. If he is lucky he can lift half a hundredweight or more and pick up a tidy sum for this night's work. If he isn't, as happens far more often, he can spend half the night standing in the cold mud left by the passage of the bore and go home empty-handed.

During these nights of bore tides the barge *Frenchay* is bright with lights which occasionally cast shadows of bucket-laden elvermen across the walls of the deserted warehouses. The catches are weighed and tipped into the tanks, and the elvermen go home to bed for a few hours sleep before starting their regular day's work.

Aboard *Frenchay* the elvers are later scooped out of the tanks and packed in special containers, either for deep-freezing or for live transport. Some are air-freighted live out of nearby Staverton Airport or from Heathrow to end up in countries as far apart as Poland and Japan.

WILFRED HARPER

Trent Trade was Marriage Making

Every name tells a story is an old adage, and for waterways enthusiasts early surveys of the Trent Navigation offer plenty of scope for research into such distinctive names as Hully's Gully, Hooton's Nose, Mose's Mouth, Juggler's Holt, Needless, Beggarly Rack, Goose Gaps and Blotah Dyke. Some, such as No Man's Friend, and Misbegotten Shoal appear to reflect only too well the feelings of eighteenth-century boatmen.

But the origin of one name – Sweetapple's Dyke – near Fledborough is both known and notorious. There really was a Mr Sweetapple and he really had a dyke – a dyke which still exists today although no longer navigated, but he flourished on a trade in marriages!

The first record of Fledborough is that of a gift of the manor with that of Newark, by Lady Godiva wife of Leofric, Earl of Mercia, to the church at Stow. This gift was subsequently confirmed by William I to Remigius, first Bishop of Lincoln, under the name of Flatburch.

After the Norman Conquest the family of De Lisieux held the manor and were probably builders of the church dedicated to St Gregory whose tower still stands.

Several antiquities are boasted by the church, including a coffin lid believed to be from the resting place of one of the fourteenth-century chancery priests; an unusually foliated cross with branches all down the stem; fragments of an Easter sepulchre showing sleeping soldiers with the risen Lord and ascending angels; and some remarkable fourteenth-century glass.

One of the windows is particularly unusual since its centre light is filled with masonry and forms a canopied niche. The two side lights will produce the effect which all the panels must have had in their original beauty. All the old glass is a greenish colour; no colour is used except yellow or yellowish stain and the tone is all smear shadings.

In the shadow of gnarled old trees and almost overgrown is the tiny parish church of St Gregory at Fledborough, which was once on the main route of a curious 'Trent trade'

Yet, despite these treasures, Fledborough's main claim to a place in history is in the annals of love as 'the Gretna Green of the Waterways'. The church registers, although imperfectly kept for nearly two centuries, date from 1562 and record a normal village life.

Even after 1712 when the Reverend William Sweetapple was appointed vicar of the parish, life was undisturbed and the adjoining dyke and nearby Trent merely served as a water highway for the infrequent barge of coal or to set down the occasional visitor.

From 1712 to 1727 only six marriages were solemnized in St Gregory's including Sweetapple's own, and only one is recorded for 1728. The following year four couples were united in matrimony but from 1730 to March 1754 there were 490 marriages! Of these, in only fifteen did one or both persons reside in the parish and, therefore, all the rest were irregular marriages.

To the editor of *Nottinghamshire Parish Registers*, it appeared 'unaccountable why persons should flock to be married in a small out of the way place as Fledborough was, from almost every parish from Newark to Worksop, and from Lincoln to the Derbyshire border; it seems unreasonable to suppose that they were all clandestine marriages.' In two cases it is said that the banns had been published in the respective parishes in which the persons lived.

One answer was supplied by Lydia Penrose, daughter of a subsequent vicar from 1783, who said: 'It was owing to its retired situation that Fledborough was much resorted to as a fit place for marriages.' She added: 'Mr Sweetapple was a surrogate which made it particularly convenient for the parties as they could have the licence and the marriage ceremony together.'

At this time, 'the roads were appalling' and as yet the railways had not thrust across the river with the fifty-nine-arch bridge which consumed some nine million bricks and 800 tons of steel. This £65,000 giant nearby had not even been conceived and so, unlike Gretna Green which was served by both road and rail, Fledborough relied well into the eighteenth century on the Trent as a highway for incoming and departing couples.

Picture the scene as the young couple quietly row a small craft along the Trent, probably at evening time, searching for the entrance to Sweetapple's Dyke and eventually tying up alongside the church.

Here, in the outer wall blocking the arch at the east end of the south aisle, they would see an effigy of a lady, originally recumbent, probably a widow. With her head resting on two cushions, a veil or kerchief falling to her shoulders, she wears around her throat a wimple covering the chin and carried forward up the sides of her face. A gown with tight sleeves has a mantle fastened across the neck by a cord and gathered up with each arm so as to hang in folds, while in her hand she holds what is probably a heart – symbol of love and affection.

After the ceremony, which according to Sweetapple was by 'a license granted by me', the couple would return to their craft to be borne romantically away on the Trent.

William Sweetapple died on 31 August 1753, his departure curiously coinciding with Lord Hardwicke's Act making drastic conditions for the prevention of clandestine marriages and effectively stopping the trade in licenses on which the worthy clergyman had thrived.

Paradoxically, the fact that weddings could no longer be held at short notice or in private houses, provided the impetus which propelled Scotland's Gretna Green from an obscure village where fishing, weaving and smuggling were the only industries into the cynosure of the elopement-marriage trade which prospered there for another century.

By Tanker to Leeds

In May 1978 I wrote in *Waterways News* about the increased freight traffic on the Aire and Calder Navigation. The tonnage of traffic carried on this navigation was over two million in 1977 and expected to be more in 1978. Of this tonnage about 400,000 is liquids, mainly oil and petroleum products. The West Yorkshire County Council has stated in its Transport Policies and Programme in July 1978 with regard to canals the following: 'Support will be given to maximize use of canal facilities by encouraging wharves and major waterside-related industries to locate at suitable sites, alongside the canal, and to the protection of such suitable sites which accord with the County structure plan.'

There is, therefore, considerable support for greater use of the Aire and Calder Navigation for freight. Many councillors have complaints from their constituents about the noise of passing heavy lorry traffic, and recently a road tanker carrying a dangerous chemical developed a leak in the ward I represent.

I was concerned to see for myself possibilities of using water to carry freight. In July 1978 I travelled down the Leeds and Liverpool Canal with David Lowe of Apollo Canal Carriers on the shortboat *Irwell*, carrying 45 tons of treated sewage effluent on a contract for Effluent Services Limited. This was an interesting journey and showed me that the Leeds and Liverpool could be used for freight, despite the seventeen locks and seven swing bridges which needed to be operated by the crew.

In September 1978 Bill Scott, the Board's freight manager (North), arranged with Whitakers Transport for me to join one of their tanker ships for a journey up the Aire and Calder to Leeds. I was told to be at the lock at Whitley Bridge near Knottingley, for 7.30 a.m. to pick up one of their boats.

To reach Whitley Bridge for 7.30 a.m. I caught the 6 a.m. train from Leeds to Selby with my cycle, and cycled from Selby. At Whitley Bridge a Whitakers tanker was travelling down the canal. This was the *Battlestone* and not my tanker. I missed the new road to the lock and tried to find a public footpath marked on my map. After lifting my bike over a fence and fighting across dense undergrowth, I reached Whitley lock just as another Whitakers tanker was leaving. This was the *Humber Jubilee*, their largest vessel, with a carrying capacity of 700 tons. It was bound for Fleet, a few miles before Leeds.

I met the lock keeper, Denis Lambert, who showed me Whitakers' next boat coming round the corner. He said that this was the *Humber Enterprise*, crewed by two brothers, and that this would be going into Leeds. This was the boat I should join.

The skipper of the *Humber Enterprise* told me he was having some engine trouble and he suggested that I join the *Fusedale* which was following as this

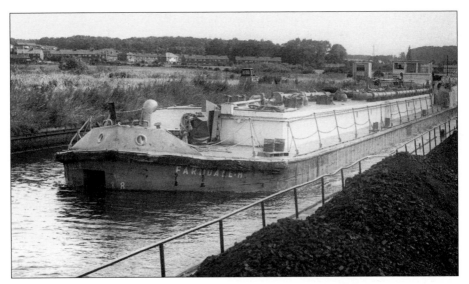

Harker's tanker *Farndale* passing a barge loaded with coal on the Aire and Calder Navigation

boat was also going to Leeds. The *Humber Enterprise* left the lock and round the corner came another Whitakers tanker, this time the *Fossdale*, and an Effluent Services vessel, which is one of eight taking sewage effluent from Leeds to be dumped at sea. Denis Lambert said that there was room in the lock for the two tankers and the effluent boat.

The crew of the *Fossdale* said that their load of petroleum spirit was not needed in Leeds until the following day so they would only go as far as Woodlesford and then leave the boat overnight. I could join them if I wished and then, at Woodlesford, join the *Fusedale* behind, which was going into Leeds. I decided to join *Fossdale*, and Denis Lambert helped me put my bike aboard.

Eventually, I left Whitley Lock at 8.25 a.m. The modernized lock was very impressive with a television camera to enable the lock keeper to see boats coming down.

The skipper of the *Fossdale* was Eric Pearson and his engineer was Ian Ledger. The boats also carried a mate, but the mate of this boat, Eric Pearson's father, was on holiday. Eric said his father and grandfather had worked on the canals. His grandfather had a horse-drawn barge. Both the crew came from Knottingley and Eric had been with John Harker's fleet until this was sold out to Whitakers.

Eric regretted the fact that the top gate at Pollington lock, further along the canal, had been removed and not replaced. The lock can only take one of their type of boat, or one of the smaller effluent boats, at once. As these boats come from Immingham, and the effluent boats also come from the Humber, they can only come through the lock at Goole for three hours on each tide. The boats are, therefore, bunched at Pollington and as only one can go through at a time, the boats at the rear are held back. If the top gates were replaced two tankers at least could pass through the lock together.

The wheelhouse of the *Fossdale* with the controls was quite different from the *Irwell*. The *Irwell* has no protection for the skipper and, like most narrow boats, has tiller steering. The *Fossdale* carries a compass for use on the Humber and has power-assisted steering. A dial shows the position of the rudder. She carries two masts, which were folded down for the canal section of the journey. I was told that when the boat is unloaded and rises in the Navigation, the canopy of the wheelhouse has to be taken down; otherwise it would hit some of the bridges. This means that on the return journey the crew are completely exposed to the elements.

From Whitley Bridge new piles have been taken into the bank to widen the Navigation, but no further work has been done because of lack of funds. I hope that eventually more money will be made available for this Navigation. The railway line from Knottingley to Goole runs close to the Navigation on this section and a number of coal trains went past on a merry-go-round working from collieries to the power stations at Eggborough or Drax. I had travelled on one of these trains to Eggborough Power Station a week earlier to see how British Rail move bulk traffic.

Soon we reached Kellingley Colliery and met the first of many coal boats of Cawood-Hargreaves. Most of these were taking coal to Ferrybridge Power Station. Some were barges and others were push-tow. From here the canal was very busy and at Castleford we met the *Misterton*, a general cargo boat coming from the Wakefield branch. Progress through the mechanized locks was fast, but in one or two money could be spent on straightening the locks and so saving time for boats.

At Kippax Lock, we found we were in a queue having caught up the *Humber Enterprise* and an effluent boat. The *Cornish*, a hire boat from Shire Cruisers of Sowerby Bridge and a Hoseasons boat were also waiting. They were dwarfed by the oil tankers. The crew of the *Fossdale* said that they both had boats of their own and enjoyed cruising on the canal system for their holidays. Eric said that he hoped to spend two weeks on the Leeds and Liverpool Canal in 1979.

The *Cornish* was stuck on the mud and we were able to pass it. I hope that people on hire cruisers on the Aire and Calder, if they find working boats behind them, will let them pass through the locks before them. Time is money for working boats!

We left the Kippax locks at 11.55 a.m. The journey from Knottingley to Leeds is through much desolate country dominated by collieries, opencast mines and slag-heaps. There are some interesting developments. At Fairburn Ings near Ferrybridge there is a large nature reserve and the County Council is helping with developments. At Castleford excavations by the County Council for a new road have revealed extensive Roman remains, including a Roman fort and a Roman bathhouse.

Much could be done in this lower Aire valley, and in a few years time it may become a larger recreational area with the Navigation a major attraction. Meanwhile coal from the opencasting in this part of the Aire valley will travel by boat from Astley Staithe near Woodlesford.

At Woodlesford the *Fossdale* tied up below the lock as the *Humber Enterprise* had tied up above the lock. Its load also was not needed until the following day in Leeds. Eric's wife had brought the car to meet her husband and so both crews were able to return home by car at 1 p.m.

The *Fusedale* soon reached Woodlesford and with permission of the Skipper, Harry Emmerson, I joined this vessel to continue my journey. Harry had worked for many years on canals particularly on the Sheffield and South Yorkshire. He had used both a horse and boats with sails. His brother Ellis Emmerson was a crew member, but he had taken his car to Leeds to meet *Fusedale*. The other member of the crew was William Middleton, who had other relatives on Whitakers boats. Whitakers is very much a family business.

The *Fusedale* was carrying 500 tons of gas oil for Esso in Leeds. We soon reached the oil depot just below Leeds Lock, at 3.10 p.m. It would take 2½ hours to unload. The crew helped me off with my cycle.

I found the whole journey very impressive. Altogether I had seen five boats carrying over 2,500 tons of oil and petroleum products travelling very safely along the navigation, causing no disturbance to anyone.

JOHN M. SULLY

Carrying Giant Castings with Confidence *on the SSYN*

The heaviest load ever to be moved in this country on the Board's waterways, a 332 ton casting, made its way in December 1982 inland by waterway from Goole to Doncaster. It was carried on a newly improved section of the Sheffield and South Yorkshire Navigation by E.V. Waddington and Sons' specially constructed barge.

The giant casting, the first of four, travelled to Sheffield to be machined at the Davy-McKee works in Darnall. It will return via the navigation to Goole for export to Mexico. After machining the weight of the casting will still be in excess of 300 tons.

The four castings are major components of a £350 million order won by Davy-McKee (Sheffield) Limited, to build a new steel rolling mill in Mexico. Though the castings themselves were too big to be poured in this country, the experience required to finish them to the required tolerances is only to be found in the United Kingdom at Sheffield.

In negotiations lasting many months Davy-McKee defeated intense competition from rival companies from Japan, France, Germany and Italy in successfully obtaining the contract to design and build a new steel rolling mill for Siderurgica Lazaro Cardenas – Las Truchas, S.A. (SICARTSA). Altogether, over £200 million of the contract will be direct exports of British-made plant and equipment.

John Anderson, the Board's freight development officer, said that the Board are proud to be involved with such a large export contract, and the fact that British Waterways were chosen to move this large indivisible load demonstrates just one of the many plus points for transporting cargoes by 'The Water Way'.

It has taken eighteen months of long and determined discussion to achieve the smooth operation reported here, which involved major co-operation between the Board's personnel and many others. It is indeed the first new business to be carried on the Sheffield and South Yorkshire Navigation and the rest of the negotiated movement will take place during and just after the official completion of the improvement scheme.

Victor Waddington's family business of master boatbuilders and waterside wharf operation is based at Swinton. Victor has shown his support for the SSYN Improvement Scheme in a positive way – by extending his wharfside premises and building a dry dock, by adding to his fleet and, just recently, by using the new dry dock to construct this special barge to carry the heavy castings.

Using two of his smaller vessels, the bow section was cut off one, and the stern section from another. Then a new specially strengthened section was welded on to form the middle of the craft. The construction of this vessel was designed by Victor himself, with the assistance of the Board's Engineering Services at Rickmansworth, with their new micro computer to check the design. Philip Orton wrote a programme giving structural details so that the computer could analyse the stresses to ensure the newly constructed vessel could take the extra heavy load.

The vessel, which Victor Waddington appropriately named *Confidence*, is 142 ft long with a 19 ft 6 in beam and an unloaded draft of 2 ft. With the heavy load, the draft was 7 ft. By the beginning of November *Confidence* was complete and floating in the canal. On 4 December she was moored at Goole to await her first heavy lift cargo from West Germany.

This 332 ton casting started its long journey when it left the factory in West Germany and was loaded onto a railway wagon to be transported by rail from Hattingen to Mulheim. At the port of Mulheim it was loaded onto *Warsleth*.

The ship sailed on 11 December and arrived at Goole Docks on 13 December. Here a lifting frame was fitted and a J.D. White TC4000 crane, lifted the casting into the hold of *Confidence*. The crane had to be counterbalanced with ballast slung on an opposing jib because of the immense weight of the casting.

At 9 a.m. on 17 December, *Confidence*, pushed by Waddington's *Kingfisher* – a specially converted push-tug – left Goole and started the journey to Doncaster. She was preceded by BWB tug *Water Haig* fitted with echo sounding equipment, which was only employed as a fail safe check at the specific request of the shipper. *Confidence* took just six hours for the trip to Doncaster, arriving at 3 p.m.

A certain amount of work had to be done at the unloading quay. This included laying hardcore and removing the fencing and bollards at the entrance to provide access for a Pickfords trailer which was taking over for the last part of the journey to Sheffield by road. Pickfords provided a sixteen-axle trailer and arrangements had to be made with the police for an escort because of the length of the trailer and weight of the casting.

The Christmas holiday intervened during the movement, and the casting was loaded onto the Pickfords trailer and left there until 6 January when it set off from Doncaster at 9 a.m.

Because of the abnormal load there were restrictions on the time of day it could be moved. There were also some problems while the load was being transported on the M1 and the trailer had to have welding repairs to the suspension. The road journey took six days and involved a change of axles by Pickfords from sixteen to twenty-four to take the load across Brinsworth Road Bridge. It was necessary for South Yorkshire County Council on behalf of the Department of Transport and the police, to make a bridge deflection test. It was decided to strengthen the bridge with steel plates stuck on with special adhesive before the loader crossed it.

Early on Tuesday morning 11 January, the casting was delivered at Davy-McKee's Darnall Works.

Many months of carefully planned arrangements involving a number of companies, including the Board, proved worthwhile when the casting finally arrived safely. But this is only the beginning of the story. This casting has to be returned to Goole, and there are three more to go before all four are exported to Mexico, and all those responsible for the various stages in the long journey can relax.

Considering the complexity of the whole movement of the casting starting in West Germany everything went according to plan and the first casting is now completing its final machining in Darnall.

four

Stairways to Heaven

Canal Inclined Planes of Shropshire

The advent of canals to the 'industrial corner' of East Shropshire was retarded by the existence of what were regarded then as almost insuperable difficulties. On the one hand, the nature of the terrain, high ridges and deep valleys, was discouraging. On the other hand there was the real problem of a serious shortage of water for lockage. Even today one rarely sees a stream in this area. The reason, undoubtedly, is that the extensive mining for coal and ironstone over a very long period caused the water to go underground.

The first and second canals in Shropshire were private ventures. In 1782, the Marquis of Stafford – a relative of the famous Duke of Bridgewater – constructed a 7-mile canal between Donnington Wood and Pave Lane, near Newport, to serve his coal and ironstone mines in the Donnington Wood District, with a branch to his Grace's limekilns at Lilleshall.

In 1769, the great Quaker ironmaster, Richard Reynolds of Ketley, visited the Duke of Bridgewater's canal, and came away deeply impressed with its efficiency. Nineteen years later, his son, William, decided that if he was to take full advantage of the excellent coal and ironstone in the Oakengates area, he must have a better means of transport than that offered by the terrible roads. The Ketley Canal, his answer to the problem, was constructed on a dead level to Ketley, in 1788. But there was still the problem of a fall of 73 ft at the Ketley extremity. The method Reynolds adopted to overcome this difficult problem made him and the Ketley Canal famous. He modernized a device which has been used with a little success on continental canals, the inclined plane.

Bringing his canal forward to an abrupt edge of the bank, Reynolds made a lock – the bottom of which was actually part of the inclined plane. This lock could be flooded and the water withdrawn (for further use) at will. Over the lock he erected a framework into which he put a large wooden drum around which was coiled a long wire rope. Down the face of the incline a double railway was laid which connected the canal at the top with a basin near the ironworks at the bottom.

On the rails ran trolleys or cradles, on which the 8-ton boats were carried up and down the incline. These trolleys had two large wheels in front and two small ones behind, to enable them to remain in a horizontal position. The cradles were drawn up and down by the wire rope, and at first the incline was self-acting; a carrier with a fully-loaded boat descending would draw up a boat almost two-thirds loaded.

The ascending cradle would be drawn into the lock at the top, the lock gates closed and the lock flooded. The boat which had just ascended would be flooded off the cradle and another one would be put on the cradle and secured, after which the water in the lock would be drawn off into a side pond, the lock gates opened and the boat begin its descent. The speed of the cradles was controlled by a brake acting on the axis of the drum.

At a later date, a small steam engine, or 'fire-engine' as it was called, was installed to provide the extra power necessary for full boats to ascend as well as descend.

In 1789 a token bearing a replica of the Ketley Inclined Plane was struck to commemorate this feat of engineering, and was used as local currency, being 'Payable at Ketley and Coalbrookdale'.

In later inclines the top lock was dispensed with, and by building a small incline into the top basin it was found possible for the cradle to be drawn over the 'sill' and the boat deposited in the deep water of the basin, saving much valuable time.

The life of the Ketley incline was of short duration. In 1817 the price of pig iron, carriage paid from Ketley to Stourport, fell from £18 per ton to £7 10s. The following year Joseph Reynolds, William's brother, blew in his Ketley furnaces and sold all his stock and equipment. Hirsch, writing in *Notice Sur Les Elevateurs*, reports that when Dutens, the French engineer, visited the spot in 1818 he found the Ketley Inclined Plane disused; that it was ever used again is extremely doubtful.

Nevertheless the success of the device was such that within six years of its inception several canals made possible by the use of the inclined plane had been constructed, and the whole of the industrial area north of the River Severn was connected with that important waterway. At least eight inclined planes were constructed on these canals, one of the first being at Coalport, a once-thriving Midland port from which in its heyday over 100,000 tons of coal were despatched annually. The last inclined plane to operate was that at Tench which, after being in service longer than any other in the country – it was used for about 125 years – was closed in 1921.

W. HOWARD WILLIAMS

Canal Tunnels

Canals were constructed before railways and so canal tunnels came before railway tunnels, although mine tunnels were the first of all. In those days they used gunpowder for blasting. And for the rest it was pick-and-shovel work by the light of tallow candles. Tunnels were driven from each end.

Engineers tried a new method with canal tunnels – shafts were sunk from the top of the hill to the line of the tunnel, which would then be extended in both directions from the bottom of the shafts. In this way more men could work at the same time. And it was easier to get rid of the spoil, which was hauled up the shafts in baskets by a horse-windlass.

The resulting heaps of spoil mark the line of many canal tunnels and are characteristic features today – if you know where to look. When the tunnel was finished most of the shafts were usually covered, but some were left to give ventilation: they usually have a circular brick top.

Five tunnels were cut for the Grand Trunk canal (Trent and Mersey) which was planned and engineered by James Brindley, the longest being Harecastle, near the Potteries – over a mile and a half long. Its dimensions were so restricted, however (the biggest part was only 12 ft high and 9 ft wide), that a 7 ft wide boat with a moderate load could pass through only with difficulty. Incidentally, all craft were taken through this tunnel by 'legging', but that's another story.

So, early in 1822, the Canal Company asked Thomas Telford to examine Harecastle Tunnel to see whether a second tunnel could be bored. In consequence of his favourable report he was authorized to do the job. During 1824 some of the fifteen pit-shafts (the deepest being 179 ft) were sunk; a large number of shafts was used to speed the work.

As the miners went down and cut through the various strata of the hill on their downward progress, they met vast quantities of water. And here, Telford's skill with pumping machinery proved of great value. He had a fire-engine or atmospheric steam-engine set up on the top of the hill, which could pump out volumes of water night and day.

This great amount of water, though it seriously hampered the work, was something that Telford had calculated for and, indeed, depended on, for it supplied water for the summit level of his canal. When the shafts had been sunk to the proper line of the intended waterway, the excavation struck out in opposite directions to meet up with other driftways (unfinished tunnels before bricking) which were in progress. When the whole line of excavation was finally joined by a continuous driftway, the water ran out freely at both ends and the pumping apparatus on the hilltop was no longer needed.

On 21 February 1825, the first brick of the tunnel was laid. The work went forward with such energy that the last brick was laid on 25 November 1826. Then the towing-path was completed and the tunnel opened to the public on 30 April 1827, not quite three years after the start of the operations.

This 'new' tunnel is parallel with the older one 26 yd away and about the same length (over a mile and a half). It is 16 ft high and 14 ft wide, of which

4 ft 9 in is covered by the towing path. That leaves 7 ft 3 in for the passage of the boat. The tunnel is so straight that it is possible to see from one end to the other. Electric fans have been installed at one end to draw out the exhaust fumes and now boats can navigate Harecastle under their own power.

There are three other tunnels on the Trent and Mersey, the first ever built in Britain for waterway transport.

The three longest canal tunnels to be constructed in this country were Standedge, 5,415 yd, through the Pennines on the Huddersfield Narrow Canal; Strood, 3,909 yd on the Thames and Medway; and Sapperton, 3,817 yd on the Thames and Severn. The first and last are disused, while the one at Strood is now used as a railway tunnel for trains from Gravesend to Strood and Rochester.

The longest canal tunnel still in commercial use is Blisworth, 3,056 yd on the Grand Union. This is followed by Netherton, 3,027 yd on the Birmingham Canal Navigations; and Harecastle New, 2,926 yd described above.

Most long tunnels had no towpath through them. Strood and Harecastle New were exceptions while the Netherton, opened in 1858 and the last tunnel to be constructed in Britain, has two towpaths and was originally lit by gas, but now by electricity. Such tunnels have more headroom than those without paths.

Where a tug is not used for taking boats through a tunnel there are usually fixed hours at which boats can enter at either end. This happens at Preston Brook, Barnton and Saltersford tunnels on the Trent and Mersey.

In the days before self-propelled craft, boats were passed through a tunnel with no tow path either by shafting, that is by pressing on the sides or roof of the tunnel with an iron-tipped shaft, or by legging. Sometimes legging was performed by the boat's crew, later including women, but at some major tunnels professional leggers were employed.

Later, attempts were made to draw boats through the tunnels by means of an endless rope driven by a waterwheel. It was not, however, until the era of the tug, and later the self-propelled boat that craft ceased to depend on manual labour for getting through tunnels.

DENIS J. ASTON

Staircase to the South – The Story of Foxton

Leicestershire has prospered for a thousand years and although the Arms of the City may bear a complacent 'Semper Eadem' – Always the Same – the county offers a vigorously progressive 'For'ard, For'ard'!

Leicester is well known as the eastern terminus of the Swannington railway – acknowledged generally as the country's first commercially successful line – but

The upper pool of the Foxton Lift near Market Harborough shortly after it opened in 1900. It was abandoned in 1911

the city's place on what was once England's most flourishing waterway is almost forgotten.

Unlike the county town of Leicester, Loughborough is a comparatively modern settlement of small size; and when, at the beginning of the Canal Age, Loughborough stepped smartly forward with a proposal for a navigation to the River Trent, it did so on the proverbial shoe-string.

By 1778 the town had completed a series of locks and navigable channels along the River Soar, and by that route had linked its own trade with that of Nottingham, Newark, Lincoln, and the sea.

Local financiers had plunged £10,000 into Loughborough's dead-end branch-line; were their shares intended to benefit the town's commercial development, or had they a shrewd foresight of the needs of their county town? Could they possibly have foreseen Leicester's wishes for connection to the growing system of waterways? Whether they knew or not, the subsequent extension of the Soar Navigation to Leicester had multiplied the value of Loughborough's waterway several times within a decade; and future events were to establish a Stock Exchange record.

In 1828, a £142 Loughborough Navigation share changed hands at £3,850, and in one momentous year paid a dividend of 87 per cent!

Leicester's linkage with the southern waterways was slow to develop and the first flush of 'Canal Mania' had passed when, in 1809, a broad canal had reached Market Harborough. There, a newly styled Grand Union Canal terminated in a basin in which one may still moor; and the rest of the route lay

25 miles to the south, over the wide, high, and stony uplands of Northamptonshire.

Close scrutiny of the contour-lines of the modern Ordnance Survey map makes one wonder whether the proposal to reach Northampton directly was ever made seriously, for the expensive prospect of a good deal of tunnelling, cutting, and embankment would not easily part speculators from their money. So, in the declining years of the Canal Age, the canal company called a halt at Market Harborough – leaving the more prosperous portion of its route to the Trent.

Six years later, another company planned the awaited connection of Leicester to the Thames. Thomas Telford was consultant engineer on the project, and the presence of all the locks in two staircases is indicative of the practice he employed on his other canals – notably on the 'Shroppy' main-line and on the Macclesfield Canal – of concentrating the major engineering works.

Barnes and Bevan were the surveyors and active engineers of the aptly named Grand Junction Canal, and the combined efforts of the three men resulted in a curious mixture of planning. While the locks are characteristically Telford, the

A barge in a water-filled tank arriving in the lower pool of the Foxton Lift by which barges were hauled up and down a 300 ft incline

tortuous following of the contours around Yelvertoft and Crick is certainly not; these lengthy meanderings are in the best Brindley tradition!

The summit level includes two long tunnels, yet although these are both well up to 'broad canal' dimensions, the two lock staircases at Foxton and at Watford (3 miles from the junction with the Grand Union at Norton) are only of narrow boat size. Economy can be the only explanation of such an anomaly and has resulted in a bottleneck which has always throttled through traffic.

The complete route from the south was open by 1816. It included 25 miles of the original river navigation to Leicester; almost as much broad canal to Market Harborough; and 24 miles – with a 20-mile summit pond – of narrow canal from Foxton to Norton Junction.

There is an ascent of 75 ft in the ten locks of Foxton staircase; these can be negotiated within the hour, but a pair of working boats obviously takes twice as long. When, at the turn of the century, a railway competitor was being keenly fought, the Grand Junction sought a way to reduce this delay, and substituted for the locks an astonishing contrivance on the inclined plane principle.

A hundred yards to the east of Foxton Top Lock one may still find the twin termini of a short, forked, branch canal. Below these, tracks can still be traced down the hill-side to two basins at the foot. Above the tracks lie the ruins of an engine house, which once hauled two wheeled and waterfilled tanks each

Lower pools of the Foxton Lift, which enabled barges to be transported between the upper and lower pools in about twenty minutes

intended to carry a boat, and with one tank counter-balancing the other. A boat entered the tank at the top by way of water-tight guillotine doors; down below, the tracks led the tank straight to the bottoms of the two basins.

The weight of the tanks (they could hardly have weighed less than 100 tons) persistently caused the tracks to subside, and whether there were boats waiting nor not, the winding-gear engine needed to be expensively maintained under steam. The lift began to operate in 1900 and was closed barely ten years later; during this period the locks had fallen into poor condition, and were then repaired and reopened. The inclined plane was partially dismantled in 1914.

The Grand Junction never prospered to the same extent as its parent canal, reaching its peak dividend of 13 per cent in the same year as Loughborough's 87 per cent. Twenty years later its profits had fallen to a sober, but steady, 5 per cent, and in 1929 the company was absorbed into the Grand Union. On the whole, trade continued to dwindle until now there is no commercial traffic at all.

F.G. BIRDEN

Canal Lighthouses

Most people are unaware that the Board own several lighthouses. As might be expected, they are chiefly to be found at the entrances to various canals, and all the working examples are in Scotland. England has only one canal lighthouse, the charming red-brick structure at the entrance to the Shropshire Union canal at Ellesmere Port. It was designed by Thomas Telford and has an unusual harebell-shaped roof. This lighthouse came into operation in 1796, when the three locks connecting the Wirral line with the River Mersey were completed, and continued to guide ships along the river for almost one hundred years.

In 1894 the Manchester Ship Canal was opened and shipping bound for Ellesmere Port had to use the new canal. The entrance was at Eastham locks, some 3 miles downstream, and so the need for Telford's light ended, though fortunately it has been preserved.

Further north there was a lighthouse at Lees Scar, Silloth, Cumbria. This had been built by the Carlisle Canal Company to guide shipping from Liverpool to the entrance to the canal at Port Carlisle. It was working in the 1840s but had only a short life as, on 1 August 1853, the canal closed. The Canal Company had received Parliamentary assent to turn itself into a Railway Company!

In the far west of Scotland, the Crinan Canal cuts across the northern part of the Kintyre peninsula of Argyll, and provides a short-cut for small vessels between the River Clyde and the Western Isles. It has a lighthouse at each end of its 9 mile length, both being automatically operated. At Ardrishaig, the eastern terminal, the light is situated at the end of the breakwater leading from the canal

The lighthouse at Crinan Sea Lock

office. It has a very maritime appearance and, despite its relatively sheltered situation, seas have been known to sweep right over the light during gales. The tides, too, can be strong and have a scouring effect at the end of the breakwater.

Ardrishaig displays a flashing white light at night to indicate the approach channel from Loch Gilp, red and green sectors indicating when a vessel is 'off course'.

Crinan light, close by the sea lock at the western end of the canal, has a fixed light with red and white sections to ensure craft keep on the correct line while approaching from Loch Crinan. Both lighthouses are believed to date from the 1840s, when extensive repairs were made to the canal.

During the same decade the Caledonian Canal, which runs for 60 miles from Corpach near Fort William to Clachnaharry, Inverness, was under repair. For some time it had been recommended that small lighthouses be provided to mark the entrances to the canal and some of the lochs. In 1848 the Canal Engineer's report to the Commissioners of the Caledonian Canal stated: 'Previous to the approach of winter, the small lights which had been provided for the line of the canal, were fixed in their respective places, namely, one at each Sea Loch Entrance, one at each end of Loch Ness, and one at the south west end of Loch Lochy, five in all.'

Of these five lighthouses, Bona, Fort Augustus, Gairlochy, Clachnaharry, and Corpach, the one at Bona is the only one where the original structure remains, however, the iron light pedestal for the old acetylene light is still standing at Gairlochy. Bona light is perhaps the most interesting because it is the only one with living accommodation adjacent. The lamp, now operated automatically, is to be found in the upper storey bay window. Although the building is now let to a tenant, the Board retain the right of access to attend to and maintain the light.

Bona lighthouse exhibits a fixed white light, as do its companions at Fort Augustus and Gairlochy. Before Fort Augustus lighthouse could be built it was necessary to obtain special permission from the Army Board of Ordnance, who then owned the military fort from which Fort Augustus got its name. Both Fort Augustus and Gairlochy lighthouses are 'pepper-pot' shaped as, too, is the sea light at Corpach, at the western end of the canal. Corpach 'pepper-pot' is of a more modern age, having been built of concrete blocks in 1913 to replace the earlier structure. It shows a fixed white light to indicate the approach channel from Loch Eil, red sectors appearing when a vessel is 'off course'.

At Clachnaharry, at the eastern end of the canal, a lattice tower now displays the sea light, which is a flashing white light. Are these lights really necessary? The Canal Engineer's report, gives the answer:

> The lights, as now placed, have been found to be of the greatest possible benefit, to vessels freely navigating Loch Ness both ways and Loch Lochy in one direction, and thereby saving the loss of the corresponding period of daylight for passage through the locks. The lights are mostly elevated from 20 and 25 ft above the level of the water and the lamps are of an improved construction for economy and convenience.

KENNETH CLEW

Opening Day at Pontcysyllte

Thousands of people went to Pontcysyllte on 26 November 1805, but very few of them travelled by boat. They journeyed there for the grand opening ceremony of the great aqueduct, whose construction had excited widespread interest.

The length of canal to the Vale of Llangollen had not yet been completed, but the aqueduct was filled with water for the occasion. It is not certain how the water was obtained; in his very interesting biography, *Thomas Telford*, L.T.C. Rolt put forward the suggestion that a nearby brook was temporarily diverted to act as a feeder.

It has been estimated that cutting the final 6 miles of the waterway would take only twelve months, but in fact it took much longer and was not completed until 1808. However, the Ellesmere Canal Company decided to adhere to their plan to open the aqueduct in 1805.

Construction work on the aqueduct had started in 1795. The Company had originally accepted a plan put forward by a Shropshire architect for an aqueduct of only three arches which would have crossed the River Dee at a much lower level than the present structure. Locks on each side would have carried the canal down into the valley.

Charles Hadfield (*British Canals*, 6th edition, 1979) attributes the creation of the aqueduct to both William Jessop and Thomas Telford. Building it was the responsibility of Telford who was the company's general agent, surveyor, engineer, architect, and overlooker. Some of the company's committee must have had grave misgivings at the idea of boats travelling high in the air.

On 25 July 1795 the foundation stone of the first pier was laid by Richard Myddleton, the owner of Chirk Castle. While work was in progress on the Pontcysyllte Aqueduct, the Chirk Aqueduct was being constructed only a few miles away.

The fact that it was so much higher and longer than the Chirk Aqueduct was not the only reason it took five years longer to build. There was difficulty in raising the necessary cash, for the 1790s were a period of financial stringency.

A narrow boat crosses the Pontcysyllte Aqueduct

However, the aqueduct was finished for the opening ceremony on 26 November 1805. Fortunately the day was fine, and the many people who had flocked to the area were able to enjoy fully the colourful ceremony which marked the completion of an engineering marvel that had been considered one of the Wonders of Wales, even when it was still only partly built.

A contemporary account says that the aqueduct was 'opened with great ceremony'. The report continues:

Before 2 o'clock, the aqueduct having been filled, the procession began. The Earl of Bridgewater's barge led the way, in which was his lordship and countess, Sir Watkin Williams Wynne, Bart, Sir Foster Cunliffe, Bart, Colonel Kynaston-Powell and lady, and several other ladies and gentlemen. In the prow of the barge, the serjeant-major of the Shropshire Volunteers, in full uniform, carried a flag, on which was painted a representation of the aqueduct, the Dee and the valley. Next followed other members of the committee, and Mr Telford, the projector of the aqueduct and general agent of the company in Col. Kynaston-Powell's barge, carrying two union-jacks. In the third was the numerous band of the Shropshire Volunteers in full uniform, playing 'God save the King' and other loyal airs. . . .

As soon as the first barge entered the cast-iron waterway, which is 126 feet above the level of the River Dee, the artillery company of the Shropshire Volunteers fired 16 rounds from two brass field-pieces.

The Company from the barges landed, and the Earl of Bridgewater, as chairman of the committee, conducted the ladies and their friends to a house belonging to the company, where they partook of a cold collation. . . . The Company went back to their barges, and the procession returned in the same order as it came. The two boats laden with coals followed the procession, the first having a handsome flag, thus inscribed: 'This is the first trading-boat which passed the aqueduct of Pontcysyllte loaded from Plaas-Kynaston collieries, on the 26th day of November 1805.' The discharge from the guns, as the procession returned, the plaudits of the spectators (calculated at full 8,000), the martial music, the echo reverberating from the mountains magnified the enchanting scene.

Such was the spectacle when boats crossed the great aqueduct for the first time. Another report said that between the cheering and exulting there were 'intervals of silent astonishment'.

Even today, 175 years later, most people experience a feeling of awe when they first see this magnificent structure.

COURTNEY DAINTON

Stairway to Heaven

This October [1984] sees the fiftieth anniversary of the grand opening of the majestic flight of twenty-one locks at Hatton, otherwise known as the 'Stairway to Heaven'. The flight was opened by Royalty as part of an optimistic and ambitious scheme to upgrade the Grand Union Canal between Braunston and Brimingham.

The scheme was never fully realized. Only the concrete overbridges, miles of familiar concrete piling, and striking locks with large encased paddle gearing, remain to remind us of what could have been, but wasn't.

The route between Braunston and Birmingham originally consisted of three different undertakings, the Oxford Canal (Braunston to Napton), Warwick and Napton, and Warwick and Birmingham canals. The two Warwick canals were built as narrow canals, and were bought by the Regent's Canal Company in 1928, forming the Grand Union Canal Company on 1 January 1929.

The company's line from London to Braunston, a broad canal, enabled narrow boats in pairs to work quickly and efficiently, and it was obvious that the route to Birmingham, a major source of trade, should be improved accordingly. A barge route would then be created between the country's two major cities on the elimination of the fifty-two narrow locks between Braunston and Birmingham.

In August 1929, a grant under Section 2 of the 1929 Development Act was applied for by the new company; concurrently attempts were made to buy up the Oxford Canal's Braunston to Napton section to gain control of the entire line to Birmingham.

Planning work went on, and a grant of £500,000 under an Enabling Act in 1931 was obtained for construction work to begin at Hatton, Knowle and Stockton in April 1932.

It was intended to carry out work with no disruption to traffic, so the old narrow locks remained in use while the new locks were built. The works were an 'engineering task calling for the greatest skill and knowledge', and, contrary to popular belief, there was never any intention to continue the works right into the heart of the Birmingham canals.

An early victim of the proposals was the decision not to build a new canal for 900 yd on the north side of the A425 at Shuckburgh, to eliminate the notorious bends under that road to the south side. The bends and bridges were widened instead. The canal was dredged to an overall depth of 5 ft 6 in, and concrete piling placed in many locations. This, like all the piling in the scheme, has the familiar date of installation, depth of pile, and dredging depth inscribed frequently.

The contractors were to build fifty-one new locks (five replacing six narrow locks at Knowle), with dimensions between the quoins of 91 ft (allowing 83 ft for boats) and a width of 15 ft 4 in.

The locks were built of mass concrete, with alternate courses of 9 in and

Looking down the Hatton flight of locks, known as the 'Stairway to Heaven'

14 in blue bricks for facing. Three openings from the top paddles into the lock chamber helped to equalize the flow and minimize the turbulence of water encountered in filling the lock. The difference in flows between the lock filling and emptying can be seen; the emptying process produces spectacular water turbulence below the bottom gates. The paddles themselves are hydraulic, encased in the familiar housings known as 'Daleks'!

Construction of the locks was standard, except at Hatton, where running sand forced the use of steel piling to stabilize the ground. The lock was then encased between the piles. At Knowle and Bascote (where a staircase replaced two narrow locks), side ponds (termed economizer ponds by the GUCC) were built. All the narrow locks were degated, the redundant equipment finding use on the company's narrow canals, with the chambers being retained to serve as overflow weirs with small footbridges across. A few old locks are now used as dry docks, an example being at the top of Calcutt Lock.

Bridges were rebuilt all along the lock flights in concrete, and look very much like early versions of the country's first motorway bridges! The bridges on level stretches were often left, as they were of sufficient width to admit barges. A Mr Farr built five small accommodation bridges, and Catherine de Barnes and Richmond Road bridges were built by the local councils in 1933 and 1935 respectively. All swing bridges were removed, one at Copt Heath being replaced by a 32 ft span bridge.

The climax of the scheme took place fifty years ago when HRH The Duke of Kent opened the Hatton Locks on Tuesday 20 October 1934. The Duke ceremoniously opened Hatton Top Lock at 12 noon, and then was taken down the flight in *Progress*, a 12 ft 6 in barge built by Bushell Brothers of Tring, to lunch at Warwick.

By this time, the grant of £500,000 had been used up, and the company then had to carry on at its own expense. No more was done after 1937 when it was realized that boats like *Progress* could not be used because of the expense of removing certain bottlenecks like Shrewley Tunnel and Rowington Cutting.

Narrow boats continued to be used, and moved along the canal more efficiently, reducing London-Birmingham times to as little as just over fifty hours. Additionally, narrow boats could work through to the narrow beam Birmingham Canal, avoiding transhipment at the Sampson Road basins, the terminus of the wide canal at the top of the Camp Hill flight in Birmingham. Transhipment basins for transferring goods into narrow boats destined for the Coventry and Oxford canals at Braunston were never built.

Short of building a new canal, the Grand Union Canal Company knew it could never attract business in the face of fierce competition from the roads and railways, so no more was done, thus ending the last great attempt by any canal company to gain back lost traffic.

ROGER FORD

five

Down the Slipway

The Scottish 'Puffers'

A part of the Scottish scene which is regarded with a great deal of affection and some amusement by local folk around and about the River Clyde and the West of Scotland, is provided by those unconventional little tramp ships, the 'puffers', which ply their trade between the Clyde, the Forth and Clyde Canal, the west coast of Scotland, Western Isles and the Crinan Canal. Sturdy little boats with a gross tonnage of about 165 tons, a length of about 85 ft, and a breadth of 19 ft, they carry coal and a miscellany of other cargoes to island outposts on the west coast of Scotland. Many of these islands have no harbours and the 'puffers', which are practically flat-bottomed, can be run up on the sandy beaches and at low tide left high and dry so that their cargoes can be unloaded into carts and lorries. They have a speed of about 8 knots and when fully laden have little or no freeboard, lying squat on the water. Many people in the islands and highlands on the west coast depend entirely on these unhurried little ships for the bare necessities of life.

In most kinds of weather 'puffers' can be seen (and heard – puff, puff, puff) on the upper reaches of the Clyde heading for the canal basin at Bowling, on the Forth and Clyde canal, to load coal or ground chips for various destinations on the coast, or on the open seas with a cargo of seaweed, sand or ballast timber. On many occasions their journey is made difficult by changing weather as many of their destinations are exposed to Atlantic gales, and often they are seen lying up at the Crinan Canal waiting for favourable weather.

The 'puffers' originated and were built to suit the locks of the Forth and Clyde and Crinan Canals. It was some time before they took to the sea, the first sea-going 'puffer' was the *Cyclops*, built in 1831, which traded between Port Dundas – at that time the canal port of Glasgow – Stirling and Alloa. She was probably the first iron steamship to ply in Scotland.

By 1866 some seventy 'puffers' were plying their trade, principally in the slate trade from Ballachulish, Luing, Easedale, Balnahua and Balvicar to Fort Dundas, Bowling and Glasgow.

Today [1953], they are not so numerous, but this distinctive class of vessel, peculiar to the Clyde and Scottish Canals still carries on a necessary service, and the tall, puffing funnels of the 'puffers' remain a welcome sight to the isolated people who listen keenly for that typical 'puff, puff, puff'.

The Story of Fly-Boats

'Let go for'd, slacken off aft!' A word of command from Captain Jarvis, a crack of a whip and the *Birmingham Fly* moved away from Ellesmere Port.

It was midnight on Sunday, and as the clock struck the hour fly-boat *Aristocrat*, star of the fleet, loaded with 20 tons of priority traffic, glided away to vanish into the darkness of the night. On Tuesday midday she would be promptly discharging her cargo in Birmingham.

The name 'fly-boat' will probably conjure up some strange notions in the minds of the younger waterways generation, but the word is in no way connected with the common insect nor does it concern the Royal Air Force.

Fly-boats were the express merchandise craft which traded extensively throughout the canal system until the beginning of the century, and were the counterpart of the express passenger packet-boats, the joint service forming an essential part of canal traffic operation in those days.

The service was of necessity an expensive one, but industry and the travelling public then, as today, demanded speed and within reason were prepared to pay for it.

The craft were specifically built for rapid movement in a restricted channel, and the merchandise-carrying flys operating on the narrow canals had a maximum loading capacity of 20 tons.

The crew consisted of the captain and two, three, or even four hands – all men, women being employed only on the slower family boats. The captain was paid on a ton-mile basis and he recruited and paid his own crew.

From starting point to destination, by day and night, the fly-boats worked non-stop except to change their tired horses whose stables were economically positioned along the route of the canal.

Journey-time schedules were carefully compiled to get the best effort from horse and man, and the fly began the trip promptly at the time announced in the working notices. These timings were strictly adhered to and unless interrupted by a major incident the boats reached the destination at the appointed hour. 'On time' was the proud motto which came to be adopted by a railway company years later.

Not only did the fly-boats have priority of passage over all other merchandise craft, including uninterrupted locking facility and choice of deep water channel, but they were given preference in loading and discharging so that not a moment was lost.

The Shropshire Union Canal in particular had a most extensive express merchandise boat system and a glance at the weekly schedule of the *Birmingham Fly* will reveal the high efficiency of the service.

Fly-boat *Aristocrat* left Ellesmere Port at midnight on Sunday and was discharging cargo in Birmingham at midday on Tuesday. Reloading immediately with 20 tons of urgent export traffic, it was off on the return trip without delay to arrive back at the port before midnight on Wednesday. With similar preferential discharging and reloading facility the second trip began, and by midday on Friday her cargo was again being unloaded in Birmingham. The crew remained in Birmingham on the Friday night – 246 miles and 207 locks since Sunday night. So who would deny them their well-earned tankards of ale?

Similar schedules operated throughout the Shropshire Union system for the carriage of perishable and urgent traffic. And it is said that farmers could check their clocks by the passing of the white-sheeted 'Cheese Special' which left Whitchurch on Wednesday night and unloaded its delicious 'Cheshire' in Manchester on Saturday morning.

Discipline in those days was of a very high order and it was with some astonishment on one occasion that a traffic agent spotted a 56 lb weight snugly placed among the cargo of cheeses. 'Where the hell did that come from?' shouted the agent to one of the guilty crew. 'Please, Sir,' stammered the trembling hand, hesitating for a few moments, 'we found it floating in Whitchurch Basin!'

Similarly, the express passenger packet-boats operated to a schedule which varied only by minutes.

Just as the express passenger trains of today have preference over all other rail traffic, so then had the express canal packet-boats priority over all other canal traffic.

These passenger packet-boats were built on even finer lines than the merchandise fly-boats. Although of similar length (70 ft) their beam was considerably reduced, being generally between 5 and 6 ft; the reduced cross-section enabled an even more speedy movement in the restricted channel.

The packets were usually drawn by two horses in a single line, on one of which rode a 'jockey'. Unlike the racecourse jockeys, the canal jockey was concerned chiefly in getting under obstacles rather than over them. And to flatten out on the horse's back while sweeping under the many bridges called for fine judgement.

The horses were hard ridden for a comparatively short distance of perhaps 4 or 5 miles when they were replaced by fresh horses. The change operation was accomplished so efficiently and quickly that an overall journey speed of 8 miles an hour was maintained.

The inside cabin of the *Duchess Countess*, which represented the 'first class' waterways travel of its era

The canal packet introduced a form of luxury travel previously unknown, for the stage-coach could in no way compete with the quiet smooth movement on water. Indeed, the popularity of canal passenger travel continued for long after the introduction of the railway coach.

A typical service of which records remain was that operating between Wigan and Liverpool on the Leeds and Liverpool Canal, a distance of 35 miles. Passengers embarked from Wigan Pier at seven o'clock in the morning and arrived in Liverpool at three in the afternoon, several calls being made at the various villages on the way.

One such call was at Burscough. Here, passengers disembarked to join the stage-coach for the seaside resort of Southport.

For a period of about sixty years these passenger packet-boats operated widely over the canal system throughout the country. But with the rapid development in the comfort and speed of rail travel, the canal passenger services were finally brought to a close. It is sad to recall that the last remnant of this once famous fleet, the old *Duchess Countess*, probably the last known packet-boat in operation, was until 1955 lying peacefully on the banks of the

The last packet boat to be in regular service was the *Duchess Countess*, which finished its days on the bank of the Shropshire Union Canal at Frankton Junction. At the prow was fixed, at one time, a huge curved knife blade. This was to sever any towline that might obstruct progress, for the packet boat had priority of passage

Llangollen Canal near Frankton Junction. The old lady has since been broken up although some portions of the hull have been retained in the British Waterways Maintenance Yard at Ellesmere.

The fly-boats, however, with their express merchandise service continued to operate for many years. The Shropshire Union Company retained these facilities until 1921. Then, with the termination of their carrying department, this highly officient service came to an end and the fly-boats, with their wealth of tradition, were retired finally to rejoin their sister craft the packet-boats in the quiet backwaters of the canal.

C.S.R. HALL

Vital Link – The Story of The Thames Steam Tug and Lighterage Company

'Control calling *Robertsbridge*, control calling *Robertsbridge* . . . over.'
'*Robertsbridge* calling control . . . over.'
'Where are you, Walter? . . . over.'

'Just passing Tower Bridge . . . over.'
'Will you round at Hay's Wharf and pick up the *Norman* for Brentford? . . . over.'
'Right mate . . . over and out.'

This is a typical message passed over the radio system of The Thames Steam Tug and Lighterage Company from its City office control room to one of its tugs on the River Thames. This vital link by which all tugs are in constant touch is a great help in the economical and speedy movement of traffic. By this means each tug is kept busy with a full load of barges and delays are kept to a minimum.

It is always interesting to learn of the activities or organizations outside the British Waterways network but who are associated with us in the water transport business, although perhaps in a somewhat different sphere. The Thames Steam Tug and Lighterage Company has more than a hundred years experience in the transport of general cargo on the River Thames and on our nearby canals. Its fleet covers the Thames from Shellhaven to Brentford, the Grand Union Canal up to Uxbridge, the Lee Navigation to Ware and all docks in London and Tilbury. Most of the time over a hundred of the company's barges are on British Waterways.

Established in 1856 the company is now one of the largest lighterage operators in London, with 630 craft, of which 330 are canal wide boats of 65–130 ton capacity, and the rest, river barges, some carrying up to 220 tons. All barges are dumb and are hauled by fourteen modern diesel tugs, seven of which operate in the docks and up the Lee to Tottenham, the remaining seven working on the Thames between the docks and Brentford. The largest of these river tugs have 400 hp engines, every ounce of power being needed to tow their trains of six barges – the maximum allowed on the Thames. Beyond Tottenham and Brentford the Company's own traffic is hauled by tractors, some of which are operated by British Waterways.

And what a variety of cargo the company carries. Tomato puree from Italy for sauces and soups, lime juice from West Indies and Africa for thirst quenchers, wheat from Canada and Russia, timber from the Baltic, sugar, paper, copper and zinc – all of which find a way into our homes at some time or another.

Some of the barges are insulated for the safe carriage of meat, butter, cheese and eggs, and there are also tanker barges for the transport of oil from the refineries at Shellhaven and Purfleet to the big Castrol depot at Hayes. Certain oils require specialized handling, and, besides fuel and lubricating oils, hot bitumen and grease are conveyed in tank barges fitted with steam coils. The company carries from 60,000 to 70,000 tons of traffic a year on behalf of British Waterways and is the vital link in the chain of transport between the London docks and the Midland industrial centres on the Grand Union Canal.

The traffic, which is unloaded overside in the docks, is taken to Brentford, where it is either transhipped to our own narrow boats for onward conveyance up the

Grand Union or unloaded at Brent Meadow Wharf for storage. Some is unloaded over the quay to road services for destinations which have no canal access.

There is a certain amount of export traffic, too, which travels by the same means in the reverse direction.

Although the lightermen, one to a barge, are employed through the Dock Labour Board, the tug crews are regular staff, some of whom started as boys and have well over twenty-five years service. An average of 400 men work for the Company each day.

If you are thinking of buying a tug, the company has its own tug and barge building yard down at Brentford which, as well as constructing boats for the company's own use and maintaining the fleet, builds launches for export – two recent orders came from the Sudan and Nigeria. At present-day [1961] prices a new diesel tug costs up to £60,000 and a river barge between £6,000 and £7,000. The word 'steam' in the company's title is of course a misnomer in present times – all the tugs are driven by either diesel-hydraulic, diesel-electric or diesel-mechanical power units.

Through the kindness of the Company arrangements were made for this writer to experience the joys of tugging on the Thames on a winter's afternoon. A radio call to skipper Walter King on the tug *Framfield* just leaving Deptford asked him to round at Tower Pier and pick up a passenger for Brentford. To the uninitiated a word about this 'rounding' business. All barge traffic travels up and down the Thames with the tide, and to stop in the direction of travel would result in the barges swinging around the tug. The tug therefore turns right round in the river with its train to face the tide which keeps the tow ropes taut and the barges under control.

The *Framfield* was delayed picking up two awkwardly placed barges of timber below Tower Bridge, and by the time I had leapt unceremoniously aboard at the pier we were forty-five minutes behind time. Introductions completed we turned around and headed up river at three o'clock at a steady 7 knots with our six barges – *Reindeer, Robin, Siren, Scotia, Spode,* and *Southsea* – following behind like well-trained hounds.

The winter sun was sinking behind the South Bank buildings and a cold breeze blew around the open bridge. Skipper Walter King didn't think it was as cold as all that, but then he was standing close to the slow-combustion stove which was only a few feet away from the wheel. He knew every trick of the tide as we shot the bridges, swinging our load through the arches with a precision born of many years' experience.

A skipper for ten years, he had worked his way up from cabin-boy and has been in the service of the company for thirty-three years. Both he and his mate, Peter Murray, declared they wouldn't want any other life. They liked the sense of both freedom and responsibility – you were told the load to take down to the docks and what to pick up when you got there. Subject to any alterations to orders over the radio you were left to get on with the job.

As the lights began to twinkle on either side of the river, cabin-boy Francis Dedman put in a very welcome appearance on the bridge with a brew of steaming hot tea from the after-cabin. Now, feeling warmer, the skipper got engineer Harry Preston to show me round the engine room. The noise was deafening as the 400 hp diesel-engine pounded, but the comforting warmth down there in the depths of the tug was a tempting alternative to the open bridge above.

I had to brace myself to return to the skipper and his mate, who were preparing for Hammersmith Bridge. The flood waters and our late running had made it doubtful whether we would get under the low arches ahead. The tug's fittings were stripped down until the top of the wheel on the bridge was the highest point.

The skipper shouted 'duck!' and we all bent down smartly as we shot under the centre arch with only 6 in to spare. We had lost the tide at Putney Bridge and were now battling ahead at only 3 knots with darkness descending and fog gradually thickening.

There was no other traffic on the river and we seemed to be plodding into an eerie silence only broken by the swish-swash of the water against the bows of the barges whose dark outlines we could only just see.

It was past six o'clock when the grey shapes of the warehouses at Brentford loomed out of the fog and a megaphoned voice from the shore told us where the various loads were to be positioned. Three of the barges were loaded with milk powder for Glaxo of Greenford and one with sleepers for British Railways, Hayes. These were slipped off and taken up into the Grand Union Canal by a small launch as we docked the remaining two barges of timber higher up the river, and groped our way back to the pier, where the relief crew were waiting to come aboard. As we stepped ashore brief greetings and 'good nights' were exchanged, but it was doubtful if the *Framfield* with its fresh load would get away that night. 'This weather is no good for us chaps,' declared the skipper, and I could certainly see his point as we pulled our coat collars tighter and set off to our respective firesides and a good hot meal.

K.W. ASHBERRY

When 'Tom Puddings' Took a Trip by Train

A railway line running down a ramp into the Aire and Calder Navigation; a little railway engine, making quite a splash sometimes (though not on purpose) by sliding down the slope and into the water!

Some of the older folk around Stanley Ferry, in the North Eastern Division, still remember it.

This railway line used to run from St John's Colliery, Normanton, to a point just east of the aqueduct at Stanley Ferry where, at Locke's Basin, the ramp took the line gently down below the water.

Rather a strange set-up you may think! This is how it worked.

A number of special steel railway vehicles were constructed, after the style of what is known as 'bolster wagons' in railway circles. A vehicle would be lowered down the ramp and under the water. An empty compartment boat, or 'Tom Pudding', was floated over it and then – with a triumpant hiss of steam – the little engine hauled back up the ramp the vehicle with the compartment boat resting on it.

When this operation had been repeated a sufficient number of times and there was a train of three vehicles loaded with empty compartment boats the little engine ran up to the front and chugged off with it to the colliery. There, the boats were loaded with coal and when this was complete the little engine, puffing and blowing a bit more now, hauled the train back to Locke's Basin and lowered the vehicles again, one by one, down the ramp.

In the water, the compartment boats would float off and be formed up into the sort of water-train which is still as familiar a sight as ever on North Eastern Division waterways, ready to be taken behind a tug to Goole.

An empty 'Tom Pudding' compartment boat being hauled out of the water at Stanley Ferry Basin to be taken to an adjacent colliery for loading. Each compartment boat is 20 ft long by 15 ft beam by 9 ft deep

A special braking system was in operation – a cable wrapped around a twin-barrelled drum and coupled to the loco and to the wagon – and the basin itself was carefully designed so that the compression of the water within its walls served to check the speed of a loaded compartment boat coming down the ramp.

The system ceased operation, however, in 1937, when the loading screens were failing to clean the coal sufficiently. A new washery plant was constructed but this had to be some 15 ft higher than the old screen and when the track was lifted it became unstable and could no longer be used with safety.

A pity, for it seemed to be such a neat, simple system, and surely something quite unique.

Inn Signs Tell of Forgotten Craft

Pop down to your local pub and there is a good chance it will have an artistic signboard outside proclaiming its name in colourful pictorial style. And there is a good chance that it may show one of the many different craft which have plied our inland waterways over the centuries.

Craft like the single masted vessels with fore and aft rig which were once a familiar sight on Yorkshire waterways. About 1849 there was a host of craft from 60 to 140 tons consisting of sloops, billyboys, and ketches, as well as a few schooners in use.

One expert on British craft reckons that these have a common ancestor in a long extinct English coastal vessel. That they penetrated far inland is supported by several records. A document of the Ouse Navigation Trustees comments: 'Two sloops are kept constantly employed in carrying Goods of different description to Hull and return with different articles to Malton.' Their northern destination was York but 60 ton sloops also traded regularly as far as Ripon.

Commemorating a typical craft is the sign of the Sloop Inn at Temple Hirst near the Aire Navigation. Although these various craft were almost entirely sailing vessels, they were not entirely dependent on the wind for motive power. As one historian pointed out there were 'some for horse, some for poles, some for sails, and some for draught by men and horses'. The obvious omission is any mechanical means of propulsion but perhaps it was not economical for it is recorded that one man towed 4 miles for a shilling with a horse which formerly would be done by four men at a cost of 'four shillings and a drink'.

Certainly manpower is all that appears to have been available for the venerable gentlemen who operated a ferry across the Lee at Hackney. He and his craft, curiously laden with cats, is commemorated on the signboard of the Cook's Ferry Inn there.

A similar vessel is to be found on one side of the two-sided Haw Bridge Inn sign overlooking the River Severn. Manned by a fisherman casting in the placid waters it has as its background a graceful three span bridge with slender cast iron ribs. Alas, in December 1958 a large vessel coming downstream with the river in spate, struck the arch ribs of the western span and caused a complete collapse. A replacement was not completed until 1961.

Waterways no less than men evolve a local character of their own and what may be true of vessels in one part of the country may be untrue elsewhere. Thus in Norfolk it was the wherry that evolved and is commemorated by signboards in Norwich; at Paston on the old Dillham–Antingham Canal; at Langley on the River Yare; and at Geldeston on the Beccles–Bungay Navigation. Suffolk has two, with the Wherry Hotel at Oulton Broad and Wherry Inn at Halesworth, built at the time the Blyth Navigation was opened.

All except Oulton Broad have signboards depicting wherries though executed with varying degrees of skill. One of the best is at Geldeston where the wherry *Eudora* is shown sailing among the willow trees bordering the River Waveney on one side in daylight and on the other at sunset. Painted with the bargeman's love of bright cheerful colours, the *Eudora* had a bright green masthead with yellow and blue bands with a sleek black hull and high peak sail with a 6 ft long streak of blood red bunting fluttering aloft.

Some historians suggest these craft developed from the Viking craft that raided our shores. Certainly such a vessel graces the signboard of Hobb's Boat

At one time the wherries, which are said to have evolved from Viking craft, were a familiar sight on the inland waterways of Norfolk and Suffolk. This inn sign at Geldeston shows the wherry *Eudora*

The menacing Viking vessel on the sign of the Hobbs Boat Inn was clearly not on a pleasure trip

Inn situated near the junction of the Axe and Severn. The building was once a ferryhouse and is believed to take its name from one Hubba, a Danish sea-rover who in Anglo-Saxon times raided here. Legend has it that during one raid the villagers of Uphill and Bleadon near the inn fled with the Danes in pursuit. All, that is, except one old woman. She found the Danish longships unattended and cut the mooring lines and set them adrift. When the Danes returned and found themselves marooned they were quickly defeated by the natives who had rallied.

Not all invaders came on blood-thirsty missions however as can be seen from the signboard of the Ferry Inn at Brough near the mouth of the River Trent. With their craft drawn up on the shore Roman soldiers, doubtless having sailed up the Trent on a voyage of exploration, are shown trading with the natives. Possibly this wide, broad bottomed vessel was one of the forerunners of the Trent barges.

Another type of craft – the Severn trow – is perpetuated in the sign of the Llandoger Trow Inn at Bristol. The word trow means barge and it is probable that these sailing craft carried coal from the Welsh coalfield. On the River Thames the great western barges were 'remarkable for the Length of the Vessel, and the Burthen they carry, and yet the little water they draw; in a word some of these barges carry above a Thousand Quarter of Malt at a time, and yet do not draw Two Foot of Water'.

Evidently at least one captain took this statement too literally with the result that we find The Barge Aground at Barking, where the colourful signboard depicts a once typical Thames barge which has run aground on a mudflat. In contrast the sign of The Barge at Battlesbridge beside the River Crouch shows a barge in full sail with crimson canvas adding a splash of colour. In marked contrast is the sign of The Paddington Packet Boat at Cowley Peachey beside the Grand Union. Knowing that packet boats plied regularly between Paddington and Uxbridge as long ago as 1801 and that troops were sent by canal from London to Liverpool by packet boat it was surprising not to find a colourful pictorial signboard. Perhaps its very antiquity caused its demise for I eventually tracked it down and found it being offered for sale by an Aylesbury antique dealer.

A narrow boat of later vintage makes the main subject of a pleasant sign on an inn at Alperton. This is the Pleasure Boat which seems positively puny compared with its American counterpart The Showboat which I found outside an inn at Heckmondwike near the Calder Navigation. I doubt whether this water highway was ever graced by such a paddle steamer.

Elsewhere, steam packet boats, wide barges and narrow, ketches and sailing vessels of every kind, as well as craft peculiar to any part of the country are all preserved for posterity on inn signboards and make a fascinating study of forgotten fleets for the observant traveller.

One of the Aire and Calder Navigation's Successful Operators

Operating on the Aire and Calder Navigation are many private operators; these bye-traders account for by far the biggest share of the large tonnage handled each year. One of these independents, a very forward looking company, is Messrs Cawood Hargreaves Limited.

Two independent canal carriers, namely Cawood Wharton and Company, Limited, and Hargreaves (West Riding) Limited, both large operators, each having contracts for the supply of coal to electricity generating power stations on the Aire and Calder Navigation and the Calder and Hebble Navigation, were obviously prime contenders in the fight to secure the contract for the supply of coal to Ferrybridge 'C' Power Station in the early 1960s when the station was being built. Hargreaves, for example, had been supplying coal to the Ferrybridge 'A' Power Station for nearly forty years, and therefore both the companies were well versed in the problems associated with a large contract of this nature.

Naturally, outside the administration of the companies and the nationalized bodies concerned, little is known of how the contract for the supply of coal and the method of transportation was finally decided upon, but the outcome was a sensational revolution in the formulated ideas of inland water transport in Great Britain.

A new canal carrying company Cawood Hargreaves Limited was formed. The parent companies remained independent, with their own individual canal contracts. The new company went ahead with the design and construction of 'Pusher Tugs', special tugs which push loaded compartment boats instead of using the traditional method of towing.

The design had to take into consideration the problems of navigating through locks and around bends in the navigable rivers of the Aire and Calder Navigation as well as bends in the canalized sections. Many of the problems of navigability were overcome by the use of a new system of power, manufactured by Harbormaster Limited.

Instead of the usual propeller and rudder the Harbormaster dispenses with the rudder completely. The propeller is directional and able to turn a full 360 degrees and so steers the craft by its own thrust in a most positive manner. Turning the direction of the propeller 180 degrees puts the craft into reverse immediately. The engine fitted to the Harbormaster unit is a 150 hp diesel.

The tugs fit snugly up to the compartment boats, buffer strips are fitted to ease the stress of pushing and movement around bends, and each compartment boat is fastened to its partner by a system of chains with screw fittings, to ensure rigid fastening. Each tug propels three compartment boats at a time, making a formidable total length of 195 ft.

Propelled by a 150 hp pusher tug a train of three loaded barges passes an empty train at Castleford. Each complete train is 195 ft long with barges being 56 ft long by 17 ft 3 in wide and 9 ft 6 in deep with a payload of 165 tons

The contract for the construction of the pusher tugs and the compartment boats was awarded to Richard Dunston Limited of Thorne. In all, nine pusher tugs and thirty-six compartment boats were built, the tugs being numbered *CH101* to *CH109* inclusive. The only craft to have a name in addition to its identification number is *CH107*, being named *Barbara Holbeach* at a naming ceremony held in October 1967.

The compartment boats, unlike the BACAT barges, are without hatch covers, there being no need for these with short haul work with coal; they are 56 ft long and 17 ft 3 in wide, being 9 ft 6 in deep, fitted with a cat-walk along one side over the hold. The compartment boats are numbered *CH1* to *CH36* inclusive, and each carries between 165 and 170 tons of coal. Each tug with its train of compartment boats has a total load in the vicinity of 500 tons.

The coal is collected from collieries within a 12 mile radius of the Ferrybridge 'C' Power Station and so most of the work is on the Aire and Calder Navigation; however on two separate occasions during colliery disputes, coal was collected from a loading staithe on the Calder and Hebble Navigation, the Calder and Hebble having locks for the first 3 miles which allows the passage of large craft.

Certainly one of the advantages of using compartment boats is the ease of unloading. It takes just nine minutes to unload the 150 tons of coal from each compartment boat. No cranes or grabs are used; the loaded compartment boat is 'shunted' into a receiving bay at the Power Station, which leads to a gigantic concrete and steel structure. The compartment boat is lifted bodily 40 ft out of the water and turned over, the coal emptying out into a receiver hopper. The compartment is then returned empty to the water and the next loaded one takes its place.

The contract for the supply of coal to Ferrybridge 'C' Power Station totals around 1½ million tons a year, a most formidable amount in anyone's estimation, and all by inland waterways.

There is little wonder that the Aire and Calder Navigation is so successful as a commercial waterway with a contract of such large proportions. The tugs and the compartment boats have now been operating for several years and have proved most satisfactory in every respect. The large tonnage moved each year on one contract would not be possible without modern craft and ideas, on a modernized waterway – for that is what the Aire and Calder Navigation now is.

York Had the First Iron Boat

Just over two centuries ago on the River Foss near its confluence with the River Ouse at York, the first iron boat slipped into the water – unheralded and unannounced. By so doing it stole a march on the most historic iron producer of the Industrial Revolution.

Support for this seemingly outrageous claim comes from a report in the *York Courant* of 27 May 1777 which says 'Last Tuesday a new Pleasure-Boat constructed of Sheet Iron was launched into the River Foss. She is 12 ft in length, 6 ft breadth, has sailed with 15 persons in her and may be conveyed to and from the River by two Men.'

The almost laconic nature of the report, without anything to substantiate the claim that the vessel was the first of its kind, inspired the thought that perhaps it had been preceded by others. On the other hand, the launching was referred to elsewhere. Two references to it appear in the *Gentleman's Magazine* of 1777.

The *Courant's* report is substantially repeated on page 244 in the issue dated Tuesday 20 May and again on page 291 in the 27 May issue. It is slightly rephrased but without additional information.

Both of these paragraphs are indexed under the heading 'Boat of Cast Iron'. The chances of researching further information about the vessel are seemingly non-existent since 1777 was well before reliable directories and gazetteers were published for York. Therefore the identity of the owner, builder, location of the yard and slipway are probably lost for ever – or the subject of idle speculation.

Evidence for any claim that the construction in 1757 of Naburn Lock on the Ouse heralded a spate of boat building in York seems sadly lacking.

Certainly the Trustees of the Ouse Navigation had in 1732/3 indulged in the building of a corporation barge specially for viewing the river. This cost about £200 and it was later given sash-windows and wainscot interior. This stylish vessel was subsequently instanced as an example of the inadequacies and corruption of an unreformed corporation whose improvidence caused widespread indignation.

York Corporation had toyed with the idea of improving the Foss as early as 1725 – an Act enabling them to do so was passed in 1793 – but their resources were extensively stretched due to a mass of financial irregularities associated with administration of the Ouse.

Was the launch of an iron vessel into the Foss seen as a politically inexpedient affair in view of an impending financial scandal and therefore carried out away from public gaze with the fact being suppressed as far as possible?

Was the craft really made of cast iron as stated? This seems unlikely because the metal would most likely have been about half an inch thick. Cast to the stated dimensions it would certainly have been extremely heavy and two men would have been incapable of carrying it.

Since sheet iron had been in use for half a century prior to the launching, could this have been the material used? If so it was probably used as a skin on a ribbed timber framework for the weight would have to have been around 200 lb for the two men to carry it.

Ironmaster John Wilkinson had his blacksmith turn wrought iron to $\frac{5}{16}$ in plate and is credited with launching the first iron boat on the River Severn at Coalbrookdale – ten years later than the York event.

As a news item then the *York Courant* report is extremely important, as a piece of technical writing it leaves much unwritten, and as a piece of waterways history, it seems frustratingly to defy further verification. Or does someone, somewhere, have a family record, diary, or other document which has been handed down from those far-off days, and which will establish beyond doubt that York's claim is just?

six

Aristocrats to Tiller Girls

A Pioneer of Island Waterways

Great enterprises do not always command support but unfailingly loyal are the bands of scoffers who march jeeringly with the baggage trains of progress. Canal history certainly shows no exception to the rule and the ways of the narrow boat were cut in the face of the sceptical opposition of the narrow mind.

Monsieur Voltaire, French master of satire, summing up farewell impressions of a visit to Holland, 'that waterland of Dutchman and of ditches', wrote 'Adieu, canals, ducks, rabble!' and our own Thomas Hood, also writing of the stout-hearted Hollanders and their country, said that it 'lies so low, they're only saved by being dammed'.

We may suspect that to these two great wits, unable to resist poking fun with satired pens, the fun was only fun. No such hidden goodwill softened the unpolished barbs hurled at our pioneers of inland waterways.

Taking his place in history in the van of those pioneers is James Brindley, man of genius, Derbyshire, and no learning, who in 1761 startled, even confounded the engineering world by building a canal from Worsley to Manchester, and so started the 'Klondike' rush of eighteenth-century canal prospectors.

From that rush, in which many fortunes were made, and some lost, developed the navigations and systems of inland waterways which we know today, and as they grew, so did the industrial areas of the Midlands and the north.

Previously hamstrung by the condition of road communications, industry, without a lung, had been almost local in its scope. Arthur Young, English writer to whose works can be traced much of the advance in English scientific agriculture, described the state of the roads in terms very apposite to the canals which largely neutralized them. 'In winter,' he says in *A Tour Through the North of England*, 'it would have cost no more to make the roads navigable than to make them hard.'

And so to the land-locked industries the waterways brought germination to the seeds of commerce, and great industrial branches grew out along the lines of the canals to the sea – and the ports of the world.

As these branches grew, so did the stature of the canal engineers who, in the British way, had been founded to fit the hour, men of such calibre as Telford, Rennie and Jessop. James Brindley was indeed in good company.

What kind of man was he, this unlettered commoner who started a great industrial revolution?

James Brindley, of whom Carlyle wrote 'The eloquent Brindley, behold, he has chained seas together; his ships do visibly float over valleys, invisibly through the hearts of mountains. The Mersey and the Thames, the Humber and the Severn, have shaken hands,' was born at Thornsett in 1716. Son of an indolent farmer, young James spent a profitless childhood – he taught himself to write his name – and after a spell of doing a job to augment the family income, apprenticed himself to a millwright of Sutton, near Macclesfield.

His latent talents developed slowly, there was no sudden spark of genius. He made many mistakes and was roundly berated by Bennett, his master, for leaving his proper vocation of farm labourer. But gradually the boy James became the man Brindley, and his work began to show the change.

In *Lives of the Engineers*, Samuel Smiles records how Bennett, inspecting a repair effected by his pupil, found it so well done that he even complained of the quality. 'Jem,' he said, 'if thou goes on i' this foolish way o' workin', there

James Brindley (1716–72)

94

will be very little trade left to be done when thou comes out o' thy times: Thou knaws firmness o' wark's th' ruin o' trade.'

At the age of twenty-six, James Brindley set up as a wheelwright at Leek, and with a widening reputation for ingenious and skilful work, began to be sought out as the right man for ambitious, unusual projects. He was called to the Clifton coal mines to clear them of water, and did so by using the waters of the River Irwell, obtained through a tunnel driven 600 yds through solid rock, to power an underground water-wheel. He built where others failed, he found solutions where his contemporaries found bafflement, he just employed his genius.

Living only for his job, Brindley remained an untaught man. The mathematics of complex engineering were in his head, never on paper. A truly great man, he was now moving fast to the grand passion of his life, canals – he once told a Parliamentary committee that Nature had provided rivers to serve as feeders to canals.

After the Bridgewater enterprise, he built the Grand Trunk Canal (his own name for what we know as the Trent and Mersey), the Oxford, the Staffordshire and Worcestershire, and was associated, either as consultant or as working engineer, with the Coventry, Chesterfield, Leeds and Liverpool, and the Aire and Calder.

The Grand Trunk canal! There's a ring to the name, and a suggestion of a great highway sending out byways in all directions yet never faltering in its main-line purpose.

To link by inland waterways the ports of three seas was indeed a bold conception in the eighteenth century, and it is not surprising that to James Brindley, that tireless builder of canals, the project was both his greatest interest and achievement. The busy Trent and Mersey Canal today bears witness to his work.

Although Brindley built his first canal in 1761 – the same year in which one of his greatest successors, John Rennie was born – he had already been engaged, in 1757, year of birth of that other great canal engineer Thomas Telford, in a survey for a proposal to link the Trent and the Mersey by canal.

First considered by the Corporation of the comparatively new port of Liverpool – it was still only a fishing village when Hull was a port – the proposal, sponsored by Earl Gower, afterwards Marquis of Stafford, soon became one to link not only Liverpool and Hull but also Bristol. Supported by the manufacturers of Staffordshire, opposed by the factional diehards of the northern counties (there was even a school of thought which held that a policy of canal building would so weaken the coasting trade that Britain's maritime greatness would suffer a death blow), the scheme hung fire for many years.

Into this arena of maelstrom limped a man from the Potteries, a man after Brindley's own heart, and a man whose name is now a household word, Josiah Wedgwood, master potter and hero of the Five Towns.

Youngest of a family of thirteen, Josiah Wedgwood was born in humble circumstances, and like Brindley had little education. At the age of eleven he was apprenticed in the pottery trade of his family and might well have been a practical potter all his life but for a misfortune which proved a blessing to the Potteries. Disease struck him down and he lost one of his legs.

Thus prevented from working at the potter's wheel, Wedgwood used the leisure of his illness to make a study of his trade. The white clay of the White Country had for centuries been used for potting – the Romans used it to fashion cremation urns – but there was little claim to craftsmanship, and the industry mostly kept its ware inside the county boundaries.

In Wedgwood's illness-sharpened mind the trade became an art, and an art he truly made it. He began his own small business at Burslem, and so laid the foundation of a thriving, world-renowned industry. At Etruria, named after the Etruscan ornaments which he copied so well, he built the first great pottery works.

As the demands for Wedgwood pottery grew, so did the maker's interest in improving the communications which alone could give his trade an outlet, and when the construction of Brindley's Grand Trunk Canal was again mooted, he backed the scheme whole-heartedly.

The prophets of disaster sprang to life immediately, opposing the canal with every kind of dire prophecy. The coming of canals, they predicted, would destroy the pack-horse breed of English horses, and bankrupt inn-keepers would precede the nation into ruin.

With the powerful support of the master potter added to that of Earl Gower and other backers of Brindley's genius, the Parliamentary battle was joined, fought and won, and on 26 July 1766 Josiah Wedgwood started the cutting of what we now know as the Trent and Mersey Canal by lifting the first piece of turf at Bramhills.

And so James Brindley began his greatest canal. It bristled with formidable difficulties, and in building, or planning (for he did not live to see the task finished), such great works as the Harecastle Tunnel, we see his genius at its best.

The battle was not won without concessions, and one of these, designed to serve the interests of the citizens of large towns, laid down that the canal should by-pass such towns at a distance of several miles. It cannot have been without relish that after the success of the canal had left those citizens well and truly by-passed, they were heard loudly demanding branches from the trunk. Their rueful dismay paid tribute to Brindley's own name for his canal.

But perhaps a more piquant reflection today is that to celebrate the great day of opening of the work in the Potteries, a sheep was roasted whole in Burslem market-place.

A.W. KNIGHT

A Scot Across the Borders

In Eskdale solitude and a mud-walled cottage near Westerkirk hamlet, in the county of Dumfries, Thomas Telford, son of a shepherd and father of great enterprises, was born on 9 August 1757. His father tended sheep on the remote heathered hills of the district, where the sound of the valley-bound burns was almost the only sound.

That was the early background of a great canal engineer. Like Brindley, his beginnings were humble, his trade mostly self-taught. Unlike his famous predecessor, he spread his wings, both in his profession – he built the Menai suspension bridge over the Menai Straits – and in the field of culture, he never lost a love of poetry.

Another love he never lost was that for his native Eskdale, borderland country of turbulent past, of ceaseless raids, of Scottish thrust and English parry, of English lunge and Scottish swerve. For years the district was a battle cockpit for the pillaging outlaws from both sides of the border.

The name of Johnnie Armstrong, a bandit princeling who operated from Gilknockie Tower, on the banks of the Esk, is still a name to conjure with in Eskdale. In his day it was a name which stood for terror on the English side. But his day was also that of King James V, and that puissant monarch, with a royal dislike of petty princelings, made a powerful border raid on his own account. He caught the daring Johnnie with his followers in Etterick Forest,

Thomas Telford (1757–1834)

ordered his summary execution and so helped to foster the Gilnockie legend of Johnnie Armstrong.

In this remote no-man's land of troubled history, Thomas Telford lived as sheep-herding boy, pupil of the parish school of Westerkirk, and job-seeking young man.

He became a stonemason, mostly building rough walls and bridges by and over the rougher roads of the dale. Eskdale gave him good training for a builder craftsman, but it was an unlikely breeding ground for a man destined to be buried in Westminster Abbey as a great canal man, architect, bridge, road and harbour builder and surveyor.

In 1780, he took his tools to Edinburgh, used them for two years in and around the growing Princes Street of that rising city, then followed Johnnie Armstrong across the border. But he aimed further south than that reckless brigand had dared, he was bound for London.

His chisel was soon busy on the stones of Somerset House, then building, but the young Scot was already looking up the ladders of his trade, and within two more years he obtained a commission which was the probable turning point of his career. It was merely to build a house, but the house was in Portsmouth dockyard, and there is no doubt that his later interests and consummate skill in dock and harbour building were nurtured at that time.

He was rapidly moving now to his first canal job. Appointed county surveyor for Shropshire, where he gained valuable experience and the goodwill of the county squires – his experience included the design of a piebald costume for the prison-bound felons of Shrewsbury – Thomas Telford's reputation now stood high, and in 1793 he was appointed engineer for the Ellesmere Canal, now part of the Shropshire Union.

At the time of Thomas Telford's appointment as engineer to the Ellesmere Canal, public opinion in respect of inland waterways had turned full circle. Landowners clamoured still, more noisily than ever, in fact, but now their object was to gain a share for themselves of the prosperity of a canal era, and for this new project to link the River Mersey, the River Dee and the River Severn, a project which would obviously meet many great problems in difficult country, financial support was overwhelming.

To this scene of turn-coat confidence, Thomas Telford brought the diffidence of an architect turned engineer – it was, after all, his first canal job, but he brought also his natural brilliance. Nothing more was needed.

It is a tribute to Telford's genius that in building this first canal he achieved a work which, although not used today, still stands out as a wonder of the waterways – the Pontcysyllte aqueduct in the Vale of Llangollen. The boldness of this work, and that of the only slightly lesser aqueduct at Chirk, on the same canal, typify the courage of a confident craftsman.

Telford had more in common with Brindley than genius, he had a dislike of locks, and when he faced the immense problem of taking his canal over the valleys of the River Dee and the River Ceriog, the idea of giving to the sides of each valley a watered stairway was one he soon discarded. His answer was the gigantic aqueducts of Chirk and Pontcysyllte.

Chirk came first, and across the 700 ft wide valley of the Ceriog, in lovely wooded country, dominated (until then) by the castle of Chirk, Telford threw an aqueduct of ten 40 ft arches at a height of 65 ft above the valley meadows.

In his day it was a task of colossal magnitude – it took five years to complete – but it was a job after Telford's own heart. It brought into effective play all the genius of the architect, and the mason of Somerset House, directing the chisels of his men, was on familiar ground.

Four miles to the north of Chirk, at the crossing of the Dee, Telford faced the problem of Pontcysyllte. In a valley which at its lowest part is nearly 130 ft below the canal level, the original intention had been to lock the waterway down the abrupt north bank, and up the more gradual slope on the south side.

This scheme would have meant an ellipse of probably nearly twenty locks, an expensive and water-wasting project. The supply of water for the canal was not over-abundant, and our lock-disliking engineer from Eskdale did not find it hard to dismiss the idea in favour of another aqueduct.

With both these aqueducts it was quite impossible owing to their great height to employ the Brindley method of puddling the waterbed, and Telford revolutionized canal building by using upper structures of iron. The aqueduct of Pontcysyllte took eight years to build, but in 1805, when it was opened to traffic, it added an impressive feature to the vale of Llangollen and Owen Glendower. A wonder of the waterways in Telford's day, it remains so to this day.

During these years of building, the use of iron in conventional bridge construction was sweeping the country and the versatile Telford made his own contribution to the spate of iron bridges. His first was over the Severn at Buildwas, another spanned the same river at Bewdley, and in 1801, when old London Bridge really was falling down, he submitted a bold plan to cross the River Thames with a cast iron bridge of only a single arch. It was not adopted, although the leading engineers of the day could find no flaw in it.

Returning to his native Scotland, where he made a mammoth survey of the appalling communications of that then backward country, and carried out major harbour improvements at Aberdeen and Dundee, he was consulted about the Caledonian Canal.

To link the locks of the Great Glen of the Highlands in a navigable waterway across the breadth of Scotland from the Atlantic to the North Sea, had long been regarded as a vital Scottish need, and to mariners faced with the long, dread passage of the Pentland Firth the project appeared as a boon indeed. Also, its strategic value – in days when our home guards were troubled by Napoleon – was much emphasized by the Navy.

Following Telford's survey, which itself followed surveys by Watt and Rennie, the work of linking the basin at Corpach, near Fort William, at the western end of the canal, with that of Clachnaharry, near Inverness, at the eastern terminus, was begun.

It proved a long, difficult and often frustrating job. Although only 22 miles of the 60 mile long waterway are artificial cuts between the lochs of Loch Lochy, Loch Oich and – monster of them all – Loch Ness, those 22 miles involved enormous problems of bog, rock and contour.

At Corpach, for instance, it was necessary to raise the canal up a gradient of 90 ft in less than 8 miles. Telford went up it by the eight treads of 'Neptune's Staircase' of huge locks. But they took years to build, and it was not until 1822 that the first vessel passed through the magnificently scenic canal from sea to sea.

By the time the use of steam in ships was making mock of the windy terrors of Pentland and if, in the event, the Caledonian Canal did not fully serve the purpose for which it was envisaged, the fact does not detract from Thomas Telford's genius.

A.W. KNIGHT

Colour on Canals

Most people who live or travel in areas where canals cross the country have admired the gaily painted decorations which adorn the old barges passing up and down them. This delightful art, the pictorial technique of which has remained unchanged for centuries, is one of the oldest of its kind left to us in this age of machines, and it doubtless owes its preservation to the nomadic way of life of the barge-folk.

The custom of decorating ships in this fashion dates from the earliest times, and it probably reached these islands from the countries bordering on the Mediterranean. In this part of the world it is still strong today, especially among the fisher-folk of southern Italy, Spain and Portugal. The figures of the Madonna and Saints can be seen on many Sicilian fishing boats, as well as on the little ramshackle painted carts which are the peasants' chief means of transport.

They originated in the days when it was thought necessary to put one's possessions under some powerful protection, and no doubt their immediate predecessors of pre-Christian times were the gods and goddesses of the Romans and Greeks.

One ancient design which has not changed with the times is the eye on the prow, placed there in order to enable the ship – so it was hoped – to see its way. Fishing boats in many parts of the Mediterranean still carry this device and it is also to be found in the waters of the Far East. In southern Italy and Portugal, however, its functions have been taken over by the star.

The star design is also to be found on many of the canal barges of Britain as well as those of France and Belgium. Another design which appears on the prow of many fishing boats in Sicily is the skein, or twist, and this, too, is a feature of the decorations on many of our English canal barges, particularly those on the Grand Union, which in this case takes the form of a writhing band of iron strapwork known as a 'Snake'.

The typical bargee of the English canals takes a jealous pride in the decoration of his floating home and almost always keeps to the traditional patterns. The majority of designs have now no particular significance, but are merely pleasant to look upon. The chief motifs are roses and daises and abstract patterns based on the lozenge.

Barges are generally painted every two or three years, and the job takes from one to two months to complete. More than a dozen different colours are used. Hulls are usually black, but the tiller, fore-end cabin tarpaulin stands and cabin block, which supports the gang planks, are all painted in such bright colours as ultramarine, crimson, pink and green.

The name of the owner on the side of the cabin is surrounded by a floral design and flanked by a landscape. A common example is a turreted castle set in a green meadow, through which a stream wends its way. Some of these painted fortresses have a definite Eastern European flavour, for their towers possess the bulbous domes always associated with the Slav lands.

Tarpaulin stands are frequently decorated with lozenges or triangles, and lashed about the tiller are two plaits of rope, scrubbed to whiteness, known as the 'Turk's Head' – the origin of this name is not known. On the hatch is one of the few symbolic designs to be found on English canal barges, the heart or rosette, a direct descendant of the sun face which once decorated many vessels in the Mediterranean and is still found occasionally today on the boats of Catanian fishermen.

Painting the barges is a highly skilled craft, with a particular technique similar to that of china painting. Each individual depot where the work is carried out has its own style, the painters varying the design, whilst keeping to the main theme. Uxbridge, for example, specializes in a rather simpler type of castle than the others. Another depot, at Braunston, is the principal centre for the production of painted tin-ware and such items as cabin bowls, water cans, teapots, etc. are all lavishly decorated there.

These painters are much in demand by house-owners, who send them articles to be decorated in canal-boat fashion.

PHILIP BAKER

There's Romance on Canals

Strange the effect that an unhappy love affair can have on a man. Some men join the Foreign Legion. Some shoot tigers. Some take up golf. And some go on the binge. Francis Egerton, third Duke of Bridgewater was different. He swallowed his disappointment and built Britain's first industrial canal. He made a fortune for himself, and brought fame to the illiterate son of a High Peak crofter.

In the 1750s, the Duke moved in high London society. He fell desperately in love with the beautiful Elizabeth Gunning. Alas, Cupid's aim was faulty. Elizabeth preferred the Duke of Argyll! So the young Duke of Bridgewater, in black mood, turned his back on Mayfair and applied himself vigorously to his estates at Worsley, near Manchester.

Manchester was thriving in the 1750s. Cotton had made her wealthy. But one of the big snags was the high cost and scarcity of coal, which had to be carried by pack-horse over bad roads from collieries in the district. The Duke had mines on his estate, and toyed with the idea of transporting the coal by a short canal to the River Irwell at Barton, and thence by the river to Manchester. However, he ran into difficulties with the Mersey and Irwell Company.

This is where James Brindley comes into the picture. Born in a humble home and apprenticed to a millwright (the engineering 'jack of all trades' of the eighteenth century), he had soon shown genius, and had early set up in

The Duke of Bridgewater with his canal and Barton aqueduct

business on his own – a real case of local boy making good. At the age of forty 'Brindley' was a big name around the Potteries.

The meeting in 1760 between the Duke and James Brindley must have been a strange one: the man of fashion, cultured and gracious of manner, and Brindley – self-taught, rough of tongue, down to earth – a man who, even at the end of his life, could barely sign his own name. Yet the Duke sensed the genius hidden behind the bluff, honest face.

The Duke made up his mind on the spot and commissioned Brindley to survey the route from Worsley to Manchester. Brindley recommended that instead of going down to the river by means of a flight of locks, the proposed canal should be carried over the Irwell by an aqueduct, and should proceed on its own level to Manchester. Such a proposal was a costly one. It was regarded by everyone except the Duke and his protégé as fantastic, and doomed to failure. Nevertheless, the Duke staked his whole fortune – and Brindley his reputation – on this 'crazy' project.

Brindley bent to his task with inspired confidence. He planned everything – even the boats that would use the canal. He bored into the hillside at Worsley, bringing the canal right up to the coal-face, and incidentally draining the mines and using jet water to ventilate them. At the Manchester end he bored a shaft from the hilltop so that the coal could be lifted in special boxes straight from the barge up to the town.

A day in 1761 must have been a proud one for both peer and commoner. Together they stood and watched the first barge pass over the Barton Aqueduct carrying a cargo of coal equivalent to the loads of many dozens of pack-horses. That aqueduct became the monument to Brindley's fame. People of all classes came from miles around just to stand and gaze at the miracle of barges passing at a height of nearly 40 ft above the river.

This was the forerunner of many wonderful engineering achievements on the part of Brindley.

Coal prices immediately tumbled in Manchester for it was only scarcity of transport – not of the coal itself – which had caused the high prices. Steam power for the mills in Manchester at last became a really practical proposition. Manufacturing costs were slashed, and the Industrial Revolution which was soon to bring world economic leadership to Britain, rapidly increased its pace.

CYRIL WILLS

People and Craft of the Narrow Canals

There seems little doubt that the canal boats introduced in the days of Brindley, the pioneer of British waterways, were of the simplest construction with little or no decoration, being bow-hauled by men who worked on the 'day system'.

Their direct descendants can be seen today on the Birmingham Canal.

As the waterways spread farther afield and journeys became longer, the necessity arose for living accommodation aboard and so came the family boats. These boats between 69 and 72 ft long with a beam of 6 ft 10 in to 7 ft 2 in were made expressly to fit the narrow locks and so conserve water. They had rounded bilges, which took less energy to propel, but when manual haulage gave way to horses the added power available and the need for more cargo space brought the square bilge into being.

Evolution from that day has given us successively the gay decorations of castles and roses, and brass work, mechanical propulsion to oust the horse, steel to replace wood, and now since nationalization a standardized colour scheme of blue and yellow.

British Waterways' choice of blue and yellow has led to much controversy, but it is only fair to say that the two main carrying fleets, those of Fellows, Morton and Clayton and the Grand Union Canal Carrying Co., which were merged on nationalization, did not operate such beautifully painted craft as those of Samuel Barlow Co. Ltd and The Mersey Weaver Carrying Co. There has only been a change of house colour – the cabin interiors and many items of running equipment are still painted in traditional pattern.

Early records have little to offer in the way of information on the subject of boat decoration. Many theories have been put forward, but we think the decorations may well have been developed by the boat people themselves. After all, they lived in close contact with every item portrayed – flowers, castellated towers of stately homes, bridges, and water. Telford himself used the turret to decorate some of his aqueducts and Rennie made full use of all architectural embellishments.

How the highly coloured diamonds and circles came to be used is also a matter of some conjecture, but it could be that these figures, made up from basic geometric shapes, were easily drawn with simple instruments and then coloured with readily obtained paints.

No hard and fast design exists for building the traditional narrow boat, at least not for the wooden variety. These were, and still are to a very limited extent, fashioned and constructed by a departing race of craftsmen using basic woodworking tools, such as the adze, saw, shell and auger. Every part of the boat has been developed to fulfil a precise function. The foremost tent-like structure, or cratch, supports the side cloths and sheets besides acting as a cover for spare ropes and fenders though a temporary erection, or deck board, is used sometimes. The telescopic towing mast in its large square case and the stands not only divide up the hold, but also serve to support the gang planks. These planks when in position form a cat-walk along which one reaches the fore end.

A cherished horse's tail nailed to the rudder of narrow boat *Greenshank* – a rare sight

The rudder, or 'elum' in canal language, is hung at the rear on two forged iron hooks, its large size being necessary to maintain adequate control. The tiller, gracefully curved and tapered, is painted in bright colours. It is quickly detachable in order to prevent damage when working through locks, and can be reversed in its socket to lift it out of the way for ease of access to the cabin. From the top of the rudder post or 'Ram's head' to the rear of the rudder blade stretches a 'Swan's neck', a beautifully woven piece of rope work, gleaming white with pipe clay. Flowing over the 'Swan's neck' we may find a white mare's tail; both these forms of decoration are becoming extremely rare.

No one quite knows how the latter custom came into being, but it is generally accepted that the tail was kept when a favourite horse died and was then attached to the rudder, which after all would be as good a place as any; some boat people however consider this decoration an ill omen and will not fit it. Decoration is completed by small rope fenders and strips of whitened canvas tacked along each side of the blade, and of course the many coloured geometric designs.

In the cabin of a narrow boat we see human ingenuity stretched to the limit. No space or corner is wasted, for this is the boatman's home, of which he is justly proud. In it, maybe, he was born, has lived and will die, as perhaps, have several generations before him. The bed and table fold away into side compartments, the table being a cupboard door, with a drawer cunningly placed beneath it to catch crumbs. Drawers under side-benches, a stove, a coal

A pair of pre-nationalization narrow boats entering a lock on the Grand Union Canal

store – everything is there and yet nothing gets in the way, every inch being utilized to the full.

Even in modern boats there are the open-work plates, gleaming horse brasses and crimped paper curtains completed with coloured paper bows. The cabin indeed is a veritable show-piece and in the majority of cases is spotlessly clean.

So far our description has mainly concerned the 'butty', a descendant of the very earliest horse-drawn boats. The narrow-boat as we see it today, allowing for detail changes in design and materials, has altered little over the past fifty years. It was originally evolved from the horse-drawn type of boat, the stern end being altered to accommodate an engine room forward of the main cabin and a counter added to house the propeller and rudder, mounting a gracefully curved and decorated tiller or 'Ram's head'.

106

A narrow coaming running along the outside of the cabin from counter to back-end permits easy access to the engine room, but seriously limits interior width. For this reason the generally accepted living quarters are in the wider and more spacious butty, any overflow of children being relegated to the motor for sleeping. Steam propulsion was used for a short period, but this was quickly superseded by the internal combustion engine owing to the more compact installation and simplicity of control.

The arrangements evolved for towing are very interesting and show ingenious development. There is a fore-end stud to which the tow line or 'snubber' is attached, more especially in the case of the modern towed 'butty'. In the days of horse towage the 'tackle' or harness was fitted with brightly coloured rollers to prevent chaffing. The length of the snubber can be as much as 70 ft when towing in long pounds, or it can be as short as 10 ft, according to circumstances. For towing when empty, two crossed short straps are used, thus bringing the butty under more positive control by the motor and all but making the second steerer superfluous.

'Breasting up', or running side by side, is often resorted to when travelling through flights of wide locks, saving time and making full use of limited manpower, a pair of boats often being worked by a crew of two. An interesting development concerning the towing of the butty is the use of running blocks placed on the top of the stands. A long cotton line passes through these blocks to a detachable stud situated on the roof within reach of the steerer, who can allow the line to slip when getting under way and so eliminate snatch.

Boat building grew up around the main canal centres. Although the boats conform to a general layout, every builder has his own particular curves and details. This makes it easy to pick out a 'Shroppie' or Shropshire Union fly boat from a 'Riccy' (Rickmansworth) one, or a Braunston boat built by Barlow's from a Banbury one built by Tooley. So also is the decoration distinctive, and we have the brilliant reds of a Tooley, the greens of Braunston, and so on.

The boat people are a sturdy, hard-working race, and in many instances can trace their ancestry back to the beginning of the canal era – the Hambridges, Beecheys, Skinners, Hones, etc. A typical one is Joe Skinner, who is still [1958] working the last horse-drawn long-distance boat on our Midland Canals. He is a No. 1, or 'owner worker' in his own right, and with the horse and his butty *Friendship* is a well-known figure between Atherstone and Birmingham. When he goes another chapter of canal history will pass into oblivion. We are happy to say he is still hale and hearty.

Talking of *Friendship*, what magic there is in the names of boats and what scenes the memory conjures up when we see *Sunny Valley*, *Forget-me-Not*, *Clygate*, *Aster* and other beautiful names!

Much has been written about the education of the canal-boat children. They are the product of folk who are skilled in their own job, and you should see some of the ten-year-olds handling a pair of boats!

Illiterate some of them may be by 'modern' standards, yet they have an outlook and psychology that would give a lead to many people 'off the land'.

C.P. AND C.R. WEAVER

The Leisurely Life

A lock keeper's life is all leisure
That I can never believe
We're fiction we're fact
We're half way between
Depends on the tales you can leave.

From a song by A. Lock Keeper.

A pal of mine occasionally sports a blue garb, similar in style to an astronaut's suit. He also makes no secret of the fact that he 'grows' plastic flowers in his garden, or, that he rather enjoys the novelty of asking passing strangers directions to Spaghetti Junction, and other mythical places. Another of his unique sidelines is training a toy parrot to speak (without much success to date). He is a canal lock keeper, by the way.

Some wag once offered an original explanation as to how our canal system came into being. He said: 'When "they" had finished building all those canals on Mars . . . ' rather suggesting that canal people, lock keepers included, may be of extra-terrestrial origin. That might explain why a number of earthlings are unable to equate us waterways folk with modern society, and why some of our actions seem to border on the fringe of lunacy.

With several years of lock keeping experience under my belt, confronting and being confronted by canal users and THEIR inexplicable actions, I can truthfully say that my sense of humour has developed (or degenerated) along similar lines to my friend with the toy parrot – OUT OF THIS WORLD.

I don't think that the public image of a canal lock keeper has altered a great deal over the years, despite the increased usage of canals for recreation. To many folk he may be imagined as a weather-beaten isolationist, with an aptitude for blending in with the scenery of his length of canal, yet who can appear, without warning, usually at the wrong moment for misusers of canal property.

Others see him as living proof of the existence of an idyllic 'leisurely life': relaxed, easy-going, leaning on balance beams in time-passing debate with holidaymakers. None of these definitions is wholly inaccurate, but all are far from complete.

I'd long subscribed to the view that people believe only what they want to. On that basis it seemed futile to try to alter the *facts* about lock keepers, and their duties. But that attitude changed when I was invited to give a talk about my work to members of the BBC Club – Inland Waterways Division. At last here was an opportunity to enlighten a section of the boating public with some well-chosen truths.

However, I was pleasantly surprised to be welcomed by an audience seeking to understand a little more of what goes on behind the glossy blur that supposedly depicts the canal scene.

Canals exist. Their beauty and tranquillity are there for everyone to enjoy, but what of the people who work to maintain those artificial water tracts for your pleasure?

On researching for the talk, I was disappointed to find scant information about the men without whom canals would soon become dried-up dykes – the bricklayers, carpenters, lengthsmen, labourers, lock keepers. Of those authorities who made an attempt to evaluate the importance of canalworkers, Charles Hadfield is the only name that immediately springs to mind. But most written observation, I found, approached the subject historically. There seems to be little mention of today's workers.

'I would like to say', I began my talk, 'that if we are seen to use a scythe or fagging hook, then we are also capable of using the latest power tools. If we pedal ancient bicycles, then we also ride motor cycles or drive cars. And, if we possess a countryman's knowledge of weather and local lore, then that is not the limit of our intelligence.'

Canalmen have always been drawn from many walks of life. Today, though, that statement has more poignancy. I've heard of an ex-bank manager who became a lock keeper: poets, artists and writers are included in the present-day ranks of British Waterways Board employees. Escapism may have something to do with it, but one thing ALL seem to have in common is a love for canal life.

I became a lock keeper in 1971, after 'surviving' for a couple of years as a labourer on the Grand Union Canal. Surviving just about sums up my 'apprenticeship' since I had formerly been occupied as a credit controller, and the transition from 'office wallah' to canal man was not entirely smooth. However, learning through error definitely encourages a retentive memory.

The title lock keeper, I discovered, is a red herring. The job involves nothing so simple as looking after several locks and a length of canal. (By the way, in case you didn't know, on most canals lock keepers are not obliged to work locks for boaters, but to supervise their correct usage.) In fact, the work has so many permutations attached to it that 'troubleshooter' might describe our activities more aptly.

Lock keepers have held positions of responsibility since the earliest canal days. Initially, I suppose it was enough that they were literate and could command respect from canal boatmen and canal people. In those days their duties were a little more clear cut. They would probably be responsible for collection of tolls, helping work boats through their length of canal, and whenever possible, trimming hedges or cutting grass.

These days, however, hedge trimming and grass mowing form only tiny aspects of our work. For instance, depending on the season, a lock keeper can undertake tree felling, leak stopping, minor lock gate repairs, painting and tarring lock gates and fences, ice breaking, and recovering bodies (usually animals) from the canals.

All this is aside from a strict daily routine which includes taking rainfall readings, recording the passage of boats, patrolling one's length of canal, making certain that it remains navigable, checking on the validity of canal licences and, where necessary, assisting police with canal orientated enquiries. In addition one may be called upon to deliver impromptu lockside lectures to visiting schoolchildren or other visitors.

When a period of duty ends, a lock keeper remains on standby in case of an emergency. At times, especially during the boating season, a lock keeper's life literally revolves about the canal.

Whether it sounds hackneyed or not, lock-keeping is not a job, but a way of life. An aspirant to the work soon learns to accept the fact that he is available to canal users at ALL TIMES. This can take some getting used to.

Inevitably the work infringes on homelife. During the spring and summer, meals become hurried snacks taken at odd times in a usually futile effort to avoid interruption. Frequently a lock keeper may be detained away from home for long periods and, if he is married, his wife may find herself 'holding the fort' in an unpaid capacity during her husband's absence. If the lock keeper has children, then they are on trust to act responsibly if they happen to be near a lock, to set a shining example to other children who may be on a holiday cruise.

However there are compensations for the harassing times during the holiday season. Lock keeping is a healthy open air life, subject to few of the pressures that seem to beset modern society. And, yes, the opportunity does arise for a leisurely natter. But do bear with our eccentricities; they are a safety valve.

By the way have you tried my pickled pulverized potatoes?

RON WHATLEY

seven

Flotsam and Jetsam

Commemorating the Canal Cutters

Wander through that quaint built-up area of London loosely labelled Paddington, and you will find yourself surrounded by reminders of the men who carved for themselves a niche in history with the building of the Grand Junction Canal which was to become part of the Grand Union Canal.

Here, nearly a century ago when the canal was built, you would have been in open country and passed no more than a few detached cottages strung out alongside the south bank beside the rough track that was to become Kensal Road. Then came the canal, giving its name to what was later changed to Sussex Gardens. Brindley Street was probably called after the great canal engineer James Brindley and a clerk of the company gave his name to Sale Place.

Philip Bouverie, another company official, is commemorated by Bouverie Place and Praed Street is a constant reminder of William Praed, first chairman of the company. It was he who, whilst representing the Cornish borough of St Ives in several Parliaments, played a major part in obtaining and carrying into effect the Act of Parliament for making and maintaining the canal.

Imagine his feelings at the official opening at 9 a.m. on the morning of 10 July 1801 when all the officials associated with the project set sail with colours and streamers flying in two pleasure boats, each hauled by two horses. About 20,000 people are said to have lined the banks whilst the craft made the journey to Bull's Bridge and back to Paddington where, 'after three huzzas the company landed and walked to the *Yorkshire Stingo* . . . and sat down to a convivial dinner'.

Praed lived to see the canal bring a great deal of trade to Paddington. A great straw, hay and vegetable market developed in the district. Agricultural produce and manufactured goods were brought down from the Midlands and from Paddington went groceries and much of London's manure.

Immense heaps of dust and ashes stood on the canal banks and created what one writer of the period described as 'stinking Paddington'.

On 9 October 1833, aged eighty-four, Praed died at his native Trevithoe in

Cornwall and was buried in the nearby parish of Lelant. But his wife, Elizabeth, was also sole heiress of Barnaby Backwell of Tyringham, Bedfordshire – an ancient family in the locality – so it was natural that she should wish to be remembered there.

Both husband and wife therefore are commemorated by a marble tablet in the small secluded church some 6 miles from the canal which through amalgamation became the Grand Union, covering 94 miles from Brentford to Braunston and necessitating 102 locks. Appropriately then, locks dominate the sculptured relief of the commemorative plaque which also includes part of a narrow boat.

In stark contrast is the size and grandeur of Bradford Cathedral in which there is a commemorative marble tablet to Joseph Priestley who died fifteen years before Praed, on 11 August 1817 when seventy-four years of age. Priestley superintended the construction of the Leeds & Liverpool Canal for nearly fifty years. In the sculptured tablet the canal is shown passing through a countryside as yet unsullied by the advancing Industrial Revolution and the scene is set between two canal bridges. Wielding pick and shovel on the bank are two navvies watched by a top-hatted figure (Priestley himself no doubt) whilst two of the first barges float past.

The inscription reads:

This marble is inscribed by the company of the proprietors of the canal navigation from Leeds to Liverpool to the memory of Joseph Priestley, Esq., as a mark of regard for his able, zealous, and assiduous attention to the interests of that great and important undertaking, his knowledge and great talents, his inflexible integrity and his determined and faithful discharge of duty in the most important and arduous situation of superintendent which he held under the company for nearly half a century.

On the Wave of a Crest

Stand watching the coal-carrying 'Tom Puddings' bound for Goole on the Aire and Calder Navigation as they pass under the hump-backed bridge carrying the road from the north into Castleford, and you will readily understand why much of the town's prosperity is founded on coal and canals.

To your right, overlooking the waterway, is a large sign marking the borough boundary and carrying the civic coat of arms in which pictorial tribute is paid to the town's water highway.

Castleford is one of England's youngest boroughs, for its Royal Charter was granted by Queen Elizabeth II as recently as 1955. On the coat of arms the

Castleford proudly proclaims its waterway links in the distinctive civic arms displayed at various approaches to the town

name of the town is indicated by a gold castle on a ford of white and blue waves. A white rose indicates the location and links with the Romans are represented by a golden eagle. From its red collar hangs a miner's safety lamp and at the foot of the arms is the Latin motto 'Boldly and Frankly'.

Nearly every civic coat of arms is to some extent a historical document though most of them have purely local associations. The use of armorial crests by corporations is not new although about three-quarters of the 500 or so used by local authorities in England and Wales have been granted during the past century. Thus civic heraldry is largely of modern growth though firmly rooted in antiquity and tradition.

Even in the Middle Ages, when heraldry was mainly a personal and family matter, certain towns and cities such as Shrewsbury, Norwich, London and Kingston-upon-Hull, placed in their seals heraldic shields which are still their civic arms. By 1700 some ninety English towns and cities boasted coats of arms.

Civic arms are granted by the Kings-of-Arms and derive ultimately from the Sovereign who is 'the fount of honour' and although they are not an 'honour' like a peerage, they are certainly 'tokens of honour'.

Carefully defined in heraldic terms, the arms usually contain pictorial emblems relating to industry, tradition, and history.

A popular method of representing waterways is with blue and silver wavy bands. For example, Watford astride the Grand Union Canal and River Colne, features a wavy blue on silver emblem. Alongside the Leeds and Liverpool Canal at Todmorden is the borough boundary sign with a blue wavy band bisecting the coat of arms bearing the Lancashire and Yorkshire roses. Beverley, Burton-on-Trent, Doncaster, and Nuneaton, also embody blue bands in their civic emblems.

Two gold wavy bands in the arms of Brentford and Chiswick Borough Council represent the River Brent and canalside situation while six wavy silver and gold bands feature in the arms of Newark-on-Trent which are supported by an otter and beaver. Six pieces of gold and silver also appear in the base of Nuneaton civic arms. These represent water and allude to Eaton, the town of the water.

A marriage of water and air transport produced for Southall arms a blue and silver Pegasus relating to the Grand Union canal and airport in the vicinity.

Sheaves in the arms of Sheffield refer to the River Sheaf, and Keighley tells of its waterside situation by means of the doubly significant motto By Worth.

Three bees, the emblem of skill, perseverance, and industry, are characteristic of the trade and merchants who have been the means of raising Blackburn to its present position, and B is also the first letter of the name. A black wavy band represents the Black Brook (Blakewater) on the banks of which the town is built. Burnley's wavy band is also black.

A novel representation of the waterways of the locality are two circles containing silver and gold bands which feature in the arms of Uxbridge. But beware, the same symbol at Wellingborough relates to chalybeate springs.

The old and new bridges at Upton-on-Severn are depicted heraldically by two cross-crosslets parting six pieces of silver and gold while a two-arched bridge rising from wavy and silver and gold bars in the arms of Knottingley relates to the old structure over the Aire and Calder Navigation at Ferrybridge.

Vessels on civic arms usually relate to sea-going craft, although Goole boasts a Viking galley, and a gold Viking ship with a silver sail on six wavy pieces of gold and silver appearing on the arms of Lindsey County Council recalls the inland forays of these marauders. Manchester seems to have anticipated the construction of its canal by the use of a ship in its arms.

Oxford and Hertford, and the counties of which they are centres, have punning insignia. An ox fording a river and a hart in a ford are the symbols they use and Knutsford has a seal containing a representation of King Knut fording a stream.

Though far inland, Bewdley is connected to the sea by the Severn Navigation and commemorates the association with an anchor in its arms, but anchors in the arms of Brierley Hill and Dudley relate to the iron industry.

Cambridge has sea-horses supporting the civic arms, recalling that the River Cam once brought sea-going craft to the town, while at Boston the civic arms are supported by a pair of crowned mermaids. Legend has it they were crowned to commemorate the town's association with Anne Boleyn and Princess Mary, Duchess of Suffolk but the salmon fly in the arms of Redditch tells a more believable fishy story.

Canal Curio Tells of Coal Tax

Whether reeling under the impact of Value Added Tax or nervously contemplating coal, electricity, and fuel cuts, we should perhaps spare a thought for our forebears of three centuries ago who were even taxed on warmth. The Kings of old – not unlike the Governments of today – were never slow in finding new ways to raise revenue. A reminder that even coal carried by canal once contributed to the exchequer is the curious obelisk almost hidden on the towing path of the Grand Union Canal between Stockers Lock and Springwell Lock.

It is one of a series to be found beside railways and roads approaching London and marking the point at which dues were levied on coal and wine bound for the metropolis.

After the Great Fire of London in 1666 it took several years to re-build the City, at an enormous cost, which proved so great that the Corporation was unable to carry out a responsibility that it held from the fourteenth century for the wardship of all orphans of its citizens.

Consequently in June 1694 in the fifth year of the reign of William and Mary, the Orphans and Other Creditors Act was passed, which permitted the application of coal and wine dues to eliminate the City's debt. The duty was to be '4d per chaldron on coals, culm, and cinders, and 4 shillings a tun on all wine of whatever sort over and above already chargeable thereon'.

With the coming of the railways one of the first things visualized by the civic authorities was the likelihood that the new form of land transport would in due course take over a large proportion of the coal carryings. As a result they took steps to protect their interests by arranging for provisions for these dues in the Acts of incorporation of various railway companies.

During the early part of Queen Victoria's reign two further Acts were passed, which perpetuated the dues. This latter Act 24 and 25 Victoria Cap 42, which is inscribed on many of the obelisks, authorized the Corporation to erect at its own expense 'boundary stones or permanent marks on the point where the canal, inland navigation, or railway, or any turnpike or public road, first entered into or comes within the Metropolitan Police District'. It was at this point that the majority of the obelisks and markers were erected.

Nine pence of the duty was abolished on 5 July 1889, and the balance of 4d. on 3 July 1890, when the City of London's rights to collect duties on all coal brought to the 'London District' expired.

The money gained from these levies was paid into the Thames Embankment Metropolitan Improvement Fund which was used to finance the making and improving of Cannon Street, the Victoria, Albert and Chelsea Embankments, as well as the re-building of St Pauls. Although the City obtained some benefits from the proceeds of the taxes, the effects of the dues were felt over a wide area which had no share in the revenue. So much so that one writer of the period declared 'London consumes not the eighth part of the coals that pay to the tax'.

By the turn of the century more luxurious commodities were attracting the eye of the money-hungry Exchequer and nowadays quaint canalside columns with a purpose long since forgotten, no longer have any influence on fuel for the fire or wine to warm the heart.

Mystery Monument at Ripon

Who can solve the puzzle of the Ripon mystery monument which is inscribed 'Ripon Navigation, 1820. Level of Skell Crooks Dam seven feet below this'? For, despite the inscription, its origins and purpose are shrouded by the mists of time.

Does the little stone obelisk commemorate a reservoir which once held waters to feed the Ripon Canal which links to the River Ure or, as some authorities suggest, was it built to supply the city's water mills?

After all, they point out, the canal terminates on the east side of the city while the mystery memorial stands beside the River Skell on the western outskirts. And perhaps the word 'navigation' is used here in its general sense of a man-made watercourse whether it be for the passage of craft or just a water-carrying conduit for some other purpose.

Maybe a clue lies in the date? An Act of 1767 authorized the improvement of the River Ure and the construction of a couple of miles of canal to the city, and this was opened in 1772. By 1820 arrears of interest totalling £11,450 had accumulated on the £16,400 of debt which the sponsors had incurred and apparently nobody remained qualified to act as commissioner for the undertaking.

As a result the works, lacking proper maintenance and control, were in a dilapidated state. Because 'the trade and carriage . . . hath of late years greatly increased . . . and it has become necessary to provide . . . additional wharfs, warehouses, landing places etc.', reported one contemporary in 1819, a fresh approach was needed. So, in October of that year some of the creditors formed a corporate body and subscribed an additional £3,033 before obtaining a new Act which was passed in 1820.

Was the Skell Crooks Dam one result of the new enterprise? It might have been felt necessary to hold the waters of the Skell above the confluence with the River Laver and to take as much of this water as possible before 'topping up' from the dam. Such a surmise would be helped if the stone was inscribed with the new name style – 'The Company and Proprietors of the River Ure Navigation to Ripon'.

But perhaps this was both too pompous and too long? Like many other places, Ripon developed rapidly because of the Industrial Revolution and doubtless also as a result of the canal link by which 'coals and merchandise are brought up in vessels of about 30 tons burthen from Hull, York and other places and return loaded with lead, butter, etc.'.

Undoubtedly, summer droughts must have caused some concern about the maintenance of this waterway link for even today the joint efforts of the Rivers Skell and Laver produce little flow through the city. In addition, five water mills imposed demands on water supply and it was this requirement, suggest some people, that resulted in the creation of three dams – High Dam, High Cleugh Dam and Skell Crooks Dam.

Another reservoir existed at the Dutch Hill Pond. As early as 1800 a pumping engine had been erected here to pump water into some score or more standpipes around Ripon, for the city was one of the first to have piped water.

Some years later, the pumping of water was moved to the River Ure but in the meantime there must often have been an outcry about the shortage of water in the summer months.

Was the head of water created by the Skell Crooks Dam diverted across the intervening land to merge with High Cleugh Dam on the Laver and to flow into the mill race which is today identified by roads embodying the word 'Skell'?

Undoubtedly, the mill race was vital for the mills located on it and the water eventually found its way into the canal by the diverted route. Certainly the head of water was substantial, for about every twenty years the High Cleugh Dam would burst and it was finally abandoned in 1896 by which time all the milling had changed to steam power.

Curiously enough, on a map dated 1892 both High Dam and High Cleugh Dam are shown as well as the associated mill race but Skell Crooks Dam is not identified. But neither of the other two have a permanent memorial – even if it is a puzzler.

Missive with a Message

Easter marks the start of the traditional annual exodus from town and city for a few days to 'get away from it all'. And what better way of doing this than meandering afloat on the tranquil waterways? An ever-increasing number of people are doing just that as they discover the serenity, seclusion and scenic charms of hidden corners of the country.

Just as holiday makers on beaches, in parks, on piers, or wherever, succumb to that irresistible urge to send back home news about the weather, food, accommodation, or travelling, so wayfarers on the waterways seek the indispensable postcard.

As an accepted essential of any holiday over 500 million postcards flutter through our letterboxes each year compared with the 75 million handled by the postal authorities when the habit was born just over a century ago.

The first ordinary postcards in Britain were issued for sale on 1 October 1870, published by the GPO and costing 6½d. a dozen. They were only 4½ in by 3½ in and it was not until 1897 that they were enlarged to the 5½ in by 3½ in we are familiar with today.

Their introduction was by no means universally popular. Some people considered it discourteous to send a message worth less than the normal penny postage and they argued that servants or anyone else for that matter would be able to read private messages. Despite all these protests, on the first day of sale alone 575,000 cards were dealt with by postal authorities.

Yet the picture postcard, which has truly been described as one of the most useful creations of all time, was not really invented. It evolved. The addition of a picture on a plain card had its origins in the pictorial visiting cards of the eighteenth century and many early postcards were primarily advertising material.

For example, I believe Pickfords issued some to promote their canal carrying activities. And the London firms of Hinton and Horne and Locket and Judkins issued coloured postcards showing views of 'St Pauls from our Royal George Coal Wharf' with craft plying on the river. On the back they quoted prices for summer coals with Best Silkstone at the exorbitant price of 20s. 6d. – per ton!

Such was the interest in the new creation that newspapers of 1903 were bewailing: 'In ten years Europe will be buried beneath picture postcards'.

As might be expected the range of subects was both vast and varied. But canals, rivers, aqueducts and viaducts all featured. Even repair works featured as is evidenced by a couple of postcards of a gang working – or posing between working – on Bingley Five Rise Locks.

Canal scenes are often charming examples of pictorial rusticity but sometimes they portray valuable records of commercial activity and craft of bygone days. Scenes showing laden barges negotiating locks and docks were sent with happy messages just as enthusiastically as restful stretches of canal. A Valentine card of 1910, for instance, shows a colourful scene with locks on what is probably the Monmouthshire Canal at Newport.

River and canal scenes are often shown crowded with cheerful boating parties, with parasols much in evidence. Henley, Marlow, and Hampton Court on the Thames were just some of the fashionable riverside resorts. And, of

'On the Canal, Thorne' is the title of this old postcard, which shows a sailing vessel being unloaded

course, there was Tuck's series which featured popular songs of the era. Songs like the 'Jolly Young Waterman', illustrated with a tasteful scene showing the ardent lover at a landing stage with its admiring belle.

Not all the cards were purely pictorial or serious. An amusing cartoon of 'Eight Weeks in the Stone Age' by E.T. Reed was first published in 1903 and continued to be sold for many years after. And a whole 'Eights' series was published in 1907.

'Shall I mind the shop while you go out?' asks the cloth-capped passer-by of a storekeeper on a comic card which amused some visitor to Scarborough in 1927. 'No thanks, I'm not going out', comes the reply. 'Yes, you are – yer wife's just fell in the canal,' is the quick retort.

A prolific illustrator of the early postcards was 'Cynicus' who commented on a wide range of subjects. As his cognomen implies he poked malicious fun at sacred British institutions. Of particular interest is one card which showed remarkable foresight on a subject that was not to cause national concern for another sixty years or more – pollution. His illustrations show a waterway on whose bed lies rotting hulks and animal carcases with a pipe bearing the notice 'Sewage by Order'. On the banks are factory chimneys pouring out clouds of filthy smoke.

In more recent times colourful scenes of narrow boats and scenic vistas have proved more popular and attractive subjects for postcard illustrations. It is, of course, easy to overlook the informative value of the view card.

A typical example of postcard humour applied to waterways

As an editorial of the first edition of the *Picture Postcard Magazine* in July 1900 pointed out 'Ostensibly but a mere miniature view of some town or place of interest to the passing traveller, a picture postcard is yet capable of possessing an interest and significance undreamed of by those who have not yet troubled to look into the matter'.

With the growing interest in antiques, the sale of old cards in second-hand bookshops and the present-day mania for Victoriana, cartophilia – the hobby of postcard collecting – is being rediscovered.

Tragedy of the Christmas Carollers

Just a few feet from the magnificent Norman door of St Helen's church at Stillingfleet, near York, stands a communal grave commemorating a horrific Christmas tragedy on the nearby River Ouse.

On one of the headstones is the inscription:

Those whose names are here recorded were accidentally drowned in the River Ouse whilst returning from singing the praises of their Saviour in the neighbouring townships on December 26th 1833. God's Will Be Done. As a tribute to the memory of the sufferers and of deep compassion from their sorrowing families, their common landlord Bielby Thompson of Escrick Park has erected this monument.

At the opposite end the headstone records the names of eleven victims who were aged between fourteen and fifty-six.

Filled with seasonal goodwill the village choir had been in their places on Christmas morning to give the traditional service added zest with an enthusiastic rendition of popular carols and hymns.

That evening too they were in good voice, singing a selection of appropriate melodies in the Rectory where they had been entertained to supper by the Revd D.F. Markham. Afterwards they went home full of seasonal fare, pleasant memories, and happy emotions.

Boxing Day was a Thursday and fourteen of them gathered in the village street by half past one ready to continue the annual custom of visiting Moreby, Acaster, Selby, and Kelfield, to sing carols at the principal farmhouses in and around these villages.

After visiting at Moreby near the river, the carollers embarked in John Turner's boat for the river crossing to Low Acaster. After more hymns here, they embarked once again, a little after four o'clock, to re-cross the river at Stillingfleet Landing, which necessitated sailing down river about half a mile. Here they planned to disembark and continue on foot to Kelfield.

Close to the main entrance of the grey-turreted church of St Helena at Stillingfleet and marked by twin headstones is the communal grave of the drowned carollers

By now it was dusk as John Fisher and George Eccles rowed the little vessel which was being carried along by a swift ebb current at the rate of 5 miles an hour.

About a quarter of a mile from Acaster Selby, at a place called Mill Mouth, they met a coal-laden barge which was being hauled upstream on the Acaster side by a horse driven by a Cawood haulier called Stephen Green. Owned by Jon Jewitt of York, barge *Perseverance* was captained by William Rogerson of South Hindley who was anxious to make York before dark and had his sails up to take advantage of favourable following winds.

Eccles and Fisher intended to keep on the Stillingfleet side of the barge but Turner told them to row to the other side. As he was a fisherman and they were agricultural labourers in his boat they assumed he knew what he was about and duly complied.

What happened next seems a little unclear.

Apparently Turner shouted to Green asking him to slacken his tow-rope but Green thought he was being asked to tighten it. In fact Fisher later said he called for it to be tightened, but doubtless the cries were distorted and blown back by the wind.

In any event, Green shouted back that it was impossible to tighten the line without throwing them over, but he would slacken it to enable the boat to pass over.

He immediately slackened the rope and ran to his horse's head and held him. Although the rope was considerably slackened and astern of the vessel some way before the boat reached it, because of the strength of the current the line did not sink.

Bearing down at speed in the little boat John Fisher sensed danger and seized hold of the line, attempting to throw it over the heads of his companions. In this he failed and the line caught the stern of the boat, which being thrown on her broadside, instantly capsized in seconds, pitching everyone into the swirling water.

Fisher still clasped the line and thought he heard one of the bargemen call out: 'Hold thy hold, lad,' which he did and was rewarded with his life, as was Richard Toes who also managed to cling to the line. These two were rescued by Rogerson and his men on the barge which had meanwhile run aground. In saving the two men, the boat belonging to the barge was unfortunately loosened from its moorings and cast adrift on the opposite side of the river.

The whole catastrophe occupied but a few minutes and amid the confusion, the screams, the struggles, the battle for life, and the darkness, nothing could be done to rescue the unfortunate battle.

Fisher said afterwards:

After I had got on the vessel, I thought I saw three men's heads, as though they were on the bottom of the boat; they were some distance down the river, and I saw no more of them, it was getting dark; we had drunk a little ale during the day, but we were all perfectly sober, and everyone was as capable of helping himself or herself, as though we had not had any.

Rogerson too saw the upturned boat with survivors clinging to it before it disappeared behind a bend called Ness End. Probably what both men saw was Eccles who had hung on to his oar and managed to get to the upturned boat and cling on with William Bristow, the parish clerk.

The boat turned over several times in the turbulent waters but both men managed to get in even though it was full of water. But after about 200 yds the boat turned over once again and both men lost their holds, although Eccles still clung to his oar. Fortunately a second oar floated within his reach, giving him extra support.

Sighting another vessel coming upstream he cried out for help and was rescued. Turner's boat was eventually recovered at Cawood by a waterman called George Liddle but Bristow had drowned.

When the news reached Stillingfleet the villagers were stunned, struck with consternation, horror, and grief. By four o'clock on Friday morning several parties had arrived at the fatal spot from Cawood, Low Acaster, Nun Appleton, and the neighbouring villages in boats to start dragging the river.

Six hours passed before the first body was recovered in a place called Willow Hole about half a mile from where the accident happened. Nine bodies were eventually recovered. Those drowned were: Henry Spencer, a labourer, aged 44, together with his two daughters, Sarah, 16 and Elizabeth, 14; Christopher Spencer, labourer, 36; John Turner, fisherman and his daughter Jane, 16; William Bristow, parish clerk, 55; Sarah Eccles, daughter of the survivor, 17; Elizabeth Buckle, daughter of the inn keeper, 15; Clarissa Sturdy, daughter of the schoolmaster, 17; and Thomas Webster, a labourer, 44.

The river was dragged all day on Saturday for the bodies of Sarah Eccles and Sarah Spencer but they were never recovered. The current had carried them away and despite valiant and persistent efforts at dragging, only a shawl belonging to Sarah Eccles was found.

Should the boat have maintained its station on the Stillingfleet side, where there was plenty of room to pass, or would it have passed over the tow-line in the water without mishap? Opinions varied.

A coroner's inquest and searching investigation, lasting five hours, was held on the Friday evening before John Wood of York. No blame was attached to the watermen and a verdict of 'Accidental Death' was recorded by the jury who also declared a deodand on the boat which was the cause of the accident. (Until 1846, a deodand was a personal chattel which, having been the immediate occasion of the death of a person, was forfeited to the Crown to be applied to pious uses.) The amount fined was 1s.

The heart-rending episode concluded with an interment on Saturday 29 September, attended by nearly 2,000 mourners from the neighbourhood. Two days later the *York Courant* headed a lengthy report of the 'Shocking Event' with a three-verse hymn to remind its readers that 'God moves in a mysterious way, His wonders to perform. . . .'

Maud Heath's Causeway

Where the River Avon is crossed by the Great West Road, as it divides for Bath and Bristol, lies the market town of Chippenham. And it was here that a certain Maud Heath came to weekly market and annual fairs with her basket of eggs and butter some five centuries ago.

Her route in summer was dusty, apart from one section of swampland adjacent to the Avon, but in winter the whole valley was frequently inundated as the river burst its banks. Avon's waters made visits to the market a perilous undertaking so after the death of her farmer husband Maud decided to do something about the unruly waterway.

She found a solution in the endowment of a causeway. It starts at the top of Wick Hill some 4½ miles from Chippenham and goes down the hill to

A panoramic view of a section of Maud Heath's raised walkway at Kellaways where it crosses the River Avon

Tytherton, crossing the now unused Wiltshire and Berkshire Canal before going up over the Avon at Kellaways. On it goes through Langley Burrell and continues as a footpath along the Swindon Road to the corner by St Paul's church.

The causeway has been cut by the road at Tytherton and at several other points but, when the railway was made, the Great Western Railway Company constructed a narrow archway just to accommodate Maud's gift to the locality.

Early chroniclers called a raised path a *causey*, which they probably derived from the French *chausée*, a pitched road which, like Maud Heath's causeway, was a path raised above flood level.

Although originally pitched with cobblestones, parts of this causeway were later constructed of limestone brash placed on edge. This may not have been the most comfortable path on which to walk, but on the many occasions when the river was in flood or the road a sea of mud it was doubtless a blessing to many a reluctant traveller.

During the past two centuries the stones, which were originally set at right-angles to the line of the path, have been lifted and placed longitudinally before being covered by gravel, tarmacadam or concrete.

In 1811, according to the Minutes of the Trustees, the causeway was carried 'over the lowlands above the channel of the Avon on a course of 64 brick arches', and in 1853 they constructed an iron bridge over the river.

The legend of Maud Heath as a market woman is emphasized and perpetuated by a giant statue of her, complete with basket and staff, which dominates Wick Hill overlooking a wide and beautiful view of the Avon valley. On the base of the monument is the inscription:

> Erected at the joint expense of Henry, Marquis of Landsdowne,
> Lord of the Manor and Wm. L. Bowles, vicar of the parish of Bremhill.
> Thou didst pause on this aerial height
> Where Maud Heath's Pathway winds in shade or light
> Christian wayfarer in a world of strife
> Be still and ponder on the path of Life.
>
> WLB

On the opposite side of the road to the monument there is a stone inscribed:

> From this Wick Hill begins the praise
> Of Maud Heath's gift to these Highways.

At Kellaways, in the vicinity of which Maud had her home, a pillar about 12 ft high stands beside the river. This carries a three-faced block sundial inscribed:

To the memory of the worthy Maud Heath of Langley Burrell, widow who in the year of grace 1474 for the good of travellers did in charity bestow in lands and houses about eight pounds a year for ever to be laid out on the Highway and causey leading from Wick Hill to Chippenham Cliff. This pillar was set up by the feoffees in 1698. Injure me not.

By today's standards £8 a year may seem a ridiculously small price to pay for keeping your feet dry, but in those far-off times it was an indication of considerable wealth. Alas, inflation has taken its toll and now the upkeep of the causeway is divided between the Trustees and the County Council. A new bridge over the Avon was erected by the County Council between 1962 and 1963 and the waters are no longer troublesome for travellers.

A far cry indeed from the days when 3s was paid 'to John Galle for one days work to the Bridge with his plowe'.

eight

Streams of Wails

The Black Jack Mystery

I am often asked by folk who know the extent of my travels on British Waterways, 'What is your most memorable experience?' Now that's a difficult question to answer because somehow I seem to find excitement and adventure all the time. But there's no doubt that the story I am going to tell you comes high on the list.

Let's go back a few years – to my first trip along the Grand Union Canal. After a hard day I had moored for the night above a lock, out in the country, and was enjoying a coffee in the cool of the evening. I remember thinking how peaceful it was after the hurly-burly of London. A slight mist rose from the water after the heat of the day. The stillness was almost uncanny and I felt my mind drifting back through the years to the days when skill and sheer dogged guts enabled gangs of navvies to carve the vast water network on which Britain's prosperity was founded.

What had become of these stalwarts when their work was finished, and the miracle of making rivers run over hills and across valleys was an accomplished fact? Some must have remained in the service of the water they had tamed, becoming boatmen, bridgemen, lock keepers. Perhaps you'll think my story concerns one of them. . . .

It was almost dark when my reverie was interrupted by the sound of approaching boats, and as a good 'pleasure boatman' I hurried to set the lock for them. I stood by the gates watching the water roar over the sill – a sight which even today sends a thrill of excitement up my spine. But this time the thrill suddenly became a chill. As I gazed into the lock I saw – or thought I saw – a man's hand, *a black hand*, clutching the air as the turbulent foam cascaded from the open paddles. It must be a trick of the shadows – a foolish fancy. Or was there indeed a body down there amidst the rush of water? I was rooted to the spot – paralysed – trying to force myself to shut the paddles and obliterate the horror I now knew was below me. I could not move!

The drumming in my ears became more insistent but now it no longer spoke of the terror below, but seemed to beckon me, I felt myself take a step forward

. . . then another . . . seemingly impelled by some force . . . some power, maybe, released by the pent-up fury of the torrent. I was now on the very edge of the parapet and surely would have fallen into the lock had a voice not called sharply, 'Come away from there!'

I turned, the awful spell broken: indeed, feeling rather foolish as I faced the new arrival. 'You'll get drowned if you stand on the edge like that,' he said, and I noted with relief it was a boatman, one of the older types it appeared from his clothes. He was not wearing the jeans and bright shorts favoured by the younger lads. I was fascinated by his beautifully polished windlass telling of years and years of use up and down the canals. I think I must have started to explain what had caused me to go so near the edge, but, seeming not to hear me, he went on. 'You wouldn't be the first he's lured in. It's just the right time.'

Well, as you can imagine, my questions came fast. His answers were calm and factual at first. 'Black Jack' was the name of the apparition in the lock, and some of the old-time boatmen would not pass the lock after dusk, believing the ghost of this villainous negro still haunted the scene of his violent end. 'He was a bad one,' my boatman said. 'All the canal folk hated him, but he was so big and strong, no one could stand up to him.'

Then, in his curious, almost foreign voice, the old man went on to tell me how drink began to sap the negro's strength, and the bolder boatmen planned revenge. One night Black Jack began to abuse one of them, who, worn out after a long troublesome day, pulled a knife at the huge figure on the lock side. Taken by surprise, the drunken negro stumbled, fell into the lock, and was literally flayed to death by the force of the water crashing on to his body.

'What of the man who pulled the knife?' I asked.

Slowly, the reply came, 'He was horrified at the thing he'd brought about. And later, he was seen to leap into this same lock – the first of Black Jack's victims.'

I was about to ask my friend more about the 'haunting' when I saw that the boats were now entering the lock. It was not until I'd helped close the gates and open the paddles that I remembered the old boatman. He was not to be seen!

The skipper of the boats and his blonde wife had exchanged greetings with me, so I asked them if 'the old boy' had jumped back on board whilst I'd been busy with the windlass. 'What old boy?' asked Frank Fisher, for such I learned was his name.

'The old boatman I was talking to as you came up. Wasn't he your wheeler?'

'We've no wheeler,' Frank replied. 'There are only the two of us on board.'

I felt myself go cold, for I knew what his next words would be . . . 'We were watching you as we came up, and you were all alone on the lock – quite alone.'

Well, there's the tale. There may be some rational explanation for the queer

Springheeled Jack. This apparition was likely to knock boatmen on the head and make off with their windlasses

happenings. But although I've covered almost every inch of the waterways since that night I've never again run across the old boatman who knew such details of Black Jack's end. I've since been told there is a legend that a negro named Black Jack was indeed employed by a big land owner in the early days of the canal – his job to harass boatmen. It is said that he was murdered by some of the canal folk in revenge for interfering with the locks and stealing their windlasses.

So my ghostly boatman's story differed slightly from the legend, which I'd not then heard. I wonder which – if either – is the true version? I'm afraid I'll have to leave you to be the judge! Accident – or murder? Or was it all a fancy born of the autumn mists and shadows?

JACK HOWARD

Lock Bubbles for Sale

'The bubble-catcher, Mister? Oh! yes, I knew the bubble-catcher,' said the old boatman as he drew on his pipe. Clear innocent blue eyes looked at me from the brown walnut of his face. He watched silently as I reached and sent the float on another hopeful journey.

Then he went on: 'Matter of fact he was nephew to the Slipton lock keeper. Maybe that's what started the business – his spending holidays helping his uncle. Jepson, I remember, was his name – John Jepson – a smart enough young chap. Always had the gates open ready for you, not like some of them. And always grinning – though he never said a lot. Deep he was, I reckon – deep.'

The old man paused to refill with tobacco.

'But the bubbles, what about the bubbles?' I asked him.

He looked at me patiently and said: 'Now hold your horses, I'm coming to that.' He struck a match, then: 'It were like this. Running back empty from Leeds I was, when just after Wigan along comes young Fred Hampson's boat. Fred seems fair worked up about something so I shouts him over for a cup of tea. He ties up, over he comes and no sooner the cup's in his hand than he outs with – 'Have you 'eard the latest?' And without giving the chance to say owt, he goes on: 'That young chap back at Slipton's collecting bubbles.' 'He's what?' I says, and then Fred comes out with the whole story.

'It seems that Fred had got to Slipton and found the gates against him. Now this were a bit strange, for, as I just said, they're sharp off the mark there most times. So Fred wanders along to the lock and there he finds – guess what?'

The boatman paused dramatically.

'Well,' I replied, 'what?'

'Bubbles,' the old man said. 'Thousands of bubbles. A lock full and this young whipper-snapper filling them polythene bags full of bubbles as fast as he can go. "And what the 'ell are you doing?" says Fred. The kid looks up. "Oh, alloa", he grinned. "I'm afraid you can't come through yet awhile, not until I've got rid of this lot." And he pointed at the foaming lock. Well, Fred's a bit touchy at the best of times and you can imagine this weren't one of them. "I don't know what the 'ell's going on," he shouts, "but I've got work to do. Time's money to me and I'm coming through. Anyway where's your uncle?"

'"Oh! you can't disturb him" the young cocker goes on, giving a sly grin, "he's busy sorting out the right kind of bubbles, ready for the consignment tonight." And with that he goes on filling up his polythene bags as fast as he can.

'Well, Mister, I can tell you Fred was proper fogged. But he watches for a bit and then storms off back to his old woman to take it out on her. Anyways, at last they got through and ten minutes after was when I spied him.

'Well, I starts on my way wondering what it's all about. But when I get to Slipton, everything is as nice as pie, so I begin to think Fred's got a touch of the sun – till I remember it's only a month to Christmas. It were in the weeks that followed that the stories really got round. Boats getting held up for hours at Slipton, arguments, free fights, oh! I can tell you a rare to-do and all the time the bubble-catcher, as he became known, working away as fast as he could, filling up his bags, and never a hint as to what it was for. All he'd say were that he'd cornered the market.

'News, as you know, don't take long to travel on the waterways, Mister, and before a fortnight's out, along comes the Section Inspector and from what I heard there was the dickens to pay. Anyway, when I went through Slipton again soon after, it was as quiet as the grave and back to normal, save there was a new lock keeper.'

The boatman stopped talking and looked reflectively at some vagrant mallard.

'But the bubbles,' I pleaded, 'where did they come from and what were they collected for?'

'Well, I can tell you where they came from,' he replied, 'that's easy. Just above Slipton is one o' them factories what use detergents and they dump the waste once a week in the cut. If you want some bubbles, you just empty the lock, then fill her up; the churning water through the sluices does the rest for you – see?'

'Yes,' I said, 'but I still don't understand what they were used for.'

'Ah, well,' replied the boatman, 'nor did we. We never fathomed it out until about a month ago when me and my missus and Fred and his wife were having a drink in the Rose and Crown. We'd been talking the bubbles over, as usual, when a posh-looking old bloke comes in. And after a bit he comes over. "Excuse me, gentlemen," he says, "but I couldn't help overhearing your interesting conversation, I hope you don't mind."

'"You're welcome," chips up Fred, and the old boy goes on: "I think I can throw a little light on the problem." Fred said, "We hope very much you can, sir, for it's been puzzling the whole waterway from Leeds to Liverpool ever since it happened. Why they've even heard about it on the flippin' Grand Union!"

'"It seems to me," he went on, "that we have to ask ourselves the fundamental question, namely, for what purpose would bubbles be used in our present civilization?"

'"Well," continued the old gent, "I can only think of one likely use for bubbles and I do happen to know that there's been a shortage of them for some time, but the market lately has much improved."

'Well? we all said, hanging on to his every word.'

'He picked up his beer and looked at it, then at us. "Yes," he said, "that's it, and a brilliant idea too. Your bubble-catcher was a level-headed young man," he chuckled and added, "and with spirit, too," now laughing fit to bust.'

'He finished his half of best bitter, picked up his hat and turned to us. "Well, it's been very pleasant to meet such interesting folk. A very goodnight to you all." And off he went.'

'"Oi!" yelled Fred. "How about them bubbles?"

'"The bubbles," said the old gent as he went through the door. "I'd quite forgot." He gave us a knowing wink. "Spirit levels," he said, and went out."'

The boatman stopped talking and gazed at me. Then, like a conjurer, he fished into his brown waistcoat pocket and brought out a short, bright silver-coloured tube.

'There's no doubt of it,' said he, pointing a stubby brown finger to the tiny glass window set into the tube. 'There – look!'

Obediently I peered down and sure enough in the limpid green liquid floated a tiny, delicate but perfect silver oval which bobbed and danced at every movement of the old man's strong fingers.

'No doubt,' he murmured, 'no doubt at all, it's one of that young bubble-catcher's, I shouldn't wonder.'

PETER HALL

The Lady in the White Gown

Not long ago they pulled down the Hall. The Big House, people called it. They called it too, *the haunted house.*

It stood close by our Waterways depot for it had originally belonged to the man who built the warehouses. When it was demolished, however, nobody had lived there for a long time and it stood hidden behind towering cedar and walnut trees in a dark garden overgrown with elder bushes and waist-high weeds. Few people went near it because it had an odd chilly air, and even children who ventured there to play seemed to find no savour in their games and soon moved on to play elsewhere.

I stood and watched the bulldozers tearing the bricks apart, grinding them into the ground to clear the way for a new trunk road to the north. Was this, I wondered, to be the end of the Lady in the White Gown who was supposed to haunt the place? Old Joe, who used to work there as a boy – he had told me tales. Dear old Martha and Manda, who had been daily helps and lived in cottages near the Big House: I remembered the strange tales they had told me, too.

It was a rough winter's night (the story went), cold and wet, when the coach drew up to the great pillared front door bringing the master home for the last time from one of his wild parties. He was dead. Old Joe knew, for he held a lantern for the coachman as they carried the limp, heavy body up the steps and into the house. Old Joe saw, too, the lady of the house standing motionless and grief-stricken in her white gown at the window of the little room above the portico. As if in a trance she had stared wide-eyed and horrified at the tragic scene.

The shock, said Martha and Manda, was too much for her and before very long she followed her husband to the grave. But her spirit could not rest, they told me, and many a night they saw her standing in her white gown at the window of the little room – just as she had stood that wild, sad night – or pacing backwards and forwards as if in anguish.

Now the demolition contractors were pulling the old house down. As their work progressed, more and more people came to watch, among them a young art student who sat and sketched the scene. Soon, however, it became apparent to us all, from the shouting and discussions going on among the workmen, that some hitch had occurred; things were not going to plan. The centre of the building seemed to be mysteriously resisting the combined efforts of bulldozers, winches and steel wire ropes. Though everything around lay in ruins, yet the little room above the portico remained firm. There came to me, then, the queer fancy that *some power was holding it, allowing the artist time to finish his sketch* – for else nothing would remain to remind people of that little room and they would forget, as time went on, the tragic lady whose unquiet spirit had haunted it.

But I should not have forgotten.

I shall remember always the dark night in 1941 when I penetrated that eerie room. It must have been getting on for midnight. Making my usual tour of the warehouse yard after an air-raid warning I happened to glance across at the 'Big House' and saw, through the branches of the trees, what looked like a faint white shaft of light moving slowly from side to side.

The reflection of a searchlight? No, I decided; that was impossible. Then what?

I was already fumbling through the nettles, high as my hand, on a short cut to the house before I asked myself what I was doing it for, why *I* was investigating. Yet something impelled me, and I pressed on through the inky blackness, under the cedar trees and, as quietly as I could, up the steps. I felt sure it could not be a tramp in the room up there, for they were scared of the place at night. Perhaps it was one of those people we all half-believed in in those days who signalled to the German planes with lights. I was glad to be armed with a stout stick and thankful for my wartime hooded flashlamp.

Noiselessly, I pushed open the great front door which hung loosely on its hinges and paused, listening. Not a sound, save the cedar tree behind me, sighing like a lost soul in the wind. I tiptoed over the hall where the thick dust silenced my steps, and crept stealthily up the wide stairway to the first floor, keeping well pressed against the wall in case someone came bolting down. The room I sought was at the far side of the landing. Tapping along the wall, I found the door.

Bracing myself, I gave it a sudden shove with my stick, keeping my body back out of the way. I expected – well, I don't know what I expected!

The door crashed open but nothing happened; nobody appeared. So I ventured in. But not a murmur; nothing but the musty smell of a room long closed. Nothing at all.

I was relieved, of course, and clattering down the stairs in my heavy ARP boots, my loud footsteps echoed to the very roof of the desolate house. I battled back through the weeds and elder bushes towards the depot and home.

Then the thought struck me – *had I disturbed the Lady in the White Gown?*

It could have been no other.

That was a long time ago, that war-time night. Now, as the young artist put the final touches to his sketch the great pillars of the portico came crashing down, and down came the window and the little room, all tumbling in a grey cloud of choking dust.

I gave him 5s. for his drawing and I keep it in memory of the Lady in the White Gown.

Nothing else remains; so now at least she may rest in peace.

F.G. TRACEY

Saturday Night Fever for Juliet's Ghost

Will 1979 prove to be a successful year for the many boating enthusiasts who make the annual pilgrimage up the Great Ouse to Holywell in Huntingdonshire to keep a midnight tryst with a ghost? Or will Saturday 17 March 1979 prove to be just another bumper night for the licensee of Ye Olde Ferry Boat Inn where the spirit of Juliet Tewsley is supposed to rise from a tombstone in the bar and to drift out to the river?

In 1952, the then landlord applied for a late extension licence so that he could stay open legally for Juliet's night, and the evening ended up being divided between drinking and boating yarns.

Over 400 people turned up in 1954 and extra police had to come from nearby St Ives to control the crowd. Next year the Cambridge Psychical Research Society sent a team of investigators equipped with electronic apparatus to watch for Juliet's ghost. Alas they eventually went home in a huff for not so much as a wisp of a wraith was detected by their grear.

Yet the setting is right. Here are the glades in which she played and the river in whose waters she swam as a girl. So too are the woods where she walked and wooed her lover. Even the tree from which she hanged herself and, finally, that cold grey slab of granite which was her only gravestone.

The story really begins in those far-off days when Hereward the Wake crossed the river here after hiding in the reeds from William the Conqueror and his invading Normans.

A popular venue for boating enthusiasts and lovers of the supernatural is Ye Olde Ferry Boat Inn overlooking the Great Ouse at Holywell

In those times, between AD 1050 and AD 1100 near these willow-lined banks lived our heroine who fell so deeply in love that it became with her a kind of illness. She found her idea of the perfect Romeo in a woodcutter called Thomas Zoul.

A gay, vivacious, happy girl, Juliet was the toast of the village, always the life and soul of every party and almost always crowned Queen of the May. Wandering through the woods one day, picking wild spring flowers in the early morning sunshine, she caught a glimpse of Tom the woodcutter striding off to work.

Now Tom was a broad-shouldered, well-built young fellow with handsome features and curly dark hair. He would have been any young girl's pin-up so not surprisingly Juliet fell deeply in love with him. Gone was the gay, laughing girl everyone loved, for Juliet brooded over her new-found emotions.

Each day she kept early-morning vigils in the woods, waiting to catch sight of her heart-throb. At last, unable to keep her peace any longer, Juliet picked a bunch of her favourite wild flowers and waited until Tom came near her hiding place behind some trees.

When he came striding along the woodland track, Juliet, in her fresh pink dress, emerged trembling with maidenly emotion and offered him the posy. Now Tom was something of a rough diamond who preferred a pint of ale and a game of nine men's morris to the charms of females. Without more ado he pushed poor Juliet aside and told her to run home to mother. The crumpled posy fell on the grass and the jilted Juliet collapsed heartbroken beside it.

After quietly sobbing until nightfall she decided that life would be unbearable without the companionship of Tom. Ashen-faced but with steady step she made her way back to the family cottage. Searching an out-house she picked up a piece of hempen rope and walked down to the trees beside the river. And at midnight on 17 March 1050 she hanged herself to end forever her unrequited love.

The frail body was found hanging from a willow next morning and the whole village mourned. However, the old women shook their heads and many tongues wagged, for suicide then was regarded as a terrible crime. Following local custom the magistrates decreed that the body should be buried near the crossroads 'as a warning to all'.

Treated like a common criminal because she had taken her own life, poor Juliet was buried near Ye Olde Ferry with a single slab of granite to mark her resting place.

Over the years Holywell prospered, more cottages were built, and more ale was drunk at Ye Olde Ferry Boat Inn so the innkeeper sought, and was granted permission to build on another wing.

Being a thrifty man he laid the new tap room floor around the slab of granite so leaving the grave undisturbed and avoiding the expense of granite. An inch or so higher than the floor and slightly larger than the other slabs, the stone is still there.

From beneath this slab Juliet's ghost is said to appear each year on Saint Patrick's Day to return to the scene of her suicide.

Yet this is no ordinary ghost story.

Teams of psychic investigators complete with all their unusual ghost-detecting gear, reporters, photographers, thrill-hunters, tourists and the boating fraternity who regularly frequent the hostelry join with the locals in keeping a midnight tryst with Juliet's ghost.

Many people claim to have seen her and some local women will not go near the inn on 17 March. Dogs bark and run from the room with the hair bristling on their necks. On one occasion a convincing seance seemed to have established contact, while a photographer claims to have obtained a genuine picture of the ghost. Even radar has been used in an effort to prove that the ghost really does exist.

Surrounded by woods on three sides with the river coming literally to the front door at times, Ye Olde Ferry Boat Inn with its beautiful thatched roof is undoubtedly an architectural gem.

At one time the landlord also provided a ferry service across the river for customers, farm stock and machinery, but this was discontinued some years ago even though it did clip about 6 miles off the road journey from St Ives to Cambridge.

The spirit of Juliet Tewsley is said to materialize from her tomb in the floor of Ye Olde Ferry Boat Inn at Holywell

Inside, the old oak beams, stuffed fish in glass cases, eel hives made with rushes, and an old fireplace with traditional implements undoubtedly provide the right atmosphere for a haunting. And the bar stock of 1,400 bottles of drink, including some of the more exotic from different parts of the world, ensures no shortage of spirits for the unbeliever.

The Human Sacrifice

Harris looked up at the creaking sign swinging wildly in the bitter wind as he pushed open the old oak door. He removed his sodden mackintosh, hung it on the rickety coatstand in the hallway and sauntered through the slightly open doorway towards the bar.

'You look fair wet, sir,' remarked the rather plump barman. 'I should sit over by the fire there and dry yourself off, I'll be over to take your order in a minute.'

Harris sat down and looked into the fire watching the warm flames darting upwards into the stone built chimney. 'You'll soon dry out sir.' Harris looked up. Sitting at a nearby table was a weather-beaten old man probably in his eighties, a jar of ale on the brown-stained table in front of him. Harris nodded and looked back towards the fire.

'Now what'll you be having sir?'

Harris turned. 'A pint of mild please. Is there a garage in the village?'

'Yes sir. Got car trouble have we?'

'Yeah,' muttered Harris. 'The car broke down about 3 miles down the road.'

'Well, Tom Barlow will be in shortly. He owns the garage in the village. I should see him about it if I was you.'

Harris nodded and the barman ambled off to return shortly with the drink.

'That'll be eleven pence sir.'

'Here,' said Harris and handed over half a crown. The barman fished in his pocket, gave back the change and wandered off.

'On holiday sir?' Harris turned and faced the man. 'The war's put paid to holidays.'

'In the Services then are you?'

'No. Bad leg put paid to that. I'm a reporter.'

'A reporter are you. Well there's nothing to interest you here.'

'Suppose not,' replied Harris. 'Say, how come this place is called The Boatman's Arms? There's no river near here.'

'No, but there used to be a canal. Long gone now though.'

'Why's that then?'

'Not my place to say sir. I know nothing about it.'

'You mind your tongue now George.' Harris turned to see the barman standing there glaring at the old man. The door opened, another customer walked in and the barman turned to the bar.

'What was all that about?'

'Nothing,' replied the old man. 'Just an old man's talk. Superstition, you know.'

Throughout the evening Harris plied the old man with ale and kept off the subject of canals until he thought that George had had enough to loosen his tongue.

'Do you fancy making a few pounds, George?' The old man looked up.

'How's that then sir?'

You tell me about this canal and I'll see you alright.'

'I dunno sir.'

'Come on George. There's no-one near us to hear you.'

'How much sir?'

'Say a fiver.'

'Ten.'

'Seven,' replied Harris. 'No more.'

The old man looked round, then stared at Harris. 'I'm an old man, sir, not long to go. Maybe it's right that the truth should come out. Pull yourself closer sir.'

Harris moved up his seat and the old man started. 'Well, in the late eighties an ironworks opened up in the village and the owners reckoned that if they built a canal to link up with the Grand Union they could use that to ship in the raw materials and take out the iron. They had the Bill passed in Parliament but they had to build a tunnel through the hill over there.'

The old man pointed to the small window near the fireplace. 'They had trouble in building the tunnel, workmen falling in, rock falls, underground streams and the noises.'

'Noises?' interrupted Harris.

'That's when the real trouble started,' continued the old man. 'You see on top of the hill stands an old Iron Age burial chamber and when some of the workmen started hearing strange noises they became scared. Some said they'd disturbed the dead. The local labourers refused to work the tunnel and the owners had to bring in outside people, from Scotland if I remember right. Anyway, the accidents continued until they finished the tunnel.

'For a while after the tunnel was opened a few strange things happened but nothing serious. A few of the boatmen said they noticed a strange sort of smell towards the centre of the tunnel, a bit like decaying flesh. Others said that while they were legging in the tunnel. . . .'

Two men 'legging' a boat through Butterley Tunnel on the Cromford Canal, *c.* 1900

Harris broke in, 'What's legging?'

'Well sir, as you know the boats used to be pulled by horses, but because the tunnel was too narrow to have a towing path in it the horses had to walk over the hill by means of a path, while the boats were pushed through the tunnel by the boatmen lying on their backs on the deck and walking the boat through by pushing on the tunnel roof with their legs.'

'Thanks,' said Harris.

'Well a couple of the boatmen reckoned that once when they were walking the boat the tunnel walls felt as if they were walking on flesh.

'At the time I was only a young lad and my old dad got me a job on the boats. I must have been working there for about two years when it happened.' The old man paused.

'Go on,' said Harris. The old man looked down at his now empty glass. Harris picked it up, moved off and returned with a full glass. The old man took a few sips and continued.

'There were two boats at the time going through the tunnel. I was on the first boat with the other following about thirty feet behind. We were about two thirds of the way through the tunnel when we noticed the smell. Horrible it was, sir, a dreadful stench.

'We pushed our legs harder and faster against the tunnel wall. We wanted to get out of there as fast as possible I can tell you, then the tunnel walls seemed to push back. Well we were right scared. It seemed as if the tunnel was a gigantic heart pulsating, trying to pump us out of its arteries. We looked down at the waters; they were bubbling and as far as we could see in the dim light of the lamps there was what I would call white worms about twelve inches long writhing in the swirling waters. And the noise, it was like a loud whisper. "Tara, tara," it seemed to be saying.

'The boat was only a few yards from the tunnel mouth when the walls closed round the boat behind us, a wall of water shot us out of the tunnel as a bullet from a gun, so fast it was sir, but we still heard the screams of our mates on the rear boat. They must have been in agony. God help them.

'When we tied up in the pound next to the tunnel, which now seemed to have returned to normal, there were only a few pieces of wreckage floating in the water. Then we found the body. It was terrible sir, terrible. It was as if he had been bitten all over by I just don't know what. Small chunks of flesh had been torn off every square inch of the body. You wouldn't believe it sir, you really wouldn't.

'We took the remains down to the village police house and had a meeting right in here in this room. We all decided that the best thing would be to keep quiet about the matter as, if we stirred things up, whatever was there in the tunnel might take revenge on the village.

'Well a few pounds of black powder caved in the top end of the tunnel. It had to be the far end for this end can be clearly seen from the old ironworks. Funny thing you know, the village policeman never found out who was to blame – not that he really tried. The ironworks went bust soon after, something to do with one of the owners disappearing with one of the foundry manager's daughters and taking a fair sum of the firm's money with him. This end of the tunnel was boarded up, but a small door was built into it later by the locals here.'

'Why was that?' asked Harris.

'Well, some of the people here reckoned that if they pushed a boat into the tunnel every year with life in it the tunnel would leave them alone.'

'A human sacrifice?'

'No, no sir. Just a sheep or goat. It seems to have worked, no disaster has struck the village yet.'

'Thanks,' said Harris. 'This should make a first rate story – not that I believe it mind. Still, you've earned your seven quid. You should have written books with an imagination like that old man.'

Harris finished his drink in one go, stood up and turned round. Facing him was the barman and a few of his heavy friends.

'I told you to keep quiet, George,' said the barman.

'You know too much mister reporter man.'

Tied to a raft, lit only by the flickering glow of a black candle, Harris floated through the tunnel entrance

'Look here,' said Harris. 'What's the harm in the old man making himself a few quid with an old fairy tale?'

Harris moved forward and everything went black.

When he woke Harris felt that someone was playing drums inside his head. 'What a hangover,' he thought. 'What a dream.' He decided to open his eyes knowing that the light would probably only make the hangover worse. He opened them, but there was no light. Just the flicker of a candle. He tried to move but couldn't. He slowly realized that he was tied on a small raft on the front of which was a tall black candle. He looked around and saw that he was just floating through a small doorway. He looked at the heaving tunnel walls and screamed.

MICK ANTHONY

nine

All Kinds of Water

The Great Frost of 1895

It was Saturday evening, and with the flickering twilight a mighty shadow crept across the sky from the north-east. A rapid lowering of temperature, accompanied by icy rain, sent Midlanders scurrying home.

Later that night the wind shrieked to a crescendo, and roof-tiles whirled like paper.

An hour later the cruel lashing wind subsided. Far away, high in the northern sky, a lone star glittered in the dark void. The great frost of 1895 was on. . . .

The following dawn broke crisp and sparkling clear, revealing a frost of unusual penetration, upon which the pallid sun made no impression.

Within two days the canals at Cakemore, and the Jim Crow between Whiteheath and Oldbury, including the Swag and Titford pools, were frozen over, and the boating of coal was suspended.

Gradually the arctic conditions became more intense. Water poured from a vessel turned to ice as it struck the floor.

The iceboat was requisitioned, and with plenty of good boat horses a determined but unavailing effort was made to keep the waterways passable, as this was of vital importance to the local collieries which depended upon the canals as their principal means of transport.

The coal mines affected were Hartlands at Whiteheath, Rowley Hall, Ramrod, and to some extent the Grace Mary and the Twin pits.

These despatched their coal at Top End wharf, a canal arm at the end of the Jim Crow Canal.

For a time it was customary to take the boat two trips a day to keep the pack ice open, but during each succeeding night the ice became thicker.

At this time a Birmingham firm sent a boat containing a huge boiler and its equipment for boiling water and pumping it back into the canal at such a rate that, expert engineers calculated, it was capable of thawing the ice at least a mile each side of the boat.

It was fixed at the junction of the canal coming from Whiteheath and the Jim Crow, at the corner of Titford pool close to the Navigation Inn.

A horse-drawn ice breaker on the canal at an unknown location

The introduction of this device caused considerable criticism. People came from all parts of the district to watch results, crack jokes, and listen to the mirth of others. Jack Judge, of 'Tipperary' fame, was one of the star jesters.

For the first time in the history of the locality the pubs ran short of beer and one wag suggested that this was due to the supply of canal water being cut off.

Skating on Titford pool was in full swing. The landlord of the New Inn at Whiteheath, Mr W. Comely, an energetic and enterprising individual, had speculated much money over a course of several years in improving the banks of Titford pool by the planting of trees, and re-stocking the water with fish, as an inducement to local angling societies to spend their weekend close to home.

But the great frost paid him much better dividends, judging by the enormous crowds of skaters. Sixpence per day was paid and braziers were kept burning into the night when there was a moon.

It became increasingly obvious that the experiment of boiling water was inadequate. Only a few feet from the boat was clear of ice.

Then something went wrong with the mechanism one night, and before the necessary repairs could be made, it was frozen up and remained so for another ten weeks.

The frost was serious for many people at Whiteheath, who were mostly miners, wharfmen or boatmen. Already some of the pits were on short time, being unable to clear the coal from the pit head.

Every available horse and cart was requisitioned, and a continual procession of all kinds of horse-drawn vehicles wended their way through Whiteheath to Oldbury in order to keep industry going.

During this journey, many of the people out of work pilfered coal from the carts. The drivers, of course, never looked back.

The coal owners issued notices that such pilfering would be severely dealt with, but that as a concession, the women could collect any coal that might roll off.

The roads were very bad, and the drivers, many of whom were sons and husbands of the women, sought the rougher way. The falls were substantial and lucrative.

Further to help, big stones and half bricks were 'planted' in the road and the drivers became so expert that they rarely missed taking one or the other wheel over them.

After about seven weeks there came a morning when it failed to get light. Neighbours asked each other in subdued tones what was coming.

They were not kept in doubt very long, for a seeping circular wind began to

Unemployed men parade a block of ice during the great frost of 1895

146

move around, followed by a scattering of very fine snow . . . so fine that it was like flour, but very crisp.

It became darker as the wind increased in velocity and the snow in volume. People who were caught in it were almost blinded. Doors were packed with rugs, and even keyholes were plugged.

For hours the freezing blizzard lashed this part of the Midlands with raging fury. Traffic was completely suspended. Towards midday, however, it was almost spent and looking out of a bedroom window it resembled the vast frozen wastes of the Arctic.

One day four men pushed a handcart through Whiteheath and paused for a rest opposite the Bulls Head. On the cart was a block of ice sawn out of the canal wharf at Whiteheath. The block was about 3 ft square and 2 ft 6 in deep.

On either side hung a big card on which was written: 'If your hearts are not as hard and cold as this block of ice, then give us help for the out-of-work.'

Judging from subsequent reports, this appeal had the desired effect.

MONICA BENNETT

Rudyard, Stanley and Knypersley

The traveller heading north by train from Stoke-on-Trent passes through one of the grimiest and grimmest landscapes in England. The Burslem Grange, Ravensdale and Chatterley are shattered relics of the first impact of industry on North Staffordshire.

Along the line of the old Grand Trunk Canal, which here emerged from the canal engineer James Brindley's posthumous triumph, Harecastle Tunnel, are the debris of worked-out coal mines, abandoned brickyards and tileries, the gaunt five-storeyed skeleton of a shale oil refinery and all the other evidence of industry retreating from a battlefield where, after a season of success, it has succumbed to time and change.

Yet the Grand Trunk Canal which 150 years ago attracted these enterprises to its banks, added some jewels to the landscape of rural Staffordshire, unwitting compensation for this abomination of desolation which lies for miles to north and south of Bridge 129 where the first sod was cut in 1766.

By 1783 the proprietors of the Grand Trunk Canal had decided to cut a 15-mile arm of the canal from Shelton, in the present city of Stoke-on-Trent, to the vast limestone quarries at Cauldon Low and the brass and copper works at Froghall.

To feed this Caldon Canal, and the main canal, reservoirs were needed. The surveyors sited them amid lovely scenery at Knypersley and Stanley. In 1797 a branch from Endon to Leek was projected and a third reservoir planned, at Rudyard.

The necessity of creating a water supply for the canal combined with the steep folded hills characteristic of the North Staffordshire landscape to produce at the Rudyard and Knypersley sites lovely tree-fringed lakes in natural valleys, and at Stanley a large expanse of water on a shelf halfway down the hillside.

The cyclist, motorist or coach passenger going from Macclesfield to Leek skirts the bottom of the Cloud, a lofty hill whose abrupt northern slopes drop some 600 ft to the Cheshire Plain, and enters Staffordshire at Rushton Marsh. On his left behind the village rise Three Shires Head, Shuttlingslow, Meal Ark Clough, and other high points of the moorlands.

Turn your back on the metalled road and the traffic, and this rugged landscape has altered little since Prince Charlie and his Highlanders straggled through here in 1745. The Enclosure Acts of the late eighteenth century have carved into stone-walled fields the western side of the valley, but on the north-east they left the uplands untouched. But travel a bare half mile from Rushton, up the hill and round the snake bend to the summit of Wolfdale, and the scene now has a focal point new since the Young Pretender's day. Two hundred feet below, the feeder spreads out into the 2 miles of the picturesque Rudyard Lake.

The nearer shore of the lake, from here to Rudyard village itself, is steep, and for half of its length pastureland rises abruptly to the road. The fields are dotted here and there with athletic cows grazing industriously on slopes more suitable for goats, giving an alpine air to the foreground.

Across the lake lies Cliffe Park, a tract of pinewood running down to the water's edge, cut into by tiny bays, for not one foot of shore has the straight edge conjured up by the engineer's word 'reservoir'. At the further end of the lake is Rudyard village.

Here a dam was thrown across this valley in 1797, to collect the waters of the rapid stream which splashed down the valley on its way to join the River Churnet nearer Leek.

Although the stream had tributaries flowing down from the 4 mile long knife-edge ridge called Leek Edge on its west, and from the larger watershed of Gun Hill and Swythamley on the north-east, its volume was not found sufficient to accumulate the 400-acre reservoir required. Accordingly, a feeder was cut in 1809, a leet running 3 miles from Dane Bride at Wincle on the upper waters of the Dane to Cliffe Park, where it joins the lake.

From its earliest days, the scenic beauties of Rudyard Lake were recognized, and it became a favourite venue for the workers of the Potteries a bare 10 miles away. From the sixties of the last century, when the Macclesfield–Leek railway line was opened, it drew visitors from as far away as Manchester and South Lancashire.

By Acts of Parliament of 1846 and 1847, the Trent and Mersey Canal merged with the North Staffordshire Railway Company; and soon afterwards the lake was acquired. Once the railway company had cut the line and built stations at Rudyard Lake and Cliffe halt, they developed the attractions. Later, there were even penny in the slot machines to show what the butler saw in the naughty nineties.

A hotel was built, pavilions, boating facilities and a golf course. Nineteenth-century directories refer with pride to the regattas at Rudyard at Easter and Whitsun which drew their tens of thousands of spectators. Happily, exciting boating days!

The habits so firmly established have now lasted almost a century. Visitors may arrive by car or bus instead of train. But each fine weekend sees hundreds at Rudyard every summer, to walk in the pine woods, fish or use the lake itself for sport.

With increasing prosperity, the fifties and onwards have seen Rudyard dotted with an ever-increasing fleet of small yachts, whose multi-coloured sails animate the view, thanks to British Waterways for their help and encouragement.

Rudyard is as rich in associations as in beauty. Its name derives from the family who owned the land from the Norman Conquest to the late seventeenth century. A later Rudyard was a legal luminary and wit in Stuart London. Yet another Rudyard built the second Eddystone Lighthouse.

A nineteenth-century visitor to Rudyard Lake was John Lockwood Kipling, a young artist who had won a national competition with his design for the terra-cottas on the Wedgwood Institute at Burslem. While supervising his work, he met and married a Miss Macdonald. Soon the young couple emigrated to India. Their first child was born in Bombay. In token of their early happiness, the Kiplings christened him Rudyard, who, later, of course, achieved fame as writer and poet.

In complete contrast to the wooded slopes surrounding Rudyard are the bare wind-swept shores of the British Waterways reservoir Stanley Pool. Created in 1783 to feed the Stanley Moss Summit of the Caldon canal, which lies 200 ft and half a mile below it, Stanley is a sheet of some 80 acres of water, at a height of nearly 600 ft above sea-level, on a narrow plateau below the 1,000 ft hills of Baddeley Edge and Bagnall. Stanley pool replaced a former mill pool, and the water on its way to the canal still [1961] serves the Hercules and Victoria Mills, where potters' colours are ground and prepared for use in Stoke-on-Trent.

Stanley's attraction lies partly in the fascination any sheet of water has for angler and yachtsman, partly in its situation. From its banks the visitor sees a panorama of three-quarters of a circle, ranging from the distant prospect of the Potteries skyline round through Norton and Endon to the hills beyond Horton, on clear days to the moorlands overlooking Rudyard, and beyond Leek to the Morridge on the further side of the Leek–Ashbourne road.

Stanley is not devoid of historical associations. Some antiquarians claim that it is from this corner that the Earls of Derby take their family name; in support of this, one may mention that a few hundred yards from the pool is Knowsley Common, sharing a name with Knowsley Hall, the Liverpool family seat.

Beyond is the tiny hamlet of Tomkin. Here, it is said, a Highland straggler in 1745 was flayed alive by order of Squire Murrall, the local Justice of the Peace.

An even older but less trustworthy tradition asserts that at Daniel's farm in Stanley, in 1680, the method of making salt-glazed stoneware was discovered in England, when a servant girl, boiling pork in brine, allowed the pot to boil over and put out the fire. Assessing the damage her master noted the semi-porous pot was now coated with a hard, lustrous and impervious glaze. One hopes the poor girl's inattention went unpunished, in face of this happy chance!

The third of the three lakes with which the proprietors of the Grand Trunk Canal embellished North Staffordshire is Knypersley. This is some 2 miles from the main Biddulph to Stoke-on-Trent road at Biddulph Moor and Brown Edge, a 1,000 ft eminence slightly to the south.

The original reservoir of 30 acres was created in 1783 to feed the Caldon Canal, and is now known as the Serpentine.

When the proprietors obtained Parliamentary sanction to cut the second (Telford's) Harecastle Tunnel in 1823, they were allowed to increase their Knypersley reservoir by a further 50 acres. Various legal restrictions safeguarded the interests of millers on the banks of the Trent which flows into the extended reservoir.

Knypersley is set in a valley some 400 yds across and half a mile long. The end nearest the dam and mill pool is crossed by a bridge over which passes a by-road from Biddulph to Brown Edge. The eastern shore is edged by Lion's Paw Wood, so called from its shape. In the little dell where the infant River Trent bisects it is a cromlech, Gawton's Stone, and nearby is Gawton's Well, a spring which once had the reputation of curing King's Evil, scrofula.

Perhaps the most notable aspect of Knypersley's history is the strong tradition which causes the able-bodied children of the two northern Potteries towns, Tunstall and Burslem and the intervening villages, to walk to Knypersley on Good Friday each year. Even in this day of bus and car, the youngsters know the only way to make this pilgrimage is on foot, preferably carrying a bottle of 'pop' or mineral water for the 4-mile journey.

No child has ever revealed to an adult why it must go to Knypersley on that one day. It is one of these spontaneous conceptions of childhood, akin to the simultaneous abandonment throughout the country of one seasonal toy for the next.

The traveller, appalled by industrial Ravensdale and Chatterley, cannot do better than imitate the children; but he should make his pilgrimage to Rudyard and Stanley as well as Knypersley.

FRANK FERNYHOUGH

Are We in Danger of Losing the Severn Bore?

Presumably almost all people connected with waterways in their various areas, whatever their duties and capacities, are aware of the Severn Bore, that high rising phenomenon of abnormal tides which occurs in these islands on the River Severn.

The Atlantic tide on approaching the Bristol Channel is funnelled between South Wales and the south-western Peninsula. As the tide wave approaches the neck of the funnel at Sharpness, where the Severn Estuary is less than 2 miles wide, the wave is 'squeezed' and hence increases in height.

The shelving nature of the sea bed and the river both conspire to slow down the base of the tidal wave, causing the main body of water to 'trip' over. The formation of three or four waves produced by this combination of factors is known as a bore and it travels on up the river to Gloucester and beyond.

The bore occurs on approximately 260 tides a year with the onset of Spring Tide; can vary from 4 to 9 ft in height and can reach a speed of up to 13 miles per hour.

Anyone wishing to obtain further information on the bore should consult *The Severn Bore* by F.W. Rowbotham, published by David and Charles.

The reason why this bore may disappear is that proposals are being made for certain areas in the Severn Estuary for the construction of one or more barrages across the river, which would effectively restrict the wide-ranging tidal movements which now give rise to the bore.

The idea was first promoted in the decade between 1925 and 1935, but the first definite plan was the Severn Barrage Scheme promoted in a Report of 1947, which was intended to use the tidal flows to operate a power station.

At that time there was a very strict control on capital expenditure, as so much had to be allocated to repair war damage and lack of maintenance to the essential industries and their capital works since the resuscitation of our export trade was so vital to us, so the scheme had to lapse, irrespective of its merits or demerits.

Over the years several schemes have been examined in depth, and the scope of these schemes considerably exceed that of the original one although in essence they are similar and devoted to the same purposes.

The latest scheme however is a very different one to those put forward in the past. This one has the twin objectives of utilizing the very high tides in the Severn estuary for hydro-electricity and also the creation of a large inland lake which would serve the purpose of a big harbour/industrial development and a water amenity area.

Should any of the schemes ever be put into practice there are several aspects which would affect the waterways system in the south-west. So far

British Waterways Board is concerned there could be some relief on river maintenance since the level of tides will be restricted; also the possibility of flooding will be reduced in that the flood water will not be impeded by the incoming tide, since that then could be controlled by the barrage.

ALFRED SAPSFORD

Day of the 'Iceberg'

Ice, 3 or 4 inches in thickness, screeched, whined, cracked, buckled and reluctantly broke as the narrow boat forced a jagged path into its chilly heart. These somewhat alien sounds mingled with the moody snarl of winter winds and the steady thump of *Cambourne's* engine producing an overall sonic assault that somehow helped us to ignore the cold as we clung to the cabin sides of the trembling boat.

Ahead, the ice was an unbroken ribbon of white challenge that seemed to reach out endlessly. And had it not been for the sentinel-like trees on either side of the craft it might have been possible to imagine that we were pioneering a passage through encrusted Arctic waters. Yet we were inland, on the Hertfordshire border, hesitantly moving in a rough southerly direction along the Grand Union Canal. . . .

Earlier, I had stood where the canal swings wide and proud – at the junction of the Aylesbury Arm and the Grand Union – and marvelled at the wintry splendour of an ice-capped Cut.

It was as if time itself had been frozen from the way pieces of driftwood – trapped in the ice – reached out from the canal at gravity-defying angles: an old motorcar tyre, relic of thoughtlessness, lay on the ice like a useless black lifebelt, surrounded by an assortment of stone and brick missiles that had probably been aimed with youthful exuberance. And then there was frosty silence where water had once slapped and gurgled with freedom.

Cambourne, loaded with essential canal maintenance equipment, ascended the seven locks of the Marsworth Flight with difficulty. Darb, a big rawboned man with carved granite features was the steerer, who fussed and cussed the old gal to do her best, to hold course when the ice argued, while Sonny and I when we weren't pushing and pulling on balance beams or winding paddles up and down, perched on the narrow boat's gunwales, hopefully trying to catch escaping warmth from the engine's cooling system.

At something less than walking speed we moved through a charmed avenue of petrified trees and reeds that dipped and bowed as the narrow boat scrunched by.

Two narrow boats 'breasting up' the Grand Union Canal approach a frozen section

The last creature I expected to see on such a day was a swan. But this one commanded our attention. It had somehow become ensnared in the ice. 'I feel sorry for the poor devils when they get trapped like that,' Darb said. He is a keen racing pigeon fancier in his spare time and possesses a rare knowledge of our feathered friends. 'Hold on, we'll free you,' he shouted to the struggling bird and worked magic with gears, throttle and helm so that *Cambourne* shattered the ice cladding that had imprisoned the bird. Awkwardly the swan clambered over the icefloes to freedom, settling gratefully into the water left by our passing. Darb grinned with satisfaction and increased the speed of the boat.

Sonny, a rotund man with a face of a retired pirate, had kept up an entertainingly ribald commentary throughout the journey. Now, bringing his irrepressible sense of humour to the fore, he pointed with mock horror; 'iceberg ahead' he yelled dramatically.

We looked . . . and laughed. A hundred yards in front of *Cambourne's* bows two plastic milk crates, coloured red, lay on the unbroken ice looking ridiculously incongruous in the light of Sonny's curt description. As we drew nearer the canal maw showed darkly and swallowed them.

It was as we ponderously cut a passage through the frozen wastes on inland England that I thought of past generations of canalmen who had made similar winter trips; from early canal days when icebreaking craft were hauled along by teams of horses to the specially built motorized icebreakers that were

Breaking the ice in Brentford Lock on the Grand Union Canal after a big freeze in February 1956

essential to keep the 'roads' free for commercial craft. Yet we were doing the job without the same kind of urgency, almost for the hell of it really.

Four miles and three hours out from the depot and *Cambourne* arrived at her destination near Dudswell. The temperature had risen slightly and it had rained heavily during the last part of the journey. We were cold and wet and rather glad when the time came to return to our homes . . . by road!

RON WHATLEY

That Water Shortage

The canal builders of 200 years ago and since have been faced with an almost unsurmountable problem, that of getting water channels up and over hills to enable boats by means of locks to climb, for instance, up the Northamptonshire heights, or into the Peak District, or over the Pennines. Some of their schemes were deemed so impractical that the pioneering Barton stone aqueduct carrying the Bridgewater Canal over the River Irwell was dismissed as a mere 'castle in the air' until it was built, when admirers came from all over the country to see it.

One visitor was inspired to call it 'perhaps the greatest artificial curiosity in the world' and another to extol it in verse:

> Seen and acknowledged by astonished crowds
> From underground emerging to the clouds;
> Vessels o'er vessels, water under water
> Bridgewater triumphs, art has conquered nature!

So it should be with great respect and admiration that we regard the work of these amazing early engineers, whose resources were their own ability and flair for engineering construction; whose structures were the successful outcome of limited measuring methods and an understanding of the elements of design. The instruments, machines and techniques simply were not there. It is interesting to speculate that a project like the Foxton inclined plane at the turn of the century could have been successfully operating today if alternative forms of power had been developed earlier.

Yet the purpose of constructing a navigable channel that contradicted and overcame the laws of nature was achieved.

Watertight walls, gates and linings had to be devised to prevent the water from flowing away into natural watercourses. Ways were found of making stone, brick, cast iron, wood and clay meet this demand. Nothing has yet been proved a better substance for long-term waterproofing of the canal bed than the original puddled clay, and although modern concrete and steel now play their part in canal maintenance, the materials of 200 years ago are still essential and extensively used today.

Not only had the water to be contained in the channel, precautions against flooding were necessary. A complex system of overspill weirs, culverts and sluices was created to take the surplus water away harmlessly into nearby streams, rivers and lakes. But where was the water to come from? Rain dropping into a canal could not alone make up the 25,000 gallons needed to operate a narrow lock just once. And while rivers begin as streams in the hills, running downwards all the way acquiring more water as they go, canals were specifically constructed to link one river valley to another.

Think of the Trent and Mersey, the Thames and Severn, the Kennet and Avon. Canals cross the watersheds and at this level have only limited sources of supply.

A typical canal route can be visualized in diagrammatic cross-section as a pyramid flattened out at the top. The canal climbs up on both sides by means of locks from a river valley, eventually reaching what is known as the 'summit level', where there is usually a tunnel or cutting through the hill above. Here or nearby, reservoirs were constructed so that water could be supplied to the canal at its highest point above sea level. Some canals have more than one summit. As locks are operated, water flows down each side of the pyramid, some disappearing via the overspill weirs, some evaporating or seeping away, and some discharging into the river at the canal's lowest point.

It may seem obvious (though it takes a fair amount of pondering) that whether a boat moves up or down in a lock, the water invariably goes down.

So a continuous flow of water from the reservoirs or other sources is needed to counterbalance the effects of lock use, of evaporation and seepage. During times of drought a greater amount is needed, creating a vicious circle. The more water a canal needs, the less is collected into the reservoirs; for, in spite of its large catchment area drawing on water from nearby streams and springs, the supply comes either directly or indirectly from the skies. If the skies give forth no rain for a prolonged period, reservoir levels inexorably fall.

Water was so precious to the old canal companies that they would go to almost any length to avoid giving it away. Hence the 'stop locks', often still to be found at canal junctions, although they are out of use. There is no change in level, merely gates which can be closed before and behind a boat, the purpose being to stop any water flowing from one company's canal to that of another. A good example is the guillotine lock at Kings Norton, where the Stratford-upon-Avon Canal joins the Worcester and Birmingham. There are others, such as the one at Worcester Bar Basin, Gas Street, Birmingham, where the Worcester and Birmingham Canal now joins the Birmingham and Fazeley.

So fanatical were the Worcester and Birmingham Canal Company about keeping their water to themselves that once they maintained a physical barrier to navigation between two canals; this is the derivation of the Worcester Bar.

The canal company bye-laws contained stringent measures to prevent wastage of water.

The canal companies enforced their rules strictly. They had to; or they would be out of business. In the heyday of commercial carrying there were plenty of lock keepers and maintenance staff to see that the bye-laws were obeyed and to carry out repairs on the spot if a structure was damaged, perhaps working through the night or in terrible conditions.

Nevertheless, stoppages were put on in a somewhat high-handed and arbitrary manner. Perhaps those were more submissive days.

It is a great disappointment to everyone that, just as the efforts the Board and other bodies to make the public aware of the scope of the waterways for their enjoyment, are bearing fruit, [in 1974] the driest April/May since 1896 has created water shortages sufficient to close a canal for a period and necessitate other restrictions on navigation.

Those who criticized the Board for not giving earlier warning of the Leeds and Liverpool closure in particular may not have realized that the gods gave the Board very little notice of their intentions. Until 22 March, the reservoirs were almost full despite the freak conditions which followed. The drought then became so severe that no water entered the canal except from the reservoirs, which themselves were not being replenished. Economies in water had to be made, and the only measures open to the Board were to restrict traffic and to wrack the locks (a method of preventing leakage throgh lock gates by sealing them with ashes).

As on the rest of the Board's system, water levels are carefully measured and regulated by the water engineer, who advises what precautions are necessary for the conservation of water. The tasks are carried out on the ground by the reservoir keepers, who are seldom full-time but do this as well as their other responsibilities, usually canal maintenance.

John Freeman, area engineer, Wigan, under whose local jurisdiction the Leeds and Liverpool Canal lies, was asked for his comments. He replied that there is nothing new about water shortages on the canal. Right from its inception there were obvious difficulties.

The canal was closed at a period when it was being heavily used for commercial traffic and the effect must have been severe. The closures took place in the following years: 1883, 9 to 11 August; 1884, 9 August to 29 October; 1885, 2 to 12 September; 1887, 25 July to 14 September; 1896, 27 July to 14 September; 1889, 11 to 22 September; 1901, 21 July to 13 November; 1902, 15 September to 14 October; 1904, 24 September to 9 November; 1959, 18 August to 9 November.

The Leeds and Liverpool Canal is fed from Whitemoor, Foulridge, Winterburn and Rishton reservoirs. There are several feeders in addition, Morton Beck and the River Douglas being the two main sources. Managing the water supply to a canal is a complex business. It consists of balancing the reservoir water with other sources, to get the maximum benefit for the navigation while protecting fish life. Certain reservoirs fill very much quicker than others in rain time, and obviously those which do this are used more extensively.

In the heyday of commercial traffic far more water came to the canal than does now. Mine water was pumped into the canal which is not obtainable now because the mines are closed. Other sources of water were accepted which could not under any circumstances be made use of now, being so highly polluted that boatmen were nauseated by the smell coming from the canal in summertime.

During the period when the canal has been closed, people have commented that they have seen water flowing over the weirs. They evidently did not realize that any length of canal begins to drop in level by virtue of natural evaporation and seepage if the feed is cut off, and water must be fed into the levels to prevent the canal completely drying up. If this happens, the clay puddle lining cracks, becomes no longer watertight and needs to be replaced at great cost.

The reservoirs have gauges, John Freeman went on, and these are read weekly in normal times and daily in drought times, so that the water engineer and the area engineer are constantly aware of the reservoir levels and the amount of feed water which is passing to the canal. On the canal itself, there are gauges for the levels and the weirs, some of which automatically record the quantity of water passing. In addition, at certain locks, there are lock counters so that every time the lock is emptied and filled, a record is automatically made. It is, therefore possible for the Board to see at any time what water has been used to operate the canal.

FRANCES PRATT

ten

For the Common Good

A Waterway Built for War

Close to the top of Box Hill, a beauty spot on the North Downs near Dorking in Surrey, is a curious little gravestone. On it you can read these words: 'Peter Labelliere, aged 76 years, an eccentric resident of Dorking was buried here head downwards, on the 11th June, 1800.'

It was at his own wish that Major Labelliere, Royal Marines, was buried there, upside down. But why? Because, he said, 'the world is topsy-turvy, yet at the end of it I shall be right!'

It was typical of the spirit of the times. The bloody French Revolution which, not long before, had turned that country topsy-turvy – and inside out as well – had shaken a lot of English people badly; they feared that something like it might break out here, too. And then, as if that wasn't enough, another menace appeared in France – Napoleon Bonaparte.

Already, before Peter Labelliere died, Napoleon was beginning to turn the whole Continent topsy-turvy, as country after country fell before his armies. Soon France's empire would extend over much of Europe and Africa and already he was turning his greedy eyes across the Channel towards England. Just as tank-traps and pill-boxes were built in 1939 and 1940 when history was repeating itself, so forts and 'Martello Towers', still familiar landmarks on certain parts of the south coast, went up as precautions against invasion in those more distant days.

But the most ambitious defensive measure was the construction of the Royal Military Canal.

Romney Marsh is a large, misty, low-lying area jutting out to sea on the south coast of England; just the place, thought the military experts, that Napoleon would choose to make a landing. And so, to isolate the Marsh from the higher ground inland, they built the Royal Military Canal as a water barrier. Thirty miles long, and with a road running beside it, this remarkable waterway was dug from Hythe, near Folkestone, in a great curving line inland, and back towards the sea beyond Winchelsea, embracing in its course part of the River Rother near Rye.

The average width of the canal is about 30 yd and originally it was 6 ft deep throughout. It was so designed that its whole length could be commanded by batteries of guns strategically positioned along the earthworks.

General Sir David Dundass, the Southern District Commander, was enthusiastic about constructing the canal when the suggestion was put up. 'Floating defences would be moveable and manageable,' he said, 'and contribute much to its strength and the quick movement of horses and troops.'

The Duke of York was keen on the idea, too. He pointed out that the existence of the canal would probably make it unnecessary to flood the Marsh, a 'measure of ruinous consequence', which had been previously the intended method of precaution if invasion seemed near. 'When completed,' the Duke wrote, 'the Canal may be fairly considered as an insurmountable Barrier against an Enemy's penetrating into the Country.'

The canal was finished in 1806 – somewhat after the immediate invasion scare was over. But whether the Duke's optimism was justified we shall never know, because fortunately the insurmountableness of the barrier never needed to be put to the test.

So there the authorities were, with a canal on their hands which began to look, as time went on, more like a white elephant than an insurmountable barrier. They did their best to encourage commercial traffic on it and to get what revenue they could from tolls. A most impressive board was set up in 1807 to look after the affairs of the waterway, consisting of the Speaker of the

A 'peace bonus' for modern pleasure cruisers is the easy availability of moorings near Rye

House of Commons, the Lord High Treasurer of Great Britain, the First Commissioner of the Treasury, the Chancellor of the Exchequer, His Majesty's Principal Secretaries of State, the Commander in Chief of His Majesty's Forces, the Lord Warden of the Cinque Ports, the Secretary for War, the Master General of the Ordnance and the Quartermaster General of His Majesty's Forces.

Even with all these estimable gentlemen in charge, however, the canal was never much of a commercial success, though there were twenty-one barges trading upon it by 1808. The War Department sold most of the canal to private owners in 1874 and commercial navigation came to an end before the turn of the century.

But somebody had the foresight, almost as soon as there was water in it, to stock the canal with lots of fish, and that is one of its chief attractions today. Carefree holidaymakers find the canal a pleasant amenity – and probably few of them, fishing or boating on the Royal Military Canal in the sunshine, spare a thought for those distant 'topsy-turvy' days when this strange waterway was dug beneath the dark shadow of threatened invasion.

TOM LAWRENCE

Life on the Canals in Wartime Britain

Here I am, very dirty, sitting in the sun on the stern of *Daffodil* drawn up alongside the pub at Hawkesbury recalling the ten days in 1944 when John Wilson and his wife welcomed me into the closely knit community of boat people and I was accepted by their contacts among power station workers and miners.

In May 1944 there was an added sense of tension in wartime Britain; our invasion of occupied Europe seemed imminent and any holiday plans irrelevant. A recruiting poster at Oxford station announced 'Women of Robust Constitution needed on the Barges' and this raised the possibility of useful physical work in peaceful surroundings in the open air.

The Ministry concerned stated that applicants must sign on for a year. This was not possible for me, but a doctor friend told me that a boatman's wife called every few months for minor treatment. Almost immediately the opportunity presented itself, and I went down to the surgery to be introduced to my future hostess.

Mrs Wilson could not have been more helpful and it was agreed that when next they came to deliver coal to Wolvercote Paper Mill, they would pick me up from the canal towing path in the early morning, and would drop me back there at the end of my visit.

This, for a journey in wartime Britain, seemed remarkably easy; I would be able to walk down from my home in north Oxford and go on board. While I was with them I would look after myself and I hoped to prove useful as crew.

This idyll – long June days spent in the beautiful and peaceful countryside, followed by nights when the boat would be moored in some isolated spot – was only partially to materialize. Unexpectedly, my plans and the routine of many of the boat people, were to be changed by the temporary closure to navigation of part of the canal system owing to falling water level.

I was told that this had not happened since 1911 and the drain on the water supply by the new aerodromes was thought to be the cause. Elsewhere, bombs had damaged the canal banks and allowed leakage. Many of the boats would be making short hauls returning to the power station at Hawkesbury near Coventry to unload and to tie up for the night. It was fortunate that I was undaunted by the prospect of spending part of my time in an atmosphere of coal dust because, in the event, this change was to provide me with an extraordinarily interesting experience, and I followed instructions to 'come on the bus'.

Only later did I realize that this meant that I missed one of the more interesting manoeuvres on the waterways. To deliver a full cargo of coal to Wolvercote Paper Mill, boats must leave the Oxford Canal at Dukes Lock, pass along the cut, and then negotiate straight across the Thames 'back down' a passage that could be hazardous when the river was in flood. The Wilson's daughter Mrs Couling remembers how as children they would scamper across the railway bridge to be ready to haul the ropes in.

On arrival at Hawkesbury I was greeted by my host and hostess. On meeting the Wilsons I recognized them as an exceptional couple. But it was only after an interval of thirty years when I visited the Waterways Museum at Stoke Bruerne, read their literature and spoke to other canal folk that I learned of John Wilson's accepted and honoured place in the fraternity and in the evolution of the narrow boat from horse to internal combustion engine as a 'Number One' or owner occupier.

Contact with their family has filled in the background of the story as told to me by Mrs Wilson during those long days together in June 1944. 'Number Ones' formed the élite on the waterways. Known as boatmen and never as bargees, they have a book to themselves (*The Number Ones* by Robert Wilson) and among them John Wilson is recorded as the first to change from horse to engine and the last to retire.

His daughter remembers him as a generous man who lent money to friends and forgave his debtors. He had the finest horse on the canal, ultimately sold to a milkman. Later, on seeing the milkman's float in an Oxford Street, he called out and the horse recognized him immediately, took off and clattered up to him, to the delight of the family.

By the time I joined the Wilsons their boats were power driven. *Daffodil* and *Mabel* were proof of the pride and care lavished upon them: they were docked every three years, stripped down and re-tarred and painted to keep them sound. In addition to their names and those of their owner, the narrow boats were decorated in the traditional manner with flowers, a castle set in a landscape and a horizontal strip in geometric pattern, all in bright colours.

Each boat carried a cargo of coal, and *Mabel* which housed the engine, was to be my bed-sitting-room from dusk to dawn each day. On returning there at the end of each working day I could sit in the open air in the stern while cooking my supper. Beyond the painted doors lay the cabins; these were spotlessly clean, inviting and remarkably comfortable. The day cabin provided seating accommodation, a coal fire, and a table was formed by a door that folded down from the food cupboard.

The contents were exactly suited to their purpose: each had its place. The large metal jug, the pan or 'hand bowl' with its rounded handle necessary to reach the water level in the canal, and even the solid little wooden 'cabin' stool that had been used to carry each baby's cot in turn, were painted in the same manner. The hanging oil lamp was of highly polished brass and the china included the traditional lace plates with perforated borders and also the attractive figures including shepherdess and dog. This china remains a cherished possession in the family: they resist the blandishments of the travelling dealers in search of collectors' pieces.

Beyond the day cabin and separated by curtain lay my sleeping quarters. The 'bunk hole' when prepared for me contained nothing but a vast feather mattress on which I could just stretch myself diagonally and where I was to sleep so happily. When in use by the family the bed boards would go away, leaving the central space surrounded by seats below which lay a row of lockers.

By day, John Wilson took over and ran the engine while I joined his wife in *Daffodil* – the second boat or 'butty' – towed astern. The routine was to cast off within half an hour of dawn, travel along the canal to collect our cargo of coal from some mine or siding, and return to the power station at Hawkesbury in time to be unloaded mechanically by 'them grabs' and get to the pub – the Spread Eagle – by opening time. On returning to the boat I would settle into the domesticity of *Mabel*, cook my one-course supper and be asleep very soon after reaching my bed.

Once on the move, no time was lost, and there was no communication between the two boats apart from the occasional shout. Even the exchange of soiled for clean laundry was made without any decrease in our steady pace. As we approached a small, straggling hamlet, John Wilson blew several blasts on a horn that I had not previously seen. It was explained to me that the widow of a boatman lived there and she did their washing.

Within a couple of minutes a small figure was to be seen, carrying a bundle, running up the street. She then ran alongside exchanging news, threw her load on board and caught ours in return. Not a moment was lost during this transaction. Nor was there so much as a pause for a meal. Food was eaten 'under the thumb' as they remarked, and I was interested to learn later that French lorry drivers used exactly the same expression 'sous le pouce' today.

The Wilsons' midday meal consisted either of bread spread with lard, covered with a thick layer of black pepper, or a chunk of cold fat bacon. A knife was the only weapon necessary and the food was held exactly as the phrase suggests. A pot of strong tea was on the hob throughout the working day. Apart from the evening beer, I saw no variation on this except for the Sunday dinner and its remains on Monday.

Only now have I learned more of the Wilsons diet when they were children growing up. The lard and pepper had been a traditional meal in John Wilson's family in the hard times in the mines when the miners worked underground for days on end, and it was dictated by poverty and the fact that it did not become rancid. They remember the cooked breakfast with bacon, sausage or a lump of steak – 'steak was cheap then' – and 'father might have a nip of whisky to keep out the cold'. But life could be very hard as when the boats were ice-bound for ten weeks and both money and supplies disappeared.

Some of the inns on the towing path are remembered with gratitude: inn keepers befriended the canal folk in hard times. These pubs beside the waterways also provided the setting for family gatherings and an uncle's wedding feast is remembered as continuing 'with dancing in the big room' through two days and nights at The Britannia (now The Jolly Boatman) at Thrupp.

As the *Daffodil* and *Mabel* moved through the water, Mrs Wilson leant against the stern, her arm resting on the tiller, steering the butty while I stood beside her watching out for locks. I had taken over this part of the work and earned the title of 'a proper lock-wheeler'. (On the strength of this honourable status I was, many years later, to be considered entitled to a free pass into the Waterways Museum.)

At what I judged to be the correct moment I would leap from the moving boat, run alongside and get ahead, hoping to have the locks ready to receive *Mabel* and her butty without causing delay. The engine was then shut off, and I would haul my load through the lock and, having left the lock shipshape, run to catch up in time to jump on board again.

It took me some time to learn to adjust my haul so as to provide just sufficient momentum without waste of energy. This was before the days of the metal bollards; the old wooden 'strapping stumps' fascinated me as they had been polished and grooved by the pull of countless ropes as the boats made fast and they had come to resemble sculpture.

164

An occasional hazard was to be found in the towing rope of horse-drawn boats as they passed diagonally across the towing path. They could act as trip wires if one failed to notice them in one's race to reach the lock.

John Wilson remarked that my friends would never believe me when I told them that I had been hauling 56 tons of coal through the locks, and I never knew whether they did, in fact, believe this unlikely tale.

It was perhaps fortunate that the canal was, for the most part, running through fairly level country, although there was one stretch with seven locks in quick succession. But once I had acquired the knack the work was not too strenuous and I enjoyed it.

Spending so many hours in the stern of the butty with Mrs Wilson, I learnt to value her company and her philosophy of life and acquired a great respect for her. Then sixty-five years old, she came of a narrow boat family, her mother going to a cottage on the towing path at Thrupp for her birth.

John Wilson's parents came from a mining background but took to the canals when he was eight years old because of unemployment in the mines, and both the Wilsons had continued to work on the canals and brought up their family on the narrow boats. At the time of my visit the sons were boatmen employed by the big companies.

I have recently been able to fill in Mrs Wilson's stories of the family's life in wartime Britain. They carried very vulnerable loads, including ammunition, to the London Docks, and might be caught, a sitting target, in the blitz. They spoke of the night when they refused to leave the boat for a shelter and it was the latter that was destroyed; and another, when moving slowly along the Regent's Canal, they watched the canal-side church collapse into a heap of rubble.

Mrs Wilson herself was an intelligent person and, as regards literacy, ahead of her contemporaries and, indeed, of many younger canal people. She had attended the Sunday School for waterways children held by Mrs Gillett – a member of a well-known Quaker family – in Banbury, and had kept in practice by reading any advertisements along the canal-side that were within her range.

Limited literacy became an increasing handicap in the next generation and it was this that led them, when considering the future of their children, to leave the life that they valued 'where everyone would help you and look after you' for the factory floor where 'no one cared', and where lack of literacy prevented them from accepting promotion they were offered and well qualified in other respects to accept.

The Wilson's daughter remembers when they were children the skill with which they could judge the exact force required to shovel coal from the hold into a barrow which was wheeled across the plank above them. Too much enthusiasm and the shovel-full would over-shoot and drop back into the hold.

Incredible as this would seem, none learnt to swim. There were several near fatal accidents including the time one child fell through a small hole that had been hacked through the ice. A baby was nearly suffocated by a smoking oil lamp in the closed cabin.

In spite of its limitations in some respects, their childhood is evidently remembered with pleasure and pride in their community, but a daughter was glad to make her escape (by way of a hospital admission) to the wider world in her early twenties.

Towards the end of my trip I wrote 'I am getting better at understanding' the conversation. Even so, I found it difficult to form any idea of my whereabouts and only registered three names with any degree of certainty. The problem was made more difficult by the fact that all signposts and place names had been removed during the war as a precaution against invasion.

As Mrs Wilson and I talked I heard much of the life history of her clan and their friend. So far as I could judge, the boat crew's health was usually good, but acute emergencies, such as appendicitis and strangulated hernias took a heavy toll because they tended to be reported and treated too late. In 1944 tuberculosis was still a serious hazard. Once established in the conditions of close contact in a boat, it spread with disastrous consequences; a family of their cousins had been affected in this way.

Because of the change in routine due to the closure of part of the canal system, Hawkesbury Junction proved to be a very busy and crowded stretch of water. Twenty or thirty boats of different types were moored each night, closely packed alongside the power station. A huge irregular heap of coal lay on one side beneath the machinery that was to move it, while the characteristic towers and chimneys and other apparatus of the electricity works overshadowed the opposite bank.

In retrospect it is surprising that so vulnerable a landmark as Hawkesbury, with its easily identifiable network of canals, had not been a target for enemy bombers; its destruction would have been even more serious for production in Coventry than the blitz on the city centre.

On working days, by the time all the boats had been unloaded, there was a thick layer of coal dust over everything, including ourselves, although the cabins remained free. After a wash we made for the Spread Eagle on the towing path, and I was happy to treat my host and hostess, joining them with my half pint.

I came to know not only the canal people but also the men working in the power station, returning one evening the proud possessor of a red rose, grown by the driver of one of the trucks; these machines were to be seen against the skyline careering at speed as they flattened the mountain of coal by means of a scoop fixed to the front of the vehicle.

On other occasions we tied up near the mines and I was struck by the way in which the miners stood out from the rest; many were tense, thin men with gaunt, exhausted faces, but not too tired to carry on heated and intelligent discussions.

Our routine was twice broken. On one occasion we arrived at Hawkesbury in time to unload and set off again the same evening. It was a glorious June night. We were moored alongside the towing path at Nuneaton and I went to sleep to the sound of footsteps passing close by my head. We cast off at dawn and reached the mine as the miners started work. They approached the pithead in single file, silhouetted as a frieze against the mist, their safety lamps throwing shadows on their helmets. A few pit ponies were to be seen in the distance.

The need to claim new ration books led to the second break in routine. We made for some unidentified canal junction where we were held up by a queue of boats and barges. Here I could make myself useful, reading the instructions, filling in the cards, and showing the owners where to sign or, in some cases, 'make their mark'. A canal shop sold stores for the boat people and I bought two 'Woolton pies', excellent wartime food intended for agricultural and other manual workers, and I might now legitimately claim my share.

On my free Saturday afternoon I persuaded Mrs Wilson to plan a jaunt that we could enjoy together. Without hesitation she voted for Coventry and we set off by bus. My appearance, in soiled working clothes, must have shamed her, for she looked splendid in a dress of some shining black material with hat to match and jewellery.

Much of the city centre had been reduced to rubble during that terrible night in the second winter of the war when, from my Oxford garden, I had not only seen the sky lit up, but the sound carried on flood water, the blitz on Coventry had been clearly audible. By 1944 the resilient inhabitants had already put up a maze of very small temporary shops and stalls. In the warm June sunshine we wandered happily up and down, missing nothing.

Later we queued, first at the door, and then inside the very hot temporary building used as a café for a meal of baked beans, strong tea and some unidentified wartime cake or pudding. We finally got back to Hawkesbury after an exhausting but very enjoyable outing.

On Sunday morning I went off for a walk along the towing path through lovely country, knowing that I must be back in time for the midday meal. I had already been given to understand that 'Sunday dinner' was a special occasion, and had been invited to join the Wilsons, their son and daughter-in-law, a grandson and another small boy whose mother had died.

I realized once again the kindness and concern of this community for its own. I had heard several women ask who was going to give the boy his dinner and it was obvious that he was never forgotten. My medical interest had been aroused by the canal folk's diet and I was looking forward to seeing my hostess eat a square meal and some form of Vitamin C. Hospitably, she presided over her guests but herself had two good helpings of Yorkshire and nothing more. 'Cabbage?' 'No.' She would warm it up tomorrow.

I have been thinking again of the life on a narrow boat as I saw it more than thirty years ago. Obviously much of what I saw has gone forever. I was indeed both fortunate and privileged in being able to join this remarkable pair and in being accepted into their community.

VICTORIA SMALLPIECE

Dad's Waterborne Army

In churches throughout Britain on Remembrance Sunday, special prayers will be said and poppy wreathes laid to commemorate those who gave their lives in two world wars. In paying tribute to those who fought and died in far-off places it is easy to overlook the fact that those at home played their part and that there were casualties on our inland waterways which also had their fighting force.

An exquisitely painted oil lamp, the work of Frank Jones of Leighton Buzzard, commemorates steerer James Peasland who was killed when enemy action sank the narrow boat *Evelyn* moored in Paddington Basin. Mr Peasland and his son were sleeping in a butty boat, *Vera*; his wife and other children were luckily away. A piece of shrapnel penetrated the side of the boat, killing James but missing his son.

Mr Jones, who was employed on the salvage of the boat was given the historic headlamp and painted it in traditional style and for a time it formed part of a waterways exhibition.

Two family-owned narrow boats operated by Fellows, Morton and Clayton were sunk during an air raid at Fazeley Street, Birmingham in November 1940. Recalling this incident Mr V.O. Gregory, former commercial officer at Gloucester said:

> I cannot be absolutely sure, but I believe the boats were *Robin* and *Kildare*, the steerer of the boats being William Roberts. On the night in question six boats lay in the Fazeley Street arm loaded with cargoes en route for London. These particular boats were loaded with cocoa from Bournville.
>
> When the raid was over the boats were seen to be sunk and some bags of cocoa and part of the fore-end of one boat were seen to be nearby on the overhanging canopy of the warehouse. So far as I recall the other boats were undamaged and there were no casualties.

A representation of the Home Guard Trent River Patrol vessel MV *Argo* is preserved for posterity in this section of a stained glass window. It commemorates Colonel Thomas Lancelot Constable and is to be found in St John the Baptist's church at South Collingwood near Newark

But what if the enemy had landed?

Well everyone has heard of the Home Guard, made famous by the television series *Dad's Army*. However, most people seem unaware that there was at least one waterborne arm of this defensive system.

Commemorating the Trent River Patrol is part of a stained glass window in memory of Colonel Thomas Lancelot Constable Curtis DL JP, who was born in 1888 and died in 1956. It can be seen in the little church of St John the Baptist at South Collingham near Newark.

Educated at Eton and Cambridge, Colonel Curtis joined the Coldstream Guards and served with them as an officer for twenty-five years, serving in France and Turkey during the First World War. He was called up as a reservist at the time of the Munich crisis and commanded the 26th Light AA Regiment until the unit was posted to Burma. Then he became Commandant of the Home Guard Trent River Patrol. Subsequently he became a member of the Trent River Board.

Information about the activities of the patrol are sketchy in the extreme, although persistent research has revealed the existence of some old photographs of the unit exercising on the river. One old-timer recalled that a Mr W.H. Haile who was engineer to the River Trent Catchment Board served as intelligence officer. The territory of the Force extended from Keadby to Nottingham. Patrol work was undertaken with a launch MV *Argo* and a

Entering a lock on the River Trent, the Trent River Patrol rehearse tactics for defence in the event of invasion

dredger MV *Panurgic* with the normal crew being supplemented by men from riverside villages.

And still surviving [in 1980] is MV *Panurgic* which operates from a depot at Owston Ferry. This 100-ton hopper barge is 90 ft long and was built in 1935 at the Beckingham Shipyard in Gainsborough. With a 21 ft beam she is equipped with a 90 bhp engine and can carry a cargo of 100 tons of silt. Unlike many dredgers, however, she gathers the silt from shallows using a mechanical crane grab situated on the bow of the boat.

Today the *Panurgic* is engaged in a relentless battle to maintain the great Trent defences, which have tamed the river since its last outburst in 1947. The previous silt is used to rebuild the embankments which contain this strong-flowing river whose depth varies from 20 to 40 ft and which is used by many vessels with cargoes ranging from grain to gravel.

Not only is the dredger crew employed to salvage silt from the bottom of the river, they also salvage other vessels which may have run aground or sunk. One task was to recover a gravel barge which went under complete with cargo. Here the *Panurgic* crew used the grab to remove the gravel to another barge

Fighting the incursions of the River Trent by constant dredging in post-war years, MV *Panurgic* sought to keep the navigation channel clear and the banks secure from flooding

and then refloated the vessel. Shortly afterwards their assistance was requested when a sailing boat sank after an explosion on board.

Occasionally there is a pleasant find to cheer up the day and the crew have brought up a variety of objects from the bottom of the Trent including a 2,000-year-old Roman vase in perfect condition, and a seventeenth-century rapier.

Clearly this is one old soldier who will never die!

An Aire and Calder Boatman of the War Years

Stan Barrass spent the years of the Second World War on craft trading between the ports of Hull, Goole and Selby and the inland waterway depots of the West Riding of Yorkshire. During this period Stan worked on both steam-powered and dumb craft, the latter moved about at various times by tug, man and horse.

The early years of the war saw Stan employed as mate on the 'big barge' *No. 81*, a dumb iron vessel 90 ft long by 17 ft beam. The barge was tiller-steered and was towed almost everywhere it went by steam-powered tugs. Between Hull and Goole the tug service was provided by the Goole and Hull Towing Company while the Aire and Calder Navigation Company had its own tug for haulage to Leeds and Wakefield from Goole.

No. 81 could carry 165 tons on a 7 ft draught, though the average load was about 130 tons. Cement was loaded at Earles, a short distance up the River Hull, and flour was collected either from Ranks, also in the 'old harbour', or from ships' berths in one of Hull's docks. These two cargoes provided most work for the barge, but wire, copper and wheat were also carried.

For the voyage from Hull to Goole *No. 81* would meet the tug either in the dock entrance lock or at the mouth of the River Hull. In the former case the crew would have poled the barge through the dock. To travel from a loading berth on the River Hull tò the meeting point, *No. 81* would have 'dropped down' the tidal river using a mudweight of two railway-track chairs bolted together to give the vessel steerage.

The tow upriver behind *No. 2* or *No. 4* was regarded as one day's work. The train, usually consisting of five or six dumb craft arranged in two lines, left Hull three or four hours before high water to arrive at Goole near the top of the tide when the flow had subsided. The tow would be turned in the river and then penned in the docks.

No. 81 would lie in Barge Dock to await the next stage of the voyage to the West Riding. During the war an A and CN Company tug left for Leeds on Mondays, Wednesdays and Fridays, and one left for Wakefield on Tuesdays, Thursdays and Saturdays. These tugs left Goole at around 5 a.m. and Stan's diary records the shortest time taken for *No. 81*'s run to Leeds as ten hours, while the longest journey began at 5 a.m. on 12 February 1941, and ended at 12.20 a.m. on 13 February.

The time taken depended mainly on the number of craft using the service on a particular day and on this February marathon there were six other barges besides *No. 81*, which involved two pennings at each of the smaller locks above Castleford. The run to Wakefield also took longer than twelve hours. The two-man crew took it in turns to brave the elements while clutching the tiller on an open deck. They were paid a basic wage plus a bonus for each trip.

The depots at both Leeds and Wakefield suffered a wartime shortage of staff and so there were delays in unloading. Boating was a reserved occupation but warehousemen and crane drivers were in short supply.

Sometimes empty flour sacks were loaded and the return voyage, as far as Goole, would again begin at 5 a.m. but was always completed before 4 p.m. The sacks would be taken to Hull on the next working (there was no Sunday working) and discharged at 'The Corner', officially Humber Dock Basin, into the flour company's horse-drawn wagons.

The visits to Hull in the early '40s were always eventful and not a little dangerous. Two barges, *Monarch* and *Brakelu*, were blown up by a mine off Alexandra Dock in February 1941 and the Humber was frequently closed for minesweeping. A black flag was flown at the Fish Dock lockpit to indicate that navigation of the river was forbidden.

In early May 1941 this north-east coast town was extensively bombed with a loss of over 400 lives. Three thousand homes were wrecked in these, Hull's worst days in the war. Stan Barass lived at Hull during this period but, after two houses had been rendered uninhabitable, he decided to move and by August his family was living within a stone's throw of Goole Docks.

No. 81 did not escape unscathed; an incendiary bomb caused a fire on the vessel's fo'csle head; the barge was covered in debris two or three times in 1941; and, while lying in Alexandra Dock in May of the following year, she was damaged by a falling structure and spent the next few weeks in Goole Repair Yard.

During the 'alerts', Stan's diary contains the entry 'no start – shortage of men' for several days. Another frequent problem was 'no loading – ship delayed'. Indeed one ship from which *No. 81* was due to load never arrived, as it had been torpedoed while en route for Hull.

In August 1942 Stan changed his style of boating when he left *No. 81* to become mate on the steam flyboat *No. 18*. This vessel was 70 ft by 18 ft 9 in, constructed of wood and carrying a three-man crew accommodated at the fore end of the barge. As well as cement and flour delivered from Hull to Leeds and Wakefield, *No. 18* carried flour from Selby to Wakefield. Cargoes of alum, wool and egg powder were also delivered. The average load was 60 tons carried on a draught of 5 ft. Being self-propelled meant that the only restriction on the vessel's movement was the sliding gate beneath No. 5 swing bridge near Goole which was drawn across the canal each evening to close the waterway between 9 a.m. and 5 a.m. The long hours spent behind a tug with *No. 81* were considerably reduced and the Goole to Leeds voyage took only about eight or nine hours.

No. 18 called at Leeds Basin, Lofthouse Basin (Stanley Ferry) or Castleford. In an emergency a few barrow loads could be taken on at Goole. On the barge the skipper and mate took turns at the wheel; instructions were given by word of mouth to the engineer standing some feet away by the control levers. The engineer also looked after the fire and had his time off when the vessel was in dock during which time the fire was extinguished and *No. 18* moved about by poling or by use of ropes.

Again visits to Hull produced some memorable incidents. One morning the crew arrived at the vessel to find a live landmine, suspended by its parachute wires swinging from a warehouse roof within yards of the barge. On another occasion there was the sight of one railway wagon which had been blown on top of another by a bomb dropped the previous night.

In the early months of 1943 *No. 18* managed to avoid visiting Hull and regularly loaded flour on the tidal River Ouse at Selby. The barge always returned to the safety of the Selby Canal as soon as possible after loading before setting off for Wakefield.

On one visit to Selby, with the river in flood, the fierce currents beneath the road swing bridge swept the vessel onto piles beneath the structure and *No. 18* lost her propeller and went athwart off the bridge. Fortunately the skipper of Wilby's barge

Stedfast, carrying coal to York, was able to free the damaged craft and tow her to a wharf between the road and rail swing bridges until the A and CN Company's one other steam flyboat could tow *No. 18* to Goole yard for repair.

After more than two years on *No. 18* Stan was asked to become captain of the wooden dumb vessel *No. 45*, a West Country size craft. *No. 45* carried up to 60 tons as far inland as Wakefield or Leeds, but in addition the barge was able to work on the Calder and Hebble Navigation, carrying wool, tobacco and cocoa to Savile Town, Dewsbury, and general cargoes to Huddersfield. At Wakefield Depot the vessel occasionally received cargoes for Dewsbury which were transhipped from larger craft.

Above Wakefield *No. 45* was hauled by one of the company's horses. The 8 miles, six locks to Dewsbury took half a day, the trickiest point being at Broad Cut on the Calder where the horse was required to give the vessel sufficient way to enter the lock on the opposite side of the river, before being ferried across to continue hauling along the canal section to Dewsbury.

On a run to Huddersfield, 9 miles and fourteen locks further on, the maximum load was 45 tons carried on a draught of less than 4 ft 6 in and then, Stan recalls, the vessel was sweeping the bottom for a good part of the way. The voyage from Wakefield to Huddersfield was rarely completed in a single day. After an early start horse and driver finished work at 4 p.m. and the boat was moored at a convenient point such as Double locks, Dewsbury, or Battye Flood Lock so that man and beast could travel back overland to stables at Wakefield, Dewsbury or Huddersfield.

After discharging at Huddersfield a rake was sometimes fitted to the barge's head and the horse fastened to *No. 45* through a double purchase block. This was to clear out from Apsley basin the enormous volume of silt washed down from the closed Huddersfield Narrow Canal. The crew earned 5s. between them for this task and they could also earn extra money if, because of the unavailability of a horse, they were prepared to bow-haul the vessel back towards Wakefield. They earned 6d. a mile for this, but Stan had a jury mast and sail on board which could be used to make this job lighter, though the numerous bridges at Mirfield were an obstruction.

Another problem on the Calder and Hebble, Stan recalls, was in training new mates to remove the tail band, take out the tiller extensions and pull the rudder hard over across the stern to avoid the sill when coming down the locks.

Stan's diary during his stay on *No. 45* has the entry 'pumped' on almost every page. The vessel leaked badly and the crew constantly had plenty of exercise in keeping the cargo dry and the barge afloat. Stan saw out the war on *No. 45* and perhaps the most memorable event in the diary is for 7 May 1945 – 'VE day'.

MIKE TAYLOR

On Reflection

Craft-y Nonsense

In ancient times, admiring strange devices,
Mankind we're told pursued the path of evil,
Practised perverse and most peculiar vices,
Ran off the rails, and played the very devil;
And somewhere round about the Middle East
Became a quite unmentionable beast.

Then came the Deluge, flooding all the land:
And man's survival on this precious Planet
Depended on the skill of Noah's hand,
Who built the Ark – and found the crew to man it,
From him descended men of every nation:
That was the first great Inland *Navigation*.

What a tradition deep in history's pages
Dates from that ancient, legendary craft.
Riparian man, voyaging thro' the ages,
By crazy coracle or loose-limbed raft,
Has sculled his way along by barge and boat
And kept his tail up and his head afloat.

Still man's inventions take gigantic strides
With landing craft transported over dry ways
Amphibious 'Ducks' which wait not upon tides,
But wade ashore and walk upon highways.
Shortly, no doubt, we'll build a barge with wings,
That flies – and nests in trees – and sometimes sings.

Vessels are built inland in separate parts,
Then taken somewhere else and stuck together;

175

And now by 'Radar' and her kindred arts
They'll see at night – in fog – and dirty weather.
Atomic rockets take the place of steam
And soon we'll brave the aether on a beam.

What noble calling then is ours, to serve
Such undertakings: cater for their uses;
Planning improvements to each line and curve,
And striving to amend their worst abuses;
To clear the channel of all hind'ring weeds
And give the service which the Nation needs.

W.H. PRYCE

A Standard Craft

Sing me a song of the standard craft,
With her shapely sheer and her clean run aft,
A moderate beam and a decent draft,
A-sail on an inland sea.
What do I care for a London barge,
With her sails so brown and her sprit so large,
Her leisurely gait and her slow discharge,
As she lies at a Thames-side quay.

I still must care for the Humber Keel,
Whether she's built of timber or steel,
Long wooden tiller or steering wheel,
She comes from an ancient race.
But whether she's fitted with sail and mast,
Her frames are strong and she's built to last,
As broad as she's long and not too fast,
She's hardly a vessel of grace.

Give me a stately standard craft,
With five yards beam and five feet draft,
A short, and sturdy propeller shaft
And rudder tucked in at the back;
With diesel engine and oil to burn,
With ample hold and with space to turn,
And ninety-two feet between stem and stern,
To travel the standard tracks.

On a new canal of a new design,
With sloping sides at a safe incline,
And an ample channel of one in nine
To furnish a passage of fleet;
A double tow-path without a stile,
And bank protection of sheeting pile,
And long straight reaches for mile on mile,
And headroom of twelve clear feet.

This is my song of the standard craft,
With a shapely sheer and a clean run aft,
A moderate beam and a decent draft
And all you could wish aboard.
On a new canal of a new design,
With lovely locks in a long straight line,
Very much better than yours or mine,
Or any you'll find abroad.

A nice little launch for the Engineer – Me,
To make my inspections and have a look-see,
With the doings on board for making your tea,
And finished in teak and gilt.
But if ever I meet with a standard craft,
I'm perfectly sure I'll go perfectly daft
And fall overboard, and get mixed in the shaft,
And have to be dredged with the silt.

W.H. PRYCE

Grand Union

There was a young boatman named Glum
And he was, you'll agree far from dumb,
He proposed to his gal
On the Regent's Canal
And he married her long before Brum!

Where's the Typist?

There was a young lady from Gloucester
Who typed all the names on the roster.
One day in a fright
She couldn't type right,
And now the docks office have lost her.

Cartwright's Grey Mare

This is the story of Cartwright the Bold,
Who drove the Grey Mare up the cut so I'm told.
Out early morning and home next day,
With a boat load of coal from out Anglesey way.

Now this old Grey Mare was just artful you see,
Wouldn't 'bacca' a bit while they supped at their tea,
In vain they could shout, was she afraid?
The old Mare knew all the tricks of the trade.

Did she know 'Bromwich Eight' and 'Gansey' did she!
Where a nose-tin of corn would be waiting you see,
Walsall Wood and Daw End where she knew she could rest,
And home the next day with a load of the Best.

But alack and alas, 'tis said to recall,
One day she went and lay down in her stall,
And all that is left of this sad little tale
Is the Old Mare's hind shoe that still hangs on the nail.

J. CHATWIN

Note: To 'bacca' is for the horse to go forward by himself. 'Bromwich Eight' and 'Gansey' are Riders Green and Rushall Locks, respectively. Walsall Wood and Daw End are tying-up points on the way to Anglesey Canal Loading Basin.

Who?

Time lacks sympathy
With those who stay and dream
Of an age, now past,
When Canals as Harbingers of Transport
Were, in words, the first, the last.

But to the Dreamer
Whose gaze is crystal bent,
Will come true thought –
The knowledge, the wherewithal
Of modern Canal Transport.

C.W. GODDEN

Thoughts at the Clubhouse Window

Welsh Harp! upon thy waters
The little yachts disport,
While watching wives and daughters
Our skilful helms export.
Afar the speeding motor,
Unheard and barely seen,
And when we've sailed our quota,
See sunset o'er Golders Green.

From Wembley down to Hendon,
North Circ. to Edgware Road,
The gallant craft depend on:
Their sails – red, white and woad.
They round the buoys together
Their burgees fluttering free:
Unless it's beastly weather,
When they go inside for tea.

Here rival forms of transport,
Roads, railways and canals,
Unite in healthy man's sport,
And lion and lamb are pals.
Oh – banish automation
That ties our brains in knots,
And let's become a nation
That sails its little yachts!

SIR REGINALD HILL

The Last 'Number One'

I was sitting by the cut one day,
With nothing much to do,
When round the banks of Cabbage Turn
A boat came into view.

A mule in harness walked before,
And ambled slowly past,
Behind, the dripping snubber lend
To the motley towing mast.

The cratch was painted blue and green,
With sprigs of roses red,
Above the curving tiller-bar,
A freshly-made 'Turk's head'.

The cabin side a sight to see,
With castles rearing high,
The owner's name in letters bold,
Was there to catch the eye.

Behind the gleaming chimney-pot,
A-gleaming in the sun,
Stood Joseph Skinner, pipe in mouth,
The last true 'Number One'.

C.P. CARRDUS

Our Lovely Heritage

The inland waterway:
– Like silver needles threaded through with green –
Embroider all they touch, with their serene
Bright loops enhancing more each unspoilt scene.
They even allow a modern factory site
To boast a trace of beauty, where the white
Swan drifts, and rushes murmur of old days.

Bridgewater, Brindley, rest content! Boats trade,
Men profit still, on the canals you made,
And time, green-fingered, auditing your page
Confirms your work, our lovely heritage. . . .

ROSE HILDEBRAND

Peace – and Plenty

We rambled the waterways
From Birmingham to Oxford;
We ate and talked and drank and walked,
And chugged and locked and moored.

We came from far Rhodesia,
From cities south and north,
From USA and Nottingham
And the land of Firth and Forth.

Tourists having lunch on narrow boat *Water Rambler*, which was specially converted and appointed for luxury five-day voyages between Oxford and Birmingham

Picnic groups we glided past
And fishermen galore;
Past dogs that barked and cows that mooed
And fat sheep by the score.

The horses neighed and flipped their tails,
Huge piggies grunted 'Hi';
Small boys grinned and hikers waved
As we glided slowly by.

Traffic problems were but few –
Locks up and down like stairs,
With swans and rats and flowering weeds
And barges big – in pairs.

We strutted round a cocktail bar
In sleepy Banbury Town,
All very gaily garmented
In Howitt's swimming gown.

Ne'er a quarrel, large or small,
No broken bone or ache;
No jewellery nor a garment lost,
No swear words (save 'Pete's Sake').

ALMA STARRETT

Can You?

Can you give me a rate from Bristol to Leeds
Can you give to this driver the sub that he needs
Can you do me ten tons on the quick from a wharf
Can you get me the 'gen' on that claim for lost swarf.
Can you find me a spare for this Bedford artic
Can you get out the rates for this job on the quick
Can you really remember each day all these things
Can you always sit tight when the telephone rings?

Have you got all those figures for the Depot's new graph
Have you got POD for that job for the RAF
Have you passed any traffic to that foreign tramp
Have you got that job covered that needed a ramp.

Have you sent off the figures for this month, you dope
Have you made out the Indent for that piece of rope .
Have you really considered the things that you do
Have you not even forgotten at least one or two?

Have you heard that the tug way downstream lost its lighter
Have you heard that Boat No. 2's back in t'water
Have you seen the instruction for dealing with Stats
Have you heard that a chap down in Watford went bats.
Have you heard that the transfer you want, you won't get
Have you seen that big claim for the load that got wet
Have you had any time to read your *Express*
Have you any idea of your own home address?

Are you checking the Ops Forms to see they're OK
Are you following instructions for dealing with pay
Are you sure that all fuel is booked on the sheet
Are you having that load transhipped in the street.
Are you getting the boats away on the dot
Are you fixing that engine this maddening strife
Are you still on good terms over hours with your wife?

Will you check with Accounts that this credit's OK
Will you note that your tonnage is down on the day
Will you see that the Mates are filling their tanks
Will you find me an escort to go to the banks.
Will you check if this ship really closes today
Will you see that the waybills are made out this way
Will you live to be old and distinguished and grey
Will you H . . . you'll be lucky to last out the day!

ANON

Rochdale Canal

In my youth, this waterway
Passed many boats by night and day,
Over the summit and far beyond,
In and out of many a pound.

Through the locks so deep and many,
Ninety-two! if there are any;
And to youth this rise and fall
Was as magic to us all.

With the line the horses hauling,
Straining, pulling, boatmen bawling,
And 'midst all this curse and twaddle,
Boatmen shouting, 'Draw that paddle!'

Passed are days to navigate,
With captain and his mate,
And when winter's icy blast,
Held his boat so firm and fast.

With lock decay and weed so gay,
On this – a lovely waterway –
Comes to me another sorrow,
Why these boats won't pass tomorrow.

REGINALD WOOD

Trent Waters

Still flow Trent's clear and winding stream,
The theme of romance and dream;
'Tis joy to hear its waters splash,
As o'er the stones they leap and dash.

How leisurely they drift along,
And echo to the boatman's song
Where willows bending o'er the stream,
Wave gently as the waters gleam.

The murmuring waters roll around,
And shine along the varied ground
Through moss-clad rocks and tangled shades,
Sweep thro' the gardener's green arcades.

The timid moorhens splash and fly,
And 'midst the reeds and rushes lie,

On waving boughs and plumey race,
Find in the reeds a nesting place.

The peaceful aspect of the scene,
As waters flow calm and serene
The fertile slopes and pastures green,
Where boats and barges glide between.

H. DUNN

Something New in London

There's something new in London Town
Near a railway station;
Slim yachts are bobbing up and down
In St Pancras Basin.

Hard by trains that roar and steam
You'll now find pleasure boating,
In a harbour cool and green;
White marker buoys are floating.

The St Pancras Basin is a convenient mooring place for pleasure cruisers in the heart of London

A wooden catwalk skirts the bay,
High walls gave close protection,
Facilities where yachts may stay,
Right on the Regent's Section.

CELIA TURNER

Fly-boats

I woke quite often in the night
Wondering if a fly-boat might
Be one able to soar and swoop
And sometimes loop-the-loop.

Or, alternatively, perhaps,
A crew of flies in gold-trimmed caps;
The captain, hand upon the throttle,
A most elegant bluebottle.

My thanks are due to those who now
Have given me some clues on how
Men with waterways devotion
Discovered perpetual motion.

BILL HUTTON

Ducking For Joe

Oh list to our tale, a tale of woe,
The sad, sad story of our lad Joe.
That day in June the sun shone brightly
And Joe set out with step so sprightly;
Anxious to reach his destination
And join in well-earned relaxation
With all his friends upon this day
In a trip along the waterway.

Joe took his perch upon the bows
And bravely glared at grazing cows;
They frightened not our lad so bold,
Though wind blew sharp he wasn't cold;

His pipe between his teeth he gripped
And then, calamity! he tripped
And fell into the waters dank,
We all thought that he had sank.
(Poetic licence!)

The boat stopped dead upon its track;
Up floated Joe upon his back.
Smiling gaily his pipe he smoked,
'It's turned out rather wet!' he joked.
We fished him out and dried him off
To stop him catching cold or cough.
Now everyone, though friend or foe,
Knows our lad as 'Drip-Dry Joe'.

PAT WALDRON

Canal Journey

The narrow boat comes chugging,
Entering the lock:
Starting on a journey
Up the Cut, from Regent's Dock.

Painted cans for water,
Brass bands all a-shine;
Blue and yellow paintwork,
The butty boat behind.

On, up through the levels,
Johnson's, Mile End, Ford,
Acton's, Sturt's and City Road,
Fifty tons aboard.

The women on the tiller
Guides them deftly through;
The boatee and his family
Are skipper, mate and crew.

A pair of narrow boats negotiating locks as they start a long journey with a cargo

Into the long dark tunnel,
Full of damp and drip;
The arch of bricks just overhead,
The worst part of the trip.

Passing by St Pancras
Where yachts will now make fast,
Looking slightly snooty
To the boatee chuffing past.

To Regent's Park and London Zoo,
A fashionable quarter:
A lovely stretch that's only seen
By those upon the water.

Maida Vale and Browning's isle,
No more locks to clear;
Past the Traffic office,
Houseboats lying near.

Past the crowded tenements
Wharves and buildings high,
And sidings, where the endless stream
Of Industry goes by.

The journey's end is now in sight
A factory is near;
The boat gives one last gasping cough,
And bumps against a pier.

The skipper wipes his oily hands,
The tiller swings and stops;
And in the sudden silence
The water makes soft plops.

The day is long and sometimes tough,
For boatee and his wife;
A world apart – a Waterway –
Their home, their job, their life.

CELIA TURNER

A Saga of the Canals

We set out early that morning
Mary, three children and I.
For we were off to visit the Zoo
'Neath the heat of a cloudless sky.

We came all the way by canal boat,
From 'Little Venice' up to the Zoo,
Where an elephant guarded the entrance
Flanked by a kangaroo.

And the great boats travelled upwards
Filled with the wheat of man's desires
From the North Sea's rough waters
Right up to the heart of the Shires.

Wild fowl lined its verges;
Ducks, moorhens, and grey geese,
Motor boats towed the barges;
It was a scene of work and peace.

For God has made this England,
But has given it us to complete
And such silver threads of water
Are places where we meet.

ELSMERE HARRIS

Will This Make 'em Think?

Poor Transport Minister
Few men would ask
To have ten minutes of your task,
For God himself could not have planned
To move so many on the land.
The cars that crash, the cars that crawl,
The cars that hardly move at all.
But, Sir, for less dispute and slaughter
See how we do things on the water.
While those who walk and those who ride
Conflict, and curse, and then collide,
The same good feeling keeps afloat
The Barge, the Battleships or any Boat.
In any craft, in any clime,
We know our duty any time.
The Liner and the Lighter share
The signal 'NAVIGATE WITH CARE'.

ALFRED THOMAS

Sale of a Boat

I should have let you know before
My boat has sailed and left your shore,
It rests aloof, on solid ground
With hens and pigs and cows around.

We sold it to a man, how sad
Who even more than us was mad
He's going to 'do it up' he said
(He must be crazy in the head).

At any rate this silly bloke
Towed it to a farm near Stoke
And put it in a farmer's field
To see what sort of crop 'twould yield.

But we have a premonition
He will succeed, and in addition
Next year he'll pay some mooring dues
So, kind sir, you will not lose.

So thanks for all your kind attention,
(the money part we will not mention)
We'll have a boat again some day
And hope to sail it 'up your way'.

. . . in reply . . .

We thank you for your charming note
Informing us you've sold your boat,
And, as the result of this sad news,
We'll not be able to charge you dues.

But worse than that, we've lost a fan
Which hurts us more than anything can.
We hope this loss is only temporary
And there'll be another *Largo* or p'haps *Mary*.

One who's messed about the boats
Will soon want something else that floats
And when the sun shines bright next spring
The urge to cruise again will bring.

We can't agree the man was daft
Who went and bought your little craft,
And when the 'doing up' is done
We're sure that he'll have lots of fun.

We hope too you'll be soon returning
Filled with that nostalgic yearning
And that perhaps we'll meet one day
Cruising up Llangollen way.

MRS BOWAN AND E. TAYLOR

On Retiring

The habits of a lifetime are just about to change
Rising when the streets are aired is just going to feel strange:
The daily journey up to town behind the folded paper,
The scamper through the subway; the escalator caper.
I'll not miss one bit of it, in fact, it will be better
To slip the yoke of custom and cast aside its fetter.
But what about the folks I know, my comrades through the years,
With whom I share our morning joke, our hopes and, yes, our fears?
I will miss you ev'ryone, and your familiar faces,
Your voices (of'n rising, when getting down to cases).
But this parting has to come without a broken heart
For as the old-time song says 'the best of friends must part.'
So friends, I'll now say cheerio, to our familiar life,
For me it is my garden, my hobbies and my wife,
And once a year we'll meet at Annual Reunion
When we taste the sylvan joys of the old Grand Union.

GEORGE E. HORTON

The River by Night

The river's softly moonbeam-kissed
From a sky of deepest amethyst:
Yonder hoots the tawny owl,
Ripple go the water fowl.
Within the bank the water vole
Prepares for his nocturnal stroll:
The frog croaks deep, and then anon
The gliding shadow of the swan.
The coot upon its nightly feeds
Heeds not the rustling of the reeds:
Upon the bank the sharp-eyed stoat
Anticipates a meal afloat.
Thus beauty, life, and death abide,
At nightfall by the riverside.

HENRY MOTTRAM

November Holiday

As it's been a wretched summer, save perhaps for ducks and weeds,
I'm embarking on a voyage from the little port o' Leeds.
The Lily, she's a power barge, a calm and placid lass:
I'll sign as supercargo and I'll travel cabin class.
What was the Aire and Calder in the days when I was young
Is very little talked about and still more seldom sung.
The waterway, with little fuss, just cuts across the grain
Of articulated lorry, bus, and motor bike and train.
And I shall take it easy, as the tow-rope takes the tug
Of the *Lily's* ugly ducklings to her soothing engine-chug.
If there is any sun about I'll lounge upon the deck
As the *Lily* glides through Lemonroyds, through Castleford, Top Heck.
When fog or rain or twilight comes, or all three, I'll retire
With the skipper to his cabin with its cherry-heart of fire
We'll brew a pint pot mug or two – well worth a passing sonnet –
Of powerful black treacle tea: a mouse could walk upon it.
Oh, you can keep Majorca as the rain drums down outside
And the *Lily* and her ducklings waddle for the Humber tide
For if the *Lily's* language might, perhaps, surprise a nun
A November voyage aboard her would redress King Lear's disorder
It's a pleasure cruise, a pipe-dream and a rest cure all in one.

R.C. SCRIVEN

Pennine Reservoir

Winter sunlight streaking
The desolate reservoir lake
High in the Pennines gleaming
Reflecting the riven skies
That soar fast changing
Sombre as the sunlight dies.

And with the dawn mist rising
The lake, in a nebulous light
Like some fragile chinese painting
Wings of hawks and diving gulls
With the golden sun emerging
Filling the air with light and song.

MALCOLM SELLERS

The Leeds and Liverpool Canal

On it winds from Leeds to Liverpool
Trailing echoes and fettered ghosts
Of dead barges reluctant to leave
Its long meandering miles past mills
Of stone and mucky brick and black
Tall chimneys rising high like crooked
Sticks that prop the sagging sky
And smear the sun with smoke
On past backs of laundries, foundries
And sombre crematoriums, Victorian emporiums
Pickle factories and bingo halls
Tilting walls of silent weaving sheds
And empty chapels where no prayers are said,
Past anglers who sit and stare
Through uneventful Sundays
Puffing fags and killing time until
Their dreary dole queue Mondays.
And on it drifts past Pennine Hills
Spinning mills and backyard washing
Railways rumbling and couples courting
Through meadows green with spring
On and on, meandering free
To Liverpool and the sea.

MALCOLM SELLERS

The Canal

Dirty, slimy waters,
Advance and retreat upon the dark canal,
Like an infantry
They pound like cannons on the lock gates,
As if they are hands knocking on a door.

Dark murky water vibrates to and fro,
Hitting the barges like shells from a gunboat
As it slowly and dreamily pulls its way along the canal,
High in the water as it is empty
It moves along the oil-ridden water.

The lock is like a witch's cauldron
When a spell is being made,
The water in the canal is so polluted
That it is impossible to see the bottom
Or even a foot from the top.

Froth swiftly flows along the canal,
Like groups of gathering women,
Suddenly they spring apart
Like a spreading disease,
As if there is a bomb in their midst.

A barge moves steadily along the canal,
Like a great prehistoric animal,
As with a great creak and groan the lock gates swing open
And the monster is in a cage
Surrounded by the dark black walls.

CAROLYN ARTIS

Narrow Boat

Narrow boat, narrow boat where are you bound
With your gliding and scrollwork so lavishly crowned?
Are you plying to Leeds or to Liverpool Docks
Via wandering water and corseted locks?
Are you loaded with grain or bright yellow clean sand
Or some exotic ore from a faraway land?
Are you carrying coal from the mountains of Wales
Or forwarding cotton imported in bales?

Narrow boat, narrow boat holiday home,
For harassed escapists with urges to roam,
Who wish to act out their nautical dream,
And knowingly boast of your draught, length and beam
Who fill you with brassware, cut crystal, red wines,
And speak of your functional, workmanlike minds
Or sing, as they steer, of sailing ship days
As if you had a stump or a sail you could raise. . . .

Narrow boat, narrow boat where go you now,
As you travel that furrow in England's fair brow?

STAN NELSON

195

Polluted Canal

Swishing, slopping, washing, rippling,
The canal winds its way.
When I am dead
The canal will run,
Swishing, slopping, washing, rippling,
Through locks and other locks,
Imprisoned in the steel sides.
Bearing the weight of many a barge,
It does not tell us of its remorse.
Grossly polluted,
By industry sewers,
And many other culprits,
Its placid waters are bullied
By barge and locks.
To the canal
Nobody hardly ever shows kindness
Hardly anybody cares,
About its suffering.
Rippling with tiny wavelets,
Reflecting what dares to peep above.
Stones sink and thud to the bottom
Disturbing the mud
Which feels the pain
Of cruelty and loneliness.

MARTIN JONATHAN ORSON

A Black Spider

The job I do in *Waterways*
Can take me far and wide.
The water where my studies are
Ranges from quite still to tide,
But recently while in the north
For fun I was bereft,
So I thought from Northwich I'd walk
To see the Anderton Lift.
I'd never seen it in real life:
Just pictures in the *News*,

So I spent an evening sat by it
Watched it with the black sky fused.
At its base I sat and craned my neck
To gaze so high in awe.

As the night draws on it seems to be
A great spider on the floor.
The only sound is trickling water
On this otherwise silent night.

Acknowledged as one of the wonders of the waterways, the Anderton Lift opened in July 1875 to link the Trent and Mersey Canal with the River Weaver Navigation. The original design, by Edwin Clark, consisted of two caissons each 75 ft long by 15 ft 6 in wide, raised and lowered by hydraulic rams through 50 ft 4 in. Electric power was substituted in 1908

This mass of deepest black now seems
To sleep, awaiting light.
I cannot write much more about
The Lift: departure's nigh,
I leave it standing proudly there
Defiant to the sky.

MARTIN COOPER

Gloucester and Sharpness Canal

May your bridges freely cant or swing,
May the lock gates always open and close,
May a trespassing angler never get caught,
May his line come tight on some poor fish which rose,
May this ribbon of water from fouling keep clear,
And may flotsam and jetsam sink deep in repose.

STAFF OF JF FARM MACHINES LTD

We Shall Return

It is with some mixed feelings
I write this note to you
A holiday afloat, no less
This should not leave you blue.

The start was nothing special
Just a small amount delayed,
I really thought at one stage
'Perhaps we have not paid.'

And then I saw the fitter
With spanner in his hand
Head down in the engine
As on the bank we stand.

At last we were allowed to load
And get her under way
With only one thing on our minds
Just which pub should we stay.

The Sunday started fairly well
And lunchtime pub was planned
The pratt upon the tiller
Went by – forgot to land.

It may have been on Tuesday
For lunch a roast we got
The cooker then fell over
And on the floor it shot.

The early hours of Saturday
A cry of great alarm
To wake us from our slumbers
And shatter morning calm.

The cry of 'We are sinking'
Did echo down the galley
With water lapping round our feet
The whole crew had to rally.

It just was not a pretty sight
Our clothes and fags afloat
And people in pyjamas
Baling water from the boat.

With shouts of 'Bloody disaster'
And frozen near to tear
There's only one thing left to say
We shall all be back next year

MARGARET EVANS

A Working Day

Armed with strimmer, rakes, hedging bills, down the banks they trudged
Through bracken, grass, horse manure and sludge,
Whistling as they plod along
One man burst out into song.
They were happy clearing rubbish and weeds,
Doing a job that the public needs.
Bringing the towing paths into good repair,
Because this summer they'll get wear and tear.

The walkers will be out in droves
Leaving the wrappers off their loaves.
A man will have to be found
To clear the litter off the ground.

ARTHUR WHEELER

Unbelievable

At last, at last, I heard a man shout
We can get on the banks and walk about.
Not before time another man said,
Whatever is happening, scratching his head.
These walkways have been neglected for years,
Pulled out his hankie and dried up his tears.
I'll bring my wife and grandchildren too,
And I'll walk on these banks for an hour with you.
We can enjoy nature like we did years ago
Come on these rambles and let life slip by slow.
Seats and picnic areas, up and down would be grand,
There's plenty of room where they are reclaiming the land.
A waterbus picking up at the locks would make our day,
It could happen who is to say.
Down to Castleford then fresh fields afar,
It's much more pleasant than going by car.

ARTHUR WHEELER

Hard Work

Dad said I could steer the tiller,
As we went past the miller.
Mum said I could paint the boat
As we were gaily afloat.
Dad told me to get the pan,
Mum said get the Buckby Can.
Dad said the horse is hungry pick some grass
Mum said to polish the horse brass.
Dad said wash the dishes,
And go catch some little fishes.
Living on a canal boat is hard work.

EMMA G.

Into a Tunnel

Travelling into darkness,
The front of the boat glides,
Creeping under the dripping roof,
Past the slimy bank sides.
The canal boat softly slides along,
Through the nightmare cave,
Using my feet to travel on,
Trying to be brave.
At last, a tiny pin prick,
So small you have to stare,
To see it, but it's growing and growing,
I'm coming through – fresh air!

EMILY CASE

Waterways

The waterways of England
how calm and restful they seem
    that anyone who cares to cruise
on them can relax and dream.
Low are the speed limits, no
dust, and always
    what a joy to call for holidays
someday
What lovely scenery, of bushes,
grasses and trees,
    also songs of the birds heard
in the breeze.
How beautiful and peaceful
along the way,
    such a grand feeling to have
throughout the day.
To all I say there is life to be
    found, through the waterways
of England all round,
So try them and prove it's right,
for all its landscape and beauty
    Oh, what delight.

SYLVIA RUDKIN